MODERN MONOPOLIES

What It Takes to Dominate the 21st-Century Economy

ALEX MOAZED and
NICHOLAS L. JOHNSON

St. Martin's Press
New York

www.stmartins.com

Design by Letra Libre, Inc.

Library of Congress Cataloging-in-Publication Data

Names: Moazed, Alex, author. | Johnson, Nicholas L., author.

Title: Modern monopolies : what it takes to dominate the 21st-century economy / Alex Moazed and Nicholas L. Johnson.

Description: First edition. | New York, N.Y. : St. Martin's Press, [2016]

Identifiers: LCCN 2015050147| ISBN 9781250091895 (hardcover) | ISBN 9781250091901 (e-book)

Subjects: LCSH: Multi-sided platform businesses. | Technological innovations—Economic aspects. | Electronic commerce.

Classification: LCC HD9999.M782 M63 2016 | DDC 338.8/2—dc23

LC record available at http://lccn.loc.gov/2015050147

Our books may be purchased in bulk for promotional, educational, or business use. Please contact your local bookseller or the Macmillan Corporate and Premium Sales Department at 1-800-221-7945, extension 5442, or by e-mail at MacmillanSpecialMarkets@macmillan.com.

First Edition: May 2016

10 9 8 7 6 5 4 3 2

APPLICO

Applico is the world's first Platform Innovation company, specializing in developing, launching, and scaling platform businesses and the technology products that enable them. Founded in 2007 by CEO Alex Moazed while he was still a student at Babson College, Applico has transitioned from a mobile app development firm to an organization that defined the platform business model and works with some of the world's leading businesses and hottest startups to build and grow innovative platforms. Our clients include Fortune 100 companies as well as startups that have raised hundreds of millions of dollars and achieved nine-figure exits. Applico's cross-functional team of business model designers, branding strategists, product managers, UI/UX designers, and engineers have successfully launched over 300 platform businesses and mobile apps. Visit http://www.applicoinc.com for more information.

For Janet and Bonnie,

the two best moms we know

CONTENTS

Prologue   The Burning Platform   1

1   Platforms Are Eating the World   17

2   Hayek versus the Machine, or Why Everything
     You Think You Know about the Twentieth
     Century Is Wrong   49

3   The Zero-Marginal-Cost Company   77

4   Modern Monopolies: Platform Capitalism and
     the Winner-Take-All Economy   95

5   Designing a Billion-Dollar Company: How the
     Core Transaction Explains Tinder's Success   109

6   The Visible Hand: The Four Functions of
     a Platform   125

7   Let the Network Do the Work   159

8   Why Platforms Fail, and How to Avoid It   189

Conclusion   How to Spot the Next Big Thing   203

A Word from the Authors   237
Glossary of Platform Terms   239
Acknowledgments   243
Notes   247
Index   263

PROLOGUE

THE BURNING PLATFORM

It was February 2011, and Nokia had a problem. Once an undisputed leader in mobile technology, the company no longer could keep up with its competitors. For over a decade, Nokia had been the world's most successful handset manufacturer. But now it was losing ground. Fast.

With Apple's introduction of the iPhone in 2007 and Google's unveiling of Android in 2008, the rules of the game had changed. These were hugely successful software platforms in what was once a hardware-centric industry, and Nokia was nowhere near that stage. Its legacy operating system, Symbian, was outdated and difficult to develop software for and its next-gen operating system, MeeGo, still wasn't ready for prime time.

How quickly things changed. Only a generation before, Nokia had been an ailing Finnish conglomerate with stakes in everything from lumber to tires. But in the late 1980s and early 1990s, the company executed what the American Management Association called one of the "50 Best Management Saves" in history—successfully shifting focus to the mobile communications industry. There was good reason for optimism that Nokia could pull off another miracle.

In September 2010, the company hired former Microsoft executive Stephen Elop as CEO and charged him with turning its business around.

Elop faced an important choice right away. Should Nokia stick with trying to develop its next-gen operating system? Or should it abandon this approach in favor of hitching its wagon to an established competitor? In January 2011, Nokia's management was still leaning toward the former until a critical meeting changed Elop's mind. Jo Harlow, Nokia's head of Symbian, told Elop that MeeGo "wasn't mature enough" and that Symbian couldn't hold Nokia over until the new operating system was ready. A partnership with Apple's tightly controlled iOS was out of the question, so Nokia was left deciding whether to pin its hopes on the nascent Windows Phone or Android.[1]

This shift in strategy, combined with the challenge of overcoming a sclerotic bureaucratic structure, convinced Elop that the company needed to change direction. On February 4, 2011, he issued to the company's employees what came to be known as the Burning Platform memo.[2] The memo, leaked to the public a couple of days later, compared the task Nokia faced to the story of an oilman standing on a burning oil platform.

"As the fire approached him, the man had mere seconds to react," Elop wrote. "He could stand on the platform, and inevitably be consumed by the burning flames. Or, he could plunge 30 meters in to the freezing waters. The man was standing upon a 'burning platform,' and he needed to make a choice." In Elop's tale, the man chose to dive into the water and, against the odds, managed to survive. But the experience radically changed his behavior. The metaphor for Nokia's troubled situation was clear. "We too, [sic] are standing on a 'burning platform,'" Elop wrote, "and we must decide how we are going to change our behavior."

The memo went on to detail many of the challenges Nokia faced. "The first iPhone shipped in 2007, and we still don't have a product that is close to their experience. Android came on the scene just over 2 years ago, and this week they took our leadership position in smartphone volume." MeeGo was supposed to be Nokia's answer to the competition, but "by the end of 2011, we might have only one MeeGo product in the market," Elop wrote. At the same time, Nokia's legacy operating system, Symbian, was "proving to be an increasingly difficult environment in which to develop" and "leading to slowness in product development." Even worse, while Android and the iPhone were attacking from above at the high end of the market, Chinese manufacturers were starting to make inroads from below with cheaper options.

These challenges were serious. But they were also all symptoms of Nokia's single biggest failure, one that Elop implicitly recognized. Nokia had missed the transformative convergence of software and hardware. It was still acting like a product company. But now the smartphone industry wasn't really about the product; it was about the *platform*.

"We're not even fighting with the right weapons," Elop said. "We are still too often trying to approach each price range on a device-to-device basis. *The battle of devices has now become a war of ecosystems* [emphasis added]."

Speaking to the *Financial Times* a month after the memo was leaked to the press, Nokia's Harlow agreed. "Our ability to change from being device-led to being software-led as the industry changed hasn't been fast enough," she said. "We could have been in a different position if we had been able to make the transition more quickly."[3]

Nokia was used to competing on specs or features. But, as Elop said in his memo, "our competitors aren't taking our market share with devices; they are taking our market share with an entire ecosystem." Elop was right. Apple and Android had taken a platform approach, building unprecedented networks of consumers and developers by connecting the two sides en masse. These other platforms didn't win because of superior features or technology. (At the time, several Nokia phones were highly reviewed.) They won because of their ability to create whole new markets and tap into new sources of value. Elop saw it coming, but not soon enough.

Two days after the memo was released to the public, on February 11, 2011, Elop announced Nokia's decision to switch to Windows Phone. Elop had spoken with Google about switching to Android, but he was wary of Nokia becoming just another hardware manufacturer in an already crowded Android device market.

Unfortunately for Elop, this decision was another mistake. Neither Nokia nor Windows Phone fared well over the next several years.

On September 3, 2013, after a few years of desperate experimentation, Elop announced that Nokia was selling its Devices and Services division to Microsoft in a deal that would be worth $7.2 billion.[4] The sale was a clear admission of failure by Nokia, which was jettisoning all of its manufacturing and supply-chain capabilities and in essence becoming a technology and IP licensing company.

By the beginning of 2014, Nokia's market capitalization had declined to $30 billion. This was a stunning fall from a decade earlier, when the company's market cap topped $200 billion. Elop had been right that Nokia was on a "burning platform." But unlike the man in Elop's story, Nokia couldn't survive.

A PLATFORM AWAKENS

The release of Elop's "burning platform" memo torpedoed Symbian. Despite being outdated and on the decline compared to iOS and Android, at the time Symbian still held the highest market share of any mobile phone operating system. Although Symbian was not likely to stand up against its new competitors for long, Elop's memo hastened its decline.

It's generally not good form for a CEO to undermine his company's signature product, especially when a replacement isn't already lined up. The market reacted accordingly, and Nokia's stock price declined precipitously. Elop later admitted that his memo hurt the company because it was made public. He was taken to task for this at a Nokia board meeting later in 2011. However, for anyone running a business today, viewing Nokia's decline simply as a case of bad management would be missing the point.

In truth, Nokia's undoing was part of a much larger phenomenon, of which there are many other victims, present and future. It's easy to think of the mobile phone industry as unlike most other businesses. It is, after all, a "tech" industry, which has an easily identifiable hub of activity in Silicon Valley, with an ethos and worldview all its own. That's why many people think of technology as fundamentally separate from much of the economy. But the smartphone wars were not an anomaly. They were the canary in our corporate coal mine. If the pressures Nokia faced don't sound familiar to you and your company now, they soon will. Entire areas of our economy already are being remade as technology has redefined the boundaries of the modern organization and shifted or even collapsed the traditional separation between industries.

From the time of Nokia's peak to now, something fundamental has changed in the business landscape. We are in a historic period where even the largest companies can rise and fall within just a few years. Sixty years ago, the average life span of a company in the S&P 500 was over fifty years. Today it's less than fifteen. This upheaval creates tremendous peril for existing businesses, but it also creates enormous opportunities. To take advantage of this change, you need to understand why it is happening. Then you need to know how to capitalize on it. Equipping you with this knowledge is the main purpose of this book.

Elop was on the right track when he took over Nokia. Unfortunately, it was already too late. "How did we get to this point?" he asked in his memo. "Why did we fall behind when the world around us evolved?" Answer: Nokia had failed to see the radical social and economic transformation that had taken place over the decade leading up to its demise. This transformation has fundamentally changed how businesses need to operate. Get it wrong, like Nokia, and even the most successful business will soon find itself on its own burning platform. Get it right, and there are billions and billions of dollars on the table.

These changes will rapidly expand the frontier of what is possible, just as the Industrial Revolution did. Many tasks that seemed insurmountable a decade ago seem routine today. The magnitude of change that this technological revolution has brought to our society and economy has largely gone unnoticed.

However, technology alone can't change the world. This book also is the story about the changing ways people interact with companies, products, and each other. This process started with the rise of mobile in the early part of the twenty-first century. But even today, the shift is just beginning.

You don't need to look far to see the difference. What may have seemed like geek fads a decade ago—mobile connections, social media, and so on—are now at the core of many thriving businesses. As a result, a new business model will continue to challenge traditional organizational structures for years to come.

This new business model is the *platform:* a business that connects two or more mutually dependent groups in a way that benefits all sides. Platforms are a radical departure from traditional business operations, most of which grew out of a twentieth-century mind-set that couldn't have imagined the level of connectedness we have today. In plain English, platforms allow consumers and producers to connect with each other and exchange goods, services, and information. By doing this, these businesses create new markets. Think of how eBay connected buyers and sellers or how iOS and Android connected consumers and developers. Uber did the same thing for passengers and drivers, and Airbnb did it for travelers and homeowners. All of these platforms created new markets and were able to grow their networks and businesses to a size that was impossible until very recently.

The platform business model is now the key to some of the most successful companies on the planet. At the beginning of 2016, the two companies with the highest market capitalization in the United States were platform businesses: Apple and Google (now listed as Alphabet Inc.). Many people think of Apple as a hardware manufacturer and software developer, and it is. But the secret behind Apple's stratospheric rise in recent years is its transition from a product company to a platform company. Apple no longer just makes hardware and software. Through iOS, iTunes, and the App Store, it also offers platforms that connect buyers and sellers of every kind of digital good you can imagine. As we explain in more detail later in this chapter, this platform was what enabled Apple to replace Nokia at the top of the mobile-phone market.

Similarly, if you think of Google as just a software developer, you'll miss the secret to its success. All of Google's core services are platforms, including Google Search and Android. As Android showed, Google is singularly adept at using its core search platform to establish new platforms in other, seemingly unrelated markets. And its recent acquisitions suggest that the company's platform ambitions don't stop with mobile phones. It has already released platforms for wearable devices and health data as well as for the connected car, and it's using Nest, a recent acquisition best known for its Internet-connected thermostat, as a beachhead for entering the connected home. There are even rumors that Google will try to create an Uber competitor. At the same time, Google also is experimenting with an online-shopping and local-delivery platform that would go toe-to-toe with Amazon.

As the success of the companies mentioned above suggests, platforms have quickly become a dominant part of our economy—and they are here to stay. In fact, platform businesses will continue to grow in influence in the years and decades ahead.

Enabled by the technological innovations of the Industrial Revolution, Henry Ford's famous assembly line changed the shape of both industry and society. By revolutionizing how we work, how we do business, and how connect with each other, platforms will do the same.

This shift in the balance of power was part of what Elop was getting at when he identified the "war of ecosystems" that was under way. Platforms build ecosystems; products don't. In the late 2000s both Apple and Google were becoming platform businesses, but Nokia was not.

As a result, Nokia's value tanked and its once-vaunted handset division was sold at a fraction of its peak value. Meanwhile, Apple and Google transformed themselves and experienced runaway success, so much so that they have launched a spree of acquisitions as both companies have expanded into other markets like the connected home, connected healthcare, and the connected car. Competitors in those industries should be ready for what's coming. Because in today's world, platforms win.

CRISIS IN MOTION

Just as Nokia was having its burning platform moment, trouble was brewing in Waterloo, Canada. BlackBerry, then known as Research In Motion (RIM), was undergoing its own leadership crisis.

Faced with a plunging stock price and shrinking market share, RIM's shareholders were calling for founders and longtime co-CEOs Mike Lazaridis and Jim Balsillie to step down. It was a stunning development for the company that had until very recently dominated the mobile market; in 2009, *Fortune* named RIM the world's fastest-growing company.[5] But in just a few years, its fortunes had greatly declined. To placate their angry shareholders, Lazaridis and Balsillie agreed to establish a committee of independent directors to review the company's management structure. Soon after, the two founders stepped down from their positions. But new CEO Thorsten Heins, who was promoted from within the company's ranks, did not provide enough of an organizational transformation. RIM continued its decline under his watch, and he was fired in November 2013.

How did RIM's decline happen? In the mid-2000s, the BlackBerry was synonymous with the smartphone. But within a few years, the company had become a punch line. As with Nokia, it is easy to blame RIM's decline on bad management. Lazaridis and Balsillie certainly didn't help their own case, making a number of public statements over the years about their industry that in hindsight were obviously wrong. For example, Lazaridis famously called QWERTY keyboards "the most exciting mobile trend" at the very moment when RIM's new touchscreen competitors, the iPhone and Android, were starting to eat its lunch.[6]

Conventional narratives about the decline of the BlackBerry are often based on this explanation. Lazaridis and Balsillie stuck around too long. The company stopped innovating. It was too slow to market with innovative products. Its bureaucratic structure was overwrought. This mismanagement is what allowed the iPhone to deeply wound the Black-Berry and Android to put the nail in the coffin—or so the analysts say.

In truth, all of these factors contributed to BlackBerry's decline. But we would propose a different, simpler theory: RIM was thinking like a product company in a platform world. BlackBerry was focused on the keyboard, but that never really mattered. The key to controlling the market was the operating system and a network of third-party app developers.

"THOSE IN GLASS HOUSES . . ."

RIM essentially invented the smartphone category when it first released the BlackBerry in 1999. As future CEO Heins would later say, the company had a very clear idea what its core product was all about.[7] The BlackBerry was focused on battery life, ease of typing, security, and data compression. And on those counts it delivered. Its BlackBerry Messenger application also was a major hit, giving the phone its "killer app."

Over the next half decade, the BlackBerry became *the* leading smartphone, famous for its reliability and security as well as its iconic QWERTY keyboard. For professionals, the BlackBerry was a must-have, and in popular culture, the phone seemed to be everywhere. Presidents, prime ministers, CEOs, and celebrities across the globe swore by their BlackBerries. There was even a term invented for the growing ranks of BlackBerry addicts—"Crackberry"—which inspired its own website.

RIM had seemingly found the magic recipe for success. By the end of 2006, the BlackBerry had nearly 40 percent market share in the United States.

But then, on January 9, 2007, Apple announced the iPhone.

Despite the hype around Apple's new smartphone, RIM's leadership initially dismissed it as an inferior competitor. RIM co-CEOs saw the iPhone as an inferior product. And, by traditional criteria, it was. Compared to a BlackBerry, the iPhone had shorter battery life. It used too much data. It wasn't secure. And, according to Lazaridis, users wouldn't like the touch keyboard.

"Not everyone can type on a piece of glass," he said. "Every laptop and virtually every other phone has a tactile keyboard. I think our design gives us an advantage."[8]

RIM's leadership truly believed that its superior hardware would win out. In particular, the company was confident that the iPhone would never be able to compete with the BlackBerry in its core market of email-addicted professionals. After all, the BlackBerry was *the* phone for businesses, and companies would never switch to an insecure device with a battery that couldn't last a day on a single charge.

So RIM, confident that the iPhone was just a novelty, decided to stick with what worked for its established audience. In truth, RIM couldn't abandon its existing successful business model, and updating its aging operating system would be a long and difficult process, as Balsillie noted publicly. In a statement that could now win awards for prophetic irony, Balsillie told the *New York Times* in April 2011 that this type of change was "almost never done" because "this transition is where tech companies go to die."[9]

However, RIM's confident co-CEOs turned out to be disastrously wrong. The iPhone was an immediate hit. RIM was right on one count: Companies didn't switch from the BlackBerry. But individuals did. They wanted iPhones. And so, before long, businesses were forced to create "bring your own device" (BYOD) policies that allowed employees to pick their own phones. Not surprisingly, employees increasingly asked their companies for iPhones.

For RIM, the bad news didn't stop there. The iPhone's runaway success led to the entrance of another would-be competitor. On November 5, 2007, Google unveiled its Android operating system for smartphones. As Andy Rubin, Google's director of mobile platforms, said in his announcement, Android was "the first truly open and comprehensive platform for mobile devices."[10] The operating system would be open source and available to anyone (as opposed to Apple's closed universe), a value proposition that would help to drive Android's stratospheric growth in the years ahead. On the same day, to support Android, Google launched the Open Handset Alliance (OHA), a consortium of over thirty companies that included leading hardware manufacturers, such as Motorola, Samsung, and HTC, as well as a group of mobile operators that included Sprint, Nextel, and T-Mobile. Google championed Android and the OHA as the foundation for an "open ecosystem" that would increase innovation and establish the industry standard for mobile operating systems—and Google would be giving it all away for free.

The difference between Google and its competition was stark. Google's approach was nearly the opposite of RIM's. Research In Motion ran a tight ship based on maintaining a closed, proprietary system. Apple's initial strategy was similar, maintaining tight control of its hardware and software. In response, Google assembled an armada—a much more radical plan than simply introducing another direct competitor to an already crowded market.

Additionally, Android was built for developers, while the BlackBerry was built for businesses. Lazaridis and Balsillie thought their core customer was the head IT guy at a large company who would never allow employees to use devices like the iPhone, which didn't have the same level of security as the BlackBerry. But Google's approach, which Apple would soon mimic with the release of its App Store, was all about building a platform that attracted developers and consumers. This platform strategy turned out to be a far more powerful lure in the marketplace, and it is where RIM went wrong. It never understood that its core customers weren't businesses. Rather, they were lowly independent software developers who built apps for the new devices and salespeople at Staples who recommended phones to the masses.

RIM, like Nokia, misread the market. It was used to fighting its competition by the old criteria of features and specs. But the new entrants from Silicon Valley changed the stakes and made the smartphone industry into a platform business they could dominate. Thanks to Google, RIM wasn't competing with just another phone. It was competing with Android's entire ecosystem of producers, which was growing exponentially.

The trouble was immediate at RIM. The company missed its earnings estimate in the first and second quarters of 2008. But rather than change course, RIM's response was to double down on its old strategy. It released the BlackBerry Bold, which featured better specs and the company's usual QWERTY keyboard and trackball. Not surprisingly, the Bold failed to stem the tide. October 2008 was the first month where the iPhone outsold the BlackBerry, selling 6.9 million units to BlackBerry's 6.1 million.[11] And there was no looking back. Business at Apple was booming. "Apple just reported one of the best quarters in its history, with a spectacular performance by the iPhone," CEO Steve Jobs said at the time. Jobs, who rarely skipped a chance to take a shot at the competition, proudly announced, "We sold more phones than RIM."[12]

Still, at the time RIM continued to hold a big lead in the overall smartphone market. In the two years since the iPhone was released, RIM had sold 23 million smartphones compared to Apple's 13 million.[13] So Lazaridis and Balsillie had reason to stay the course. But then Jobs upped the ante by releasing the iPhone 3G and, more important, opening the App Store on July 10, 2008.

The impact of the App Store on the iPhone's success cannot be overstated. But a far less heralded innovation made the App Store possible. Historically, wireless carriers had dominated the mobile-phone industry, but the success of the iPod and iTunes gave Apple considerable leverage when it was negotiating with potential wireless carriers for the iPhone. In the end, AT&T wanted the iPhone badly enough that it was willing to cede some control to Apple in return for the right to be the iPhone's exclusive carrier. The most significant of these concessions was that Apple—and not AT&T—would sell apps for the iPhone through what would eventually become the App Store. Previously, people bought the applications for their phones through their wireless carriers, and the carriers tightly controlled access to these application stores. Apple's App Store was far more open by comparison. In addition, Apple took a 30 percent cut on all App Store purchases, a deal that was considerably more generous than what developers were used to getting from wireless carriers. This incentivized app developers to focus on the iPhone over the many other mobile operating systems.

For Apple, the App Store was another instant success, with over 10 million app downloads in the first weekend that it launched.[14] RIM thought it knew what its customers wanted from a phone, but the App Store didn't even try to guess. Instead, it let them decide. The App Store's success spawned Apple's now-ubiquitous catch phrase, "There's an app for that," along with a series of ads showing off its platform's seemingly boundless potential.

The iPhone offered unprecedented flexibility. No matter what you wanted to do, there truly *was* an app for it. This was the power of the platform—the iPhone harnessed a massive community of software producers to create more and higher-quality apps than ever before.

By the end of 2008, the App Store had seen 500 million downloads. The store featured more than 15,000 third-party applications, a number that has continued to grow at a staggering rate.[15] As of the end of 2015, the App Store had more than 1.5 million applications and an even more mind-boggling 100 billion downloads.

Not to be outdone, Google opened its App Store equivalent, the Android Market, in March 2009. Google's app marketplace, now called the Google Play Store, has also seen success, with over 1.8 million apps and 50 billion downloads by the end of 2015.[16]

Compelled to respond, RIM released the BlackBerry Storm at the end of 2008. The Storm, RIM's first touchscreen phone, was billed as the "iPhone killer." However, it turned out to be anything but. For instance, one of the Storm's supposedly key features was its SurePress touchscreen technology, which made the keyboard supposedly sound and feel like clicking a real button when it was pressed. Unfortunately, users accustomed to working on regular touchscreens didn't find that feature very compelling. As a result, the Storm fizzled, with middling sales and mediocre reviews.

RIM also introduced BlackBerry App World (now BlackBerry World) in April 2009. But by then it was the third option in a crowded development marketplace. To make matter worse, the BlackBerry's operating system was notoriously difficult to develop for. So the BlackBerry app ecosystem struggled to gain traction.

BlackBerry's failure to develop a successful platform for its products is something that we witnessed firsthand. Using a few credit cards, Alex founded Applico from his college dorm room in 2009 as a BlackBerry app development company. We chose to focus on BlackBerry apps because most developers didn't want to touch them, so we saw an opportunity to build a business. This approach enabled our company to develop partnerships with existing developers who were focused on competing in the more crowded iOS and Android markets, and it helped us gain a foothold in the software development business.

All of this turned out to be good news for Applico, but not so for RIM. The BlackBerry's unfriendliness to developers doomed RIM's efforts to overcome the significant leads held by Apple and Google. Meanwhile, to app developers, the choice of whether to develop for BlackBerry came down to simple math. For most, creating BlackBerry apps was just too complex and costly for the size of the market.

WHERE COMPANIES GO TO DIE

In November 2010, RIM co-CEO Jim Balsillie demonstrated that RIM *still* didn't understand how the mobile-phone industry had changed when he spoke at that year's Web 2.0 summit.

"There may be 300,000 apps for the iPhone and iPad, but the only app you really need is the browser. You don't need an app for the web," Balsillie said. "You don't need to go through some kind of SDK [software development kit]. You can use your web tools . . . and you can publish your apps to the BlackBerry without writing any native code."[17] The problem was that Balsillie's pitch wasn't new. In fact, it was eerily similar to the one Steve Jobs had given to developers three years earlier.

At Apple's Worldwide Developers Conference (WWDC) 2007, just before the launch of the original iPhone, Jobs announced support for Web apps as Apple's solution to the growing developer demand for a way to create applications for the iPhone. Developers were not enthused, with one popular tech blogger calling Jobs's presentation a "shit sandwich."[18] Jobs changed his tune a year later with the announcement of an iPhone SDK and the App Store, but needless to say, when Balsillie made the same Web-app pitch, developers were not impressed.

By the beginning of 2011, BlackBerry World had only about 25,000 apps, compared to 200,000 on the Android Market and more than 450,000 on the App Store. At the time, when we showed a friend who still owned a BlackBerry something our iPhone or Android phone could do, he would hold up his phone and joke, "There *might* be an app for that." Not exactly a compelling slogan.

RIM's failure led to its own epistolary debacle. An anonymous senior RIM executive issued an open letter in June 2011 challenging the company's leadership. At the time, the company was planning to launch its new QNX operating system in an effort to keep up with Apple and Google, but RIM was still fighting with the wrong tools.

The exec was blunt about where RIM lagged behind. "BlackBerry smartphone apps suck," he said, while comparing BlackBerry's SDK and development platform to "a rundown 1990s Ford Explorer." Driving the point home, he wrote, "technical superiority does not equal desire, and therefore sales."[19] Apple and Google understood this. RIM, like Nokia, did not. Both companies were still bringing a knife to a gunfight—or more accurately, a smartphone to a platform fight.

Despite RIM's additional failed efforts to promote its Playbook tablet and the BlackBerry 10, and the eventual renaming of the company Research In Motion as BlackBerry, the company never regained its swagger. By the end of 2011, the BlackBerry's smartphone market share had slipped to under 15 percent. Its stock had lost nearly 75 percent of its value.

In the end, Steve Jobs's diagnosis of RIM's challenge was characteristically prophetic. Speaking on a conference call with analysts in October 2010, Jobs had words of advice for his competitor. "They must move beyond their comfort area into the unfamiliar territory in trying to become a software platform company," Jobs said. "I think it's going to be a challenge for them to create a competitive platform and to convince developers to create apps for yet a third platform after iOS and Android. With 300,000 apps on Apple's App Store, RIM has a high mountain ahead of them to climb."[20] As Jobs knew, the war of platforms and eco-systems often was winner-take-all. Apple and Google built platforms and won. RIM and Nokia did not, so they lost.

Nokia eventually recognized its weakness, but it chose the wrong partner in Microsoft. RIM tried to catch up with a new operating sys-tem, but by then it was too late. RIM was still acting like a product company, and it wasn't able to make the transition that Jobs had sug-gested. In the end, Balsillie was right about one thing: This change is where many tech companies go to die. Unfortunately for him, the next company to try it was his own.

PLATFORM INNOVATION:
THE PURPOSE OF THIS BOOK

After Applico's early success as a BlackBerry developer, we quickly left BlackBerry apps behind and moved to developing for iOS and Android. Over the next few years, we became one of the most successful app de-velopers in the country. But as the mobile industry changed, Applico evolved along with it. While many of Applico's competitors were ac-quired or went out of business, our company thrived by becoming the world's first Platform Innovation company. Each day, we work with some of the world's leading businesses and hottest startups to build and grow innovative platforms. Our clients include Fortune 100 companies like Google, HP, Intel, Disney, DirecTV, Philips, and Lockheed Mar-tin, as well as startups backed by Google Ventures, Ray Kurzweil, and top venture capital firms. While we can't list some of our startup clients due to confidentiality, startups whose platforms we've helped create, in-cluding Glamsquad and Auctionata, have raised hundreds of millions of dollars and achieved nine-figure exits. And since our entire business is focused around platform business models, we've studied them in greater depth than anyone else has. This includes creating in-depth frameworks for how to build and grow platform businesses.

That's why we understand platforms better than anyone else today. We have lived at the heart of the technological changes of the last half decade and have had to put our money where our mouths are to succeed.

We will share with you the lessons we have learned from working on the front lines with some of today's most innovative businesses. We want to impart to you the insights that drove us to transform Applico from an app developer into a company focused entirely around platforms. The first part of this book, chapters 1–4, will explain what a platform business model is and share why platforms are reinventing the economy today. The rest of the book, chapters 5–8, will dig deeply into how platform business models work and share with you some of the same frameworks and insights we use to help our clients become modern monopolies.

If you're an entrepreneur, we will help you understand what makes today's most successful businesses tick and how you can replicate their success. If you own or work at a traditional business, we will help you see the disruption on the horizon before it's too late. After reading our book, you will have the tools to help your company avoid your own burning platform and thrive in this new era.

1

PLATFORMS ARE
EATING THE WORLD

When you truly see networks, it changes the way you plan and strategize. You move differently.

—Reid Hoffman, CEO and founder of LinkedIn

Software is eating the world. That was the message from former Netscape founder and renowned venture capitalist Marc Andreessen in an op-ed he penned for the *Wall Street Journal* on August 20, 2011. In it, Andreessen made the case that software companies were about to become a cornerstone of the world economy. "We are in the middle of a dramatic and broad technological and economic shift in which software companies are poised to take over large swathes of the economy," he wrote. In short, software was "eating" a larger piece of the economic pie every day.[1]

Andreessen was right—software companies were already playing an enormous role in our economy. But classifying all of these new businesses simply as software companies would be like classifying every business in the Industrial Revolution as a hardware company. It doesn't tell you much about what these companies do or how they work. And, more important, it doesn't tell you much about how software is changing the way businesses succeed and grow.

Plenty of companies improved their margins and streamlined their supply chains by using software and connecting their businesses to the Internet. Andreessen named a few in his op-ed, including FedEx and Walmart. But he also named a litany of companies he saw as leading the charge of the new software economy. The list included Apple, Facebook, Twitter, LinkedIn, Google, Microsoft, Foursquare, Skype, Amazon, Flickr, Square, and PayPal. Yet Andreessen missed the opportunity to explain how different these companies were from the old-line businesses he named. Yes, each of these companies was built around the Internet. But more important, they are all *platforms*. Rather than merely squeezing a little more efficiency out of an existing business, these companies operate on a completely different model that truly capitalizes on the Internet's potential. Even as Andreessen wrote his op-ed, many traditional businesses were already being overtaken by their platform competitors. In fact, Apple became the most valuable company in the United States, exactly one year to the day after Andreessen's op-ed appeared.

While software may have started this economic revolution, it's platforms that are eating the world. Collectively, platforms dominate the Internet and our economy. Net neutrality proponents rightly focus on Internet service providers like Comcast, who provide and maintain the underlying technological infrastructure, as the biggest threat to a free and open Internet. And at an architectural level, the Internet is still a fairly level playing field. Anyone can start and build a business online. But as a practical matter, the open Internet is a myth. The Internet as we know it today is almost entirely dominated by platforms. For example, Facebook is responsible for nearly 25 percent of total visits on the Web.[2] Google's sphere of influence is even larger. When the company's entire platform mysteriously went down for a few minutes in August 16, 2013, it took an estimated 40 percent of global Internet traffic with it.[3] Search and social networking aren't the only areas of dominance. Platforms now play a major role in just about every area of commerce imaginable. In the United States during 2015, every one of the top ten trafficked U.S. websites was a platform, as were twenty of the top twenty-five.[4]

The dominance of platform businesses isn't restricted to the United States, either. Platforms are a truly global phenomenon. In fact, they play an even more prominent role in developing countries than they do in the United States. The economies of many of these countries were growing rapidly at the same time that Internet access became widespread. And because these countries didn't have the existing commercial infrastructure that developed economies did, their industries have been molded around the Internet. China is a great example. Outside of state-sponsored industries, such as finance, construction, and oil production, many of the most valuable Chinese companies are platform businesses, like Tencent (owner of the WeChat and QQ messaging platforms) and Baidu (China's answer to Google).

China's Internet also is dominated by platforms. Platform businesses hold each of the top eight spots in Chinese Web traffic rankings. And these companies play an even more dominant role in China's economy than platforms do in the United States. Alibaba, which went public on the New York Stock Exchange in September 2014, controls 80 percent of China's e-commerce market through its Taobao and Tmall platforms.[5] Its Alipay platform is the largest payments platform in China. Alipay also allows users to put money into its Yu'e Bao Fund. At $94 billion as of January 2015, Yu'e Bao is one of the largest money market funds in the world.[6]

Whether you're building a platform business or not, you can't succeed in this economic environment without understanding how platforms work. Want to market your business direct to consumers online? Now you can, but you better rank well on Google. Want to get people to read your content? Well, your content better share well on Facebook. Want your app to get lots of downloads? You better rank well in the App Store (or get featured). Want to sell merchandise online? You're probably going to do some selling through eBay and Amazon. Do you sell handmade goods? Then you're probably on Etsy. If you're in China, then you're almost certainly on Alibaba's Taobao and Tmall, and you probably process payments through Alipay or Tencent's Tenpay. The list could go on and on. The Internet *is* allowing an unprecedented democratization of economic freedom. Anyone can start a business and succeed online. But it isn't perfectly open. Someone has to orchestrate all of this economic activity. As a result, the Internet and our economy are dominated and run by platforms. They organize commerce and information and shape the world as we know it. If you want to understand how the Internet works today and how the economy will work for years to come, you need to start with understanding platforms.

IPO, PLEASE DON'T GO

If you were one of the millions of U.S. TV viewers who tuned into the Super Bowl on January 30, 2000, you were treated to an unusual sight.

No, we don't mean the St. Louis Rams picking up the franchise's lone Super Bowl victory. As always, the real show was the commercials. That year, they didn't disappoint. During one commercial break, an ad opened with the sad face of a dog as it watched its owner pull out of the garage to drive to the pet store. Then a crooning sock puppet came into view. It belted out an off-key version of Chicago's "If You Leave Me Now" for some 30 seconds, imploring you to buy pet food online. Why? So that you wouldn't have to leave your heartbroken pet at home when you go to the store.

The company, of course, was Pets.com, then at the pinnacle of its reign atop the dot-com pyramid. Following the football game, the *USA Today*'s Ad Meter ranked the sock puppet's Super Bowl commercial number 1 in its list of Super Bowl ads. Pets.com was the most memorable company from what would come to be known as the dot-com Super Bowl. The commercial, which cost $1.2 million, was a runaway success, as was the company's mascot. The sock puppet even made an appearance on ABC's *Good Morning America* and gave a long interview on *Live! with Regis & Kathie Lee*. And just months earlier, it had appeared as a thirty-six-foot float in the Macy's Thanksgiving Day Parade.

Founded in August 1998, Pets.com launched with an aggressive marketing plan and the goal of getting big fast. This was the M.O. of many Internet companies at the time, for which scale *was* the business model. Pets.com went public less than two years later on February 9, 2000, shortly after its Super Bowl commercial aired. Its public offering raised $82.5 million and the stock began trading on the NASDAQ at $11 a share under the symbol IPETs.

Despite its mascot's enormous popularity, Pets.com had a problem: Its business model was broken. Its assumption, one shared by many prominent venture capitalists who invested in Pets.com and similar companies, was that if the company got big enough fast enough, it would be able to turn a profit. First-mover advantage was everything, or so the theory went. This strategy gained currency as the then-vague idea of "network effects" caught on, popularized by a 1994 academic paper published by W. Brian Arthur.[7] Arthur's view of network effects suggested that whomever got big first would always win.

But for Pets.com, the numbers just didn't work. For one, at the time the market for people wanting to shop online only for pet food and related products was smaller than the company had estimated. Pets.com also invested in a large warehouse to store its products, meaning the company had high fixed costs. Even worse, Pets.com had to price low to compete with existing pet stores, even though many of these stores already had razor-thin margins on pet food. As a result, the company actually *lost* money on most of the sales it made. This combination of high costs and nonexistent margins was ultimately unsustainable. And it didn't take long for the company and its investors to figure this out.

On November 6, 2000, Pets.com declared bankruptcy—only nine months after its initial public offering. The company had burned through $300 million in investor money in less than two years. The day of the announcement, the company's stock had declined from its opening price of $11 a share down to just $0.19. It's now a perennial on "biggest investment bombs in history" lists.[8]

But while Pets.com was undergoing its meteoric rise and equally rapid fall, another dot-com company was launching its own, very different story. On Labor Day weekend in 1995, a computer programmer sat down to write code for his new website. Called Auction Web, the website was designed to be a digital marketplace where people could buy and sell anything over the Internet. The creator wanted to create a "perfect market" that could be used by everyone.

Apparently, other people wanted the same thing. A lot of other people. The company grew quickly. In 1996, Auction Web hosted 250,000 auctions. In January 1997 alone, the site hosted 2 million. Its revenue grew by 1,200 percent in its first year, from $350,000 to $4.3 million. That September, the company changed its name to eBay.[9]

Shortly thereafter, the site's founder, Pierre Omidyar, decided it was time to look for a CEO. He hired Meg Whitman in March 1998.

She took the company public six months later, on September 21. The stock debuted at $18 per share and rose as high as $53.50 in its first day. Omidyar became a billionaire overnight.

A VERY SHORT HISTORY
OF BUSINESS MODELS

For many, Pets.com is the classic example of dot-com-era excess. Those people are not wrong. The company spent millions on marketing without having a sustainable business model or a proven target market. Since many investors at the time weren't sure how to price Internet companies, lots of startups received valuations and investments that seem laughable in hindsight.

Most of these failed companies made the same mistake. Like Pets .com, they took an old business model and slapped the Internet on top. The promised benefits of network effects and lower costs never materialized. But when the bubble popped and many dot-com darlings crashed and burned, eBay was still profitable and going strong. Over time, eBay grew into a company with a market cap of more than $66 billion. It was one of the few success stories of the dot-com era. And that's no accident. The difference is the business model.

Companies like Pets.com made the mistake of choosing a linear business model in the age of the platform.

What is a linear business model? It's the model that has dominated in various forms since the Industrial Revolution, when new technologies like steam power and railways gave rise to the large, vertically integrated organization. All of the titans of industry from the early twentieth century were linear businesses, including Standard Oil, General Motors (GM), U.S. Steel, General Electric, Walmart, Toyota, ExxonMobil, and on and on.

Each of these companies created a product or service and sold it to a customer. In all of these examples, value flowed linearly and in one direction through the company's supply chain. Hence the term "linear business." In this supply chain, to the left of the company was cost and to the right was revenue. Linear companies created value in the form of goods or services and then sold them to someone downstream in the

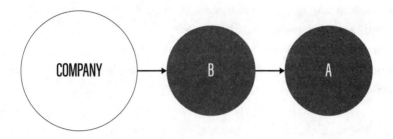

Figure 1.1.   An example of how value flows in a linear business: The company creates a product and sells it to group B (a distributor), who then sells it to group A (the customer).

supply chain. (See Figure 1.1.) Historically, there were two main types of linear businesses.

The first is your classic product company. Think Lenovo in consumer electronics. Lenovo makes and sells physical things. It builds physical assets, such as factories and distribution centers, in order to make its products and get them to consumers. Almost all manufacturing has worked in this linear fashion over the last century. So have distributors and resellers, which are companies that build or lease physical assets or technologies in order to distribute and sell physical products. Examples include resellers like Walmart, Best Buy, and Target.

Many of today's software companies also fit in this group, including most software-as-a-service (SaaS) companies. Even though their products are digital, these companies still function linearly, with value flowing from the companies to their customers. The only difference is that software companies benefit from the low marginal cost of digital distribution.

The second type of linear business model is a services company. Examples range from Oracle to JP Morgan to Jiffy Lube. These companies hire employees who provide services to customers. Generally, services companies fall in one of two camps. The first kind makes and sells physical services. Your car mechanic and plumber both fall into this category. The second builds human capital or intangible assets, like intellectual property, and uses those assets to sell specialized services. This type of services company includes everyone from tax attorneys to investment bankers or management consultants.

These models dominated the twentieth century for a good reason: They can be very efficient. Premised on top-down planning and hierarchical organizational models, these businesses create value and distribute it efficiently to their target customers. They achieved this efficiency via the supply chain, a highly structured system for organizing activities and resources that moved a product or service from the company to the customer.

The supply chain is also linear, consisting of processes that are repeated over and over again to create value. Products move from the manufacturer downstream to distributors and then to customers. For example, a car manufacturer like GM buys parts from its suppliers, which in turn may have bought parts or raw materials from another supplier. GM then takes these parts and creates a finished product, in this case a car. From there, GM sells the car to a dealership, which finally sells the product to a consumer. In this chain, value flows linearly through the supplier to the manufacturer and eventually all the way down to the end consumer of the product. At each step in the supply chain, someone adds value to the product or service and then moves it on to the next link in the chain. Information in this process has a similarly linear flow, with top-down forecasting typically filtering down to eventual production. These linear flows of value and information are what make up a company's supply chain. (See Figure 1.2.)

The supply chain was one of the major areas of competitive advantage throughout the twentieth century. The efficiency of a company's supply chain could make or break a business. That's why many of the great business innovations of the last century had to do with improving supply chains and making them more efficient.

Henry Ford's assembly line is a classic example. By adopting a continuously moving assembly line, Ford cut the typical production time of a car from 12 hours to 90 minutes.[10] This supply-chain innovation had an enormous impact on the industry. Because it enabled the mass production of cars for the first time, it drove down the price of a good that was once available only to the very wealthy and made it widely available to average consumers. More recently, Toyota's lean manufacturing

PHYSICAL PRODUCT FLOW

INFORMATION FLOW

Figure 1.2.   The linear flow of value and information in a supply chain.

process disrupted the automobile industry with its just-in-time production and focus on eliminating waste. By creating a more adaptable and efficient supply chain, Toyota was able to leapfrog previous industry leaders, like Ford and GM.

However, the efficiencies of the supply chain approach come at a cost. Linear businesses require large factories or investments in human capital and elaborate distributions channels in order to create products and move them to market.

THE PERFECT STORE

In the twenty-first century, the supply chain is no longer the central aggregator of business value. Now networks connect businesses and individuals, enabling them to exchange value among themselves. This is the essence of how platform business models work.

Linear businesses focus on creating value internally and selling that value downstream to customers. Value flows from left to right, from the manufacturer down to the customer (as in Figure 1.2). In this world, the resources a business owns and controls internally are its most valuable assets. But value exchange in a network is multidirectional—it flows

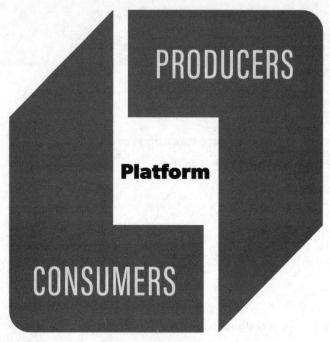

Figure 1.3.   The platform business model.

both left *and* right. (See Figure 1.3.) As a result, platform businesses work very differently from companies that run on traditional supply chains.

Networks are the new aggregator of business value. As we explore in more detail in chapter 2, when the world becomes more connected, what a company owns matters less than the resources it can connect to. Today's most valuable businesses are those that can build and orchestrate large networks, not those that can aggregate and centralize large amounts of resources under one roof. In the old model, scale was a result of investing in and growing a business's internal resources. But in a networked world, scale comes from cultivating an external network built on top of your business.

The dot-com bust was a crash course in this difference. The Internet was supposed to make dealing with customers cheaper and easier. But for businesses that didn't grasp the larger transformation afoot, this

Platforms now have a symbol to call their own. In Figure 1.3, the interlocked chevrons represent a platform's network. The connection between the consumers and producers is what creates the shape outlining the platform at the center. Just like a platform, this internal shape is defined by network that surrounds it. Without its consumers and producers, the platform at the center wouldn't exist.

You will see this symbol throughout the book whenever we take an in-depth look at a particular platform business. We will use it to introduce the platform and show you who its consumers and producers are so that you have more context as we discuss the company. As in this example, the left chevron will always represent the platform's consumers while the right chevron will represent its producers, with the platform in the center. While some platforms have multiple transaction types, we will always show the platform's original core transaction (a concept we'll get to shortly).

dream never became a reality. These businesses got big fast and then failed even more quickly. The old models simply couldn't support the scale that the Internet made possible. Unlike Pets.com, eBay didn't have any expensive warehouses or high shipping costs to deal with. That's because eBay didn't sell products from a centralized source. Omidyar wanted to make a different kind of business. "I wanted to do something different," he said. "To give the individual the power to be a producer as well as a consumer."[11] Rather than taking possession of goods itself, eBay connected individuals to other individuals so that anyone could buy from or sell to anyone else. Rather than building inventory and resources, eBay provided the digital infrastructure for this marketplace to exist and helped build the community around it. The idea was to create the "perfect market." The company would make money by charging a nominal fee to the sellers.

At the time, most people didn't "get" eBay. What was the big deal about a digital flea market selling knickknacks and other bizarre items? What did eBay even *do*, since it didn't really own anything other than a website? But that novelty was the whole point. As eBay's former president and first employee, Jeffrey Skoll, said, eBay was "a lot bigger than just a simple website."[12] Its marketplace was a boon for both buyers and sellers. For the first time, anyone could buy unique and hard-to-find goods from all over the world while also accessing an unprecedented level of information about them. One of the first events that made eBay famous was the Beanie Babies craze, yet these collectible items were only one small slice of what you could find there. At the height of their popularity, Beanie Babies were still only about 6 percent of eBay's total sales volume. Other major categories included computer-related items and antiques as well as coins, stamps, baseball cards, and all kinds of other collectibles.

For sellers, eBay was a gold mine. It allowed them access to customers from all over the world. Businesses that had been parochial and geographically limited could suddenly have global distribution at almost no cost. An antiques seller in Nebraska could find a buyer in New York or even London. You could sell anywhere you could ship. eBay's Omiydar knew his idea was a hit when he sold a broken laser pointer for $14. He followed up with the buyer to make sure the man knew what he was getting. It turned out he was a collector of broken laser pointers. As a famous *New Yorker* cartoon at the time read "On the Internet, nobody knows you're a dog." It didn't matter where you lived or what you looked like; all that mattered is that you had something to sell and someone was willing to buy it.

Some old-school sellers struggled, as the arbitrage they'd been enjoying from buying goods in one country and selling them in another dried up. But countless more were able to turn hobbies or side businesses into a living. According to the company, millions of people worldwide make a living selling on eBay.[13] As an economist would say, this outcome was socially efficient. eBay became a kind of stock market for everyday goods. By efficiently moving goods from sellers to those who value them most, eBay created enormous value for all of its users. Objects that might have languished in obscurity could now find their way to someone for

eBay—product marketplace platform

whom they would be a prized possession. eBay indeed became the "perfect store" that Omiydar set out to make.

Most tellingly, eBay was profitable from its first month all the way through to its successful IPO in 1998, and it enjoyed gross profit margins of more than 80 percent.[14] Both of these stats were almost unheard of in the spendthrift days of the dot-com era, which is why eBay left e-commerce competitors like Pets.com in the dust. More than almost any other company at the time, eBay fully harnessed the potential of the Internet.

eBay was, of course, a platform—the common thread among virtually all of the biggest Internet successes from the dot-com era, including Amazon, Angie's List, Monster.com, Microsoft, Shutterfly, and Yahoo. As would become even clearer in the years ahead, the platform was *the* definitive business model of the Internet.

THE PLATFORM:
A DEFINITION AND SOME EXAMPLES

Platforms have only continued to grow in influence and economic impact since eBay's meteoric rise. eBay's success wasn't a fluke. It was a harbinger of the next wave of economic innovation and change.

What exactly is a platform? A platform is a business model that facilitates the exchange of value between two or more user groups, a consumer and a producer (see Figure 1.3). In order to make these exchanges happen, platforms harness and create large, scalable networks of users and resources that can be accessed on demand. Platforms create communities and markets that allow users to interact and transact.

The list of platforms has swelled in recent years, as processing power and Internet access have become more widespread. Each of these businesses simply connects producers and consumers to each other and allows them to exchange value. Think about what Uber does for taxis, what Airbnb does for vacation rentals, what Apple does for apps, and what YouTube does for videos. None of these companies is a traditional, linear business. They are all platforms.

Like eBay, these businesses don't directly create and control inventory via a supply chain the way linear businesses do. Platforms don't, to

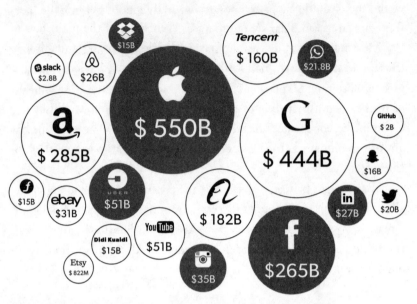

Figure 1.4.   Platform companies and recent valuations, January 2016.

use a common phrase, own the means of production—instead, they *create* the means of *connection.*

The two most successful platforms to date are Google and Apple, whose rise to the top in mobile we discussed in the prologue. But they are only the tip of the iceberg. The number of platforms at the top of our economy is growing fast. In 2015, the top three members of *Forbes*'s list of most valuable brands were platform companies, as were eleven of the top twenty.[15] All of the companies at the heart of the social media boom were also platforms, including Facebook, Twitter, and LinkedIn. In fact, most of today's biggest IPOs and acquisitions are platforms, as are almost all of the most successful startups. The list includes Apple, Google, Microsoft, Facebook, Twitter, Amazon, eBay, Instagram, You-Tube, Twitch, Snapchat, WhatsApp, Waze, Uber, Lyft, Handy, Airbnb, Pinterest, Square, Social Finance, Kickstarter, and more. (See Figure 1.4 for examples of platform startups and their latest valuations.) The growth of platforms isn't isolated to the United States either; platform companies such as Alibaba, Tencent, Baidu, and Rakuten have taken over China and much of Asia.

However, not all of these businesses will be around ten years from now. In the wake of the dot-com crash, even some of the mainstays of the modern economy, like Amazon, nearly failed. The size and durability of the opportunity for any one of these businesses depends on many factors, including the state of its industry and how quickly technology evolves in that sector. But when these companies do fail, it will be because they have been replaced by newer and better platforms. This has already been the case for years. When Apple became the most valuable company in the United States, guess who it dethroned? Microsoft, whose Windows platform was supplanted by Apple's iOS when the mobile Internet outgrew its desktop predecessor.

As always, the cast of characters will change as technology evolves. But platforms are here to stay.

Why? Because platform business models enable companies to expand at a pace unprecedented in human history. When a linear business gains a new customer, it adds only one new relationship—one buyer of products or services. When a platform adds a new user, that person doesn't add just a single relationship but rather a potential relationship with all of the platform's users. In other words, platforms grow exponentially rather than linearly. As a result, platform business models are far more cost-effective and higher scale than the old, linear models they are replacing.

NOT JUST A TOOL

To be clear, when we use the word "platform," we're talking about a *business model*. Think of a business model as a way to visualize and understand how a company creates value for customers and how money then flows back into a company. It also includes a company's cost structures and key activities, as well as where a company needs other companies or partners to implement its business. When we talk about platform business models in this book, this is what we mean: a holistic description of the way a company creates, delivers, and captures value, not just a piece of technology.

But confusingly, in the tech world, "platform" has recently become a buzzword. Just about every startup these days claims that it's building a platform. As a tactic to get funding or attention, this trick seems to meet with relative success. But very few of these businesses actually understand the model they are trying to emulate.

For example, countless companies have popped up claiming to be the new "Uber for X," by which they simply mean taking a product or service and making it available "on demand." (The definition of on demand also is quite pliable—very few "on-demand" companies offer services that will arrive within minutes the way Uber does.) These businesses may get the on-demand part to work, but without the essential business model, they won't be able to grow as quickly or successfully as Uber has. In effect, they're making the same mistake that dot-com busts like Pets.com did by locking themselves into the cost structures and resource-heavy approach of a linear business.

Not surprisingly, almost none of these Uber imitators has made it very far. And the ones from the on-demand economy that have—including not just Uber and Airbnb, but also fast risers like Instacart and Handy—are all platforms.

In most other cases, businesses that use the term "platform" incorrectly are using it to refer to a piece of technology rather than a business model. Here are a few examples:

- **Computing platform:** Underlying computer system on which application programs can run (e.g., Symbian)
- **Product platforms:** Common design, formula, or versatile product, upon which a family or line of products is built (e.g., a car chassis used across many different models)
- **Industry platform:** Products, services or technologies that serve as foundations upon which complementary products, services, or technologies can be built (e.g., Intel)
- **Platform as a service:** Category of cloud computing services that provides computing platform and solution stack as an online service (e.g., Amazon Web Services)

Each of these instances of the word "platform" refers to an underlying product or technology that allows modular components to be built on top of it. Platform business models often use this kind of modular modification, which is why the terms frequently are conflated.

Finally, probably the most common misuse of the term "platform" is when it's used to describe an integrated suite of software products. This is especially common among SaaS companies, which love to claim they have a complete "platform" for X. In such cases, the word "platform" really is just being used as a marketing term. As with all of the preceding examples, these SaaS companies are still linear businesses. They're products, not networks, and as such, they don't have the cost structure and underlying economics that make platform business models so successful today. We explore this distinction further in chapter 3, but for now, just remember: *platform ≠ technology.*

OPEN SOURCE,
NO LONGER A PAIN IN THE ASS

Linus Torvalds is a nerd hero. If you're at all involved with technology, you've heard of him. And if you haven't heard of him, your daily life has almost certainly been influenced by his work. Torvalds is best known as the creator of Linux, the open-source operating system that is the dominant operating system for Web servers and supercomputers. It's the operating system of choice for everything from cloud computing and IBM's Watson supercomputer to the New York Stock Exchange and your TiVo. Google's Android operating system is even adapted from a part of Linux.

Torvalds's creation is responsible for tens of billions of dollars in economic value. But he gives it all away for nothing. Linux is free, both free as in speech and free as in beer. You can use it without paying a dime (which is why it's so popular with big companies running lots of servers, such as IBM and Google), and you can modify it and redistribute it as you wish. Others have gotten rich off building Linux "distributions," essentially premium versions of Linux with extra features. Red Hat, a company that as of January 2016 had a market cap of over $14.5 billion, built its business by selling its Linux distribution and related services.[16] Most big platform companies today use Linux somewhere in their technology stack. Facebook is one major example—its original front-end servers were built using a LAMP configuration, in which the *L* stands for Linux. So while Linux may not make money directly, it's still big business. However, Linux wasn't Torvalds's only major contribution to the software development community.

Back in Linux's early years in the late 1990s, Torvalds struggled to incorporate all of the open-source community contributions to the operating system. In software development, the process of managing all of these different contributions and figuring out how to incorporate them into one system is called "version control." At the time, most version control systems worked off a central repository of all the code and files that were part of a project. When a developer made changes, they would be directly changing the code in the central repository of that system.

This type of version-control system set Torvalds up as the centralized gatekeeper of Linux. If someone fixed a bug, they would have to email him the changes and hope he read the email. Needless to say, as Linux increased in popularity and its development community grew, this wasn't a great way to manage the project. Large amounts of code containing potential improvements would never see the light of day. So in 2005, Torvalds did exactly what you'd expect a leader of the open-source community to do: He developed a piece of open-source software to solve his problem. The program he created was called Git. (Yes, it was named after the British slang for "unpleasant person.") It created a more decentralized version-control system that significantly streamlined the process of creating and submitting changes to Linux.

Using Git, you could download and tinker with your own version of Linux or any other project available and submit those changes to the project's owner or anyone else with the push of a button. Git made it easy for project managers to manage any new contributions or changes to a repository without having to worry about overwriting that project.

This system made it significantly easier to manage a large open-source project like Linux. But that wasn't its only benefit. Git also allowed you to easily create what's called a fork of Linux, essentially a separate version based off the original program's code. Using Git, you could easily create and maintain your own version of Linux, which is exactly what Red Hat and other companies did. You also could use Git to track changes in any kind of software project, which made it very useful for large companies managing big software projects or for developers who worked together over long distances.

However, Git did have one problem: It was a pain in the ass to use. It was a command-line tool (think MS-DOS) that required you to know a series of complex commands. For some programmers this might not be a huge barrier, but it limits the program's usability and appeal, especially for a generation raised on graphical user interfaces (GUIs). Additionally, while the distributed nature of Git (there's no central server) made it easy to work on your own projects, it still wasn't easy to discover projects you might want to work on. That's why by 2007, Git was still largely unknown outside of the Linux community.

Enter GitHub. It's Facebook for nerds, Wikipedia for programmers, or Twitter for code, depending on whom you ask. In reality, it's a little bit of all three: It's a combination of a social networking platform for programmers and a Wiki-like content platform that lets you edit files and track who changes what. Anyone can comment on your code or add to it and improve it. You can follow particular pieces of code, organized in "repositories," and get notified when any changes are made, in the same way you might follow someone on Twitter and get notified when they tweet.

Github—content platform

GitHub also made Git easier to use by adding a GUI, which is the way most people are used to interacting with a computer (through graphical items like windows, icons, and menus). And GitHub added many additional bells and whistles, such as messaging and other social features that make it easy to coordinate and maintain projects at a distance. As GitHub cofounder and former CEO Tom Preston-Warner says, Git made collaboration possible, but it didn't make it easy. GitHub significantly simplified the process. The company's first slogan was "Git hosting: No longer a pain in the ass."[17]

By default, projects on GitHub are public, meaning anyone can view your code and copy it. Companies that host large public GitHub repositories include Google, Facebook, Twitter, and Microsoft. Applico also has a number of open-source projects on its GitHub page.[18] GitHub has become *the* place to host and find open-source code. But you can also pay to create private code repositories with gated access. The fee can range anywhere from a few dollars a month for individual developers to hundreds of thousands of dollars a year for huge companies managing multiple large, complex projects. With private repositories, major companies also use GitHub to manage some of their internal projects.

Today, projects on GitHub are written in almost every programming language out there. A handful of nonsoftware projects also use GitHub, including books, in order to manage collaborative projects. One book, called *ProGit*, which aptly enough is about Git, has been translated into a number of other languages on GitHub. There's also a repository that has the entire French legal code dating back to Napoleon. If French law changes, you can track the alterations on GitHub.

PLATFORMS AND PAIN-IN-THE-ASS COSTS

In 2012, GitHub raised $100 million in funding from venture capital firm Andreessen Horowitz, then the largest investment in the firm's history. Three years later, GitHub raised an additional $250 million at a valuation of $2 billion.[19] Today GitHub has about 9 million registered users and is visited each month by about 20 million unregistered users.[20] What is it that makes GitHub so valuable and attractive to users?

First, as we described earlier, the platform makes it easier for developers to manage software projects. And if you're looking for other projects, GitHub makes it easy to find them. In economic terms, GitHub significantly reduces transaction costs for people collaborating on software projects. The term "transaction cost," coined by the economist Ronald Coase, refers to any cost incurred in making an exchange. Another term for it is a "coordination cost." In essence, a transaction or coordination cost is the cost of participating in an interaction. Transaction costs arise because markets and communities in the real world aren't like the perfect markets you learn about in Economics 101. For one thing, they lack the perfect information that these perfect-market models assume to exist. Transaction costs arise out of this and other imperfections or deviations from the ideal market scenario.

Transaction costs aren't limited to monetary costs alone. In fact, they can be entirely nonmonetary in nature. For example, even if you don't spend any money on GitHub, you would incur costs in terms of time, attention, and effort when you look for a specific project. The same applies when you "push" an update to an existing project or manage updates from other contributors. A nonmonetary cost is associated with each of these actions.

Transaction costs fall broadly into three main categories. First is search and information costs, which include the cost of finding a particular good. On GitHub, this would be the time and effort it takes to find a particular project. The second category of transaction costs is bargaining costs—the costs associated with making an agreement with another party. For example, when you push an update to a code repository on GitHub, the project manager has to decide whether to accept your changes or not. GitHub has standardized this process and has significantly reduced the time and effort it takes to manage code changes. Finally, the last category is enforcement costs—the costs associated with making sure everyone involved in an exchange of value acts appropriately. Like most platforms, GitHub monitors its community to weed out bad actors and to encourage good behavior.

GitHub significantly reduces all of these costs, providing a major value to users. As the company itself put it, GitHub removes the pain-in-the-ass cost of Git hosting. You can think of transaction costs broadly as pain-in-the-ass costs. All platforms reduce these costs in some way. For example, Google reduces the pain-in-the-ass cost of finding a website. Uber reduces the pain-in-the-ass cost of hailing a cab. Airbnb reduces the pain-in-the-ass cost of finding and booking a short-term rental. Facebook reduces the pain-in-the-ass cost of staying up-to-date and interacting with friends. PayPal reduces the pain-in-the-ass costs of sending digital payments. And so on.

In fact, if you're building a platform and trying to figure out what your core value proposition is, here's a good formula. Figure out what the main activity is you're trying to change and then put it in to this sentence: "X, no longer a pain the ass." You should probably tweak the messaging a bit (after all, GitHub didn't keep its original slogan for long), but this will get you started.

THERE'S AN APP FOR THAT

In addition to reducing transaction costs, another key part of GitHub's value proposition is that it provides an environment to manage and edit code. The platform is designed to encourage users to *create*, not just to transact. This is the second key aspect of what platforms do: They provide infrastructure that enables innovation in complementary products or services. On GitHub, these complements are code repositories. The more repositories that users create, the more valuable GitHub will be as a platform. So GitHub provides the basic infrastructure that makes it easy for software developers to host and manage open-source projects, including version tracking, editing, and communication. These tools are designed to help people create and edit code, because ultimately GitHub's fundamental value lies in how it facilitates the creation and editing of code repositories.

Apple's iOS platform is very similar. Just as GitHub needs to attract developers who will create repositories, iOS has to attract developers

Apple's iOS—development platform

who will make apps. To encourage this, Apple provides a cheap software development kit and many developer application program interfaces (APIs) that allow developers to tap into the core functionality provided by the device. A big part of the value that iOS provides to developers is that it allows them to easily access and combine the phone's many capabilities to create new experiences, from Candy Crush to Snapchat to Tinder. The developers of all of these apps used iOS as a platform to create something new. Remember Apple's old slogan: "There's an app for that." Apple knew early on that a large part of the value of the iPhone wasn't just in the phone itself but rather in the new experiences that it enabled developers to build for users. The GitHub equivalent would be "There's a repository for that." If you're looking for any kind of software project, chances are you'll find it on GitHub.

In a nutshell, all platforms do two things: reduce transaction costs and enable complementary innovation. Combined, these two value propositions can have a profound impact. They can disrupt existing industries, as Uber with taxis, or they can create entirely new ones, as Apple did with mobile apps. Before GitHub, there was no market for paid Git hosting. By building a platform, GitHub created that market.

THE ANATOMY OF A PLATFORM

A platform ultimately enables this value creation by facilitating transactions. While a linear business creates value by manufacturing products or services, platforms create value by building connections and "manufacturing" transactions. If you think of General Motors as a manufacturer that produces cars, then in a simplistic sense, Uber is a manufacturer that produces transactions between drivers and riders. Uber doesn't actually deliver the ride, but it facilitates the connection and exchange of value between drivers and passengers. The transaction that is at the heart of the platform is called the *core transaction* (see Figure 1.5). The core transaction is the platform's "factory"—the way it manufactures value for its users. It is the process that turns potential connections into transactions. Getting the core transaction right is the most important piece of platform design, as the platform will need its users to repeat this process over and over to generate and exchange value.

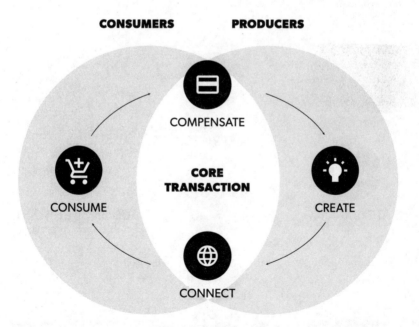

Figure 1.5   The core transaction.

However, although a platform enables the core transaction, it doesn't directly control its users' behaviors. The challenge is a unique one: how to get potentially millions of people to behave the way you want them to. First you must attract users to join, then you aid them by matching them together, providing the technology to facilitate the transaction and establishing the rules that govern the network in order to build trust and maintain quality. These are the four core functions of a platform (see Figure 1.6):

1. Audience building
2. Matchmaking
3. Providing core tools and services
4. Setting rules and standards

If a platform handles these four functions well enough, it will be able to facilitate its core transaction (and, hopefully, a lot of it). We take a look at the core transaction in much more detail in chapter 5, and, in chapter

Figure 1.6   The four functions of a platform.

6, we dive into the four core functions. For now, this summary is enough for you to understand how platforms build and maintain their networks and then turn those potential connections into transactions.

EXCHANGE VERSUS MAKER: THE BASIC PLATFORM SPLIT

Compare a platform like Alibaba to one like iOS, and you'll notice that their core values are different. Some platforms are more focused on reducing transaction costs, like Alibaba, while others actually provide the underlying infrastructure that enables their users to create. Examples of the latter include development platforms like iOS and Android as well as content platforms like Medium (a platform where anyone can post articles or blog posts) and YouTube. GitHub is another example. Each of these platforms provides the tools and infrastructure for producers to create software, written content, videos, or code, respectively. Contrast these platforms with platforms like Alibaba, Uber, and Airbnb, which are much more focused on facilitating a direct exchange, and you'll see the difference.

The key difference is between platforms that provide value primarily by optimizing exchanges directly between a consumer and a producer and platforms that generate value by enabling producers to create complementary products and broadcast or distribute them to a large audience. We call this first category *exchange platforms*. And we call the second category *maker platforms*. Although both categories share the same underlying platform business model, there are very basic differences in how exchange and maker platforms function.

MATCHING INTENTION: 1:1 VERSUS 1:MANY

One of the key differences has to do with a concept called matching intention. The matching intention is the maximum number of units of an item that a producer can exchange at a given time.

Let's look at a product marketplace, such as eBay. A seller is trying to sell one item. Once that auction ends, the item can't then be bought by another buyer. A seller may have multiple copies of an item (e.g., they might be selling five copies of the same T-shirt), but the matching intention for *each unit* of inventory still is 1. For an Uber driver, the matching intention is similar: He wants to give a ride to one passenger at a given time. He might be able to give multiple rides over the course of an hour. But when he is looking for a rider at a given moment, he is looking to be matched with one passenger or group of passengers. Once a single passenger books a driver, that driver is no longer available on the platform at that time. So the matching intention for a driver is 1.

The value of a producer's matching intention can vary depending on the type of interaction involved. But for exchange platforms, that matching intention always has a limited, discrete value. Expressed as a ratio, a producer's matching intention on an exchange platform is 1:1 or at most 1:few. A three-way Skype conversation is an example where the matching intention of the person making a call would be 1:2. However, the matching intention of a person making a Skype call still is limited by the number of people he or she feasibly can communicate with at a given time.

Maker platforms don't have this same limitation. The matching intention for a producer on a maker platform is, theoretically, infinite. Any number of people can consume the same YouTube video, download and use the same app, or read the same article on Medium. The producer publishes an app or a piece of content and broadcasts it to an audience. In these cases, the matching intention is $1:\infty$, or at least 1:Many. Contrast a live stream on Twitch (a content platform where you can watch other users play video games) with the Skype example. The person broadcasting to an audience on Twitch doesn't communicate in a 1:1 manner with every person watching the stream. Rather the person is broadcasting out to a large group of people who are viewing the stream.

Another way to think about this dynamic is that exchange platforms have limited inventory—only a certain number of people can consume the platform's available inventory at a given time—while maker platforms do not. For example, as noted previously, any number of people can consume the same piece of content on YouTube at the same time. Assuming YouTube's servers could handle it, every person on Earth could watch the same YouTube video at the same time. But only so many people can take a specific ride using Uber or rent out a single apartment at a given time on Airbnb.

PLATFORM TYPES

Within exchange and maker, we've broken down platforms into distinct types (see Figure 1.7). Each type has a core transaction built around a particular type of value being exchanged. Platforms within each type often operate very similarly—even across industries, a trend that became obvious when we were building in our database of platform companies.[21]

The nine platform types are listed next along with the type of value that defines their core transaction:

Exchange:
1. *Services marketplace:* a service
2. *Product marketplace:* a physical product
3. *Payments platform:* monetary payment
4. *Investment platform:* an investment (i.e., money exchanged for a financial instrument, be it equity or a loan, etc.)
5. *Social networking platform:* a double-opt-in (friending) mode of social interaction

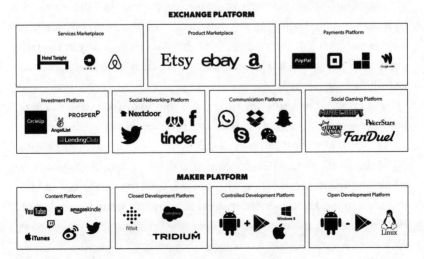

Figure 1.7. Platform types, with examples for each type.

6. *Communication platform:* 1:1 direct social communication (e.g., messaging)
7. *Social gaming platform:* a gaming interaction involving multiple users, either competing or cooperating

Maker:

1. *Content platform:* a piece of content (a text article, photo, video, etc.)
2. *Development platform:* a software program

Each platform type exists along a commoditization spectrum that defines how it should be built and designed. The level of commoditization is a reflection of the amount of complexity inherent in the core transaction. To put it another way, you can think of commoditization as a reflection of the transaction costs incurred by consumers and producers to complete a transaction. More commoditized platforms operate in industries with naturally lower transaction costs.

For example, within services marketplaces, platforms vary depending on how commoditized the service offering is. What makes a service "commoditized" in this context? Simply put, the service has only a limited number of relevant characteristics that consumers care about. Therefore, the complexity of the core transaction should be low. Consider a job like fixing a toilet or delivering a meal. In both cases, the consumer simply wants the job done well and in a timely manner. As long as the platform can guarantee a certain level of quality at the right price, all that matters to the consumer is that there is someone available to fulfill a request.

As a result, platforms that offer these commoditized services should focus on matching consumers with available producers as seamlessly as possible. And the best ones do exactly that. For example, Uber's automatic matching and even its controversial surge pricing are all about facilitating the most transactions. Compare Uber's commoditized services to a noncommoditized service, such as renting an apartment on Airbnb. In this example, many additional characteristics matter to consumers, such as where the apartment is located, how large it is, what different amenities it offers, if the host will be there, if it's a full apartment or just a couch, if the apartment allows dogs, or smokers, and on and on. Here, there are simply too many relevant characteristics for automatic matching to work well. That's why Airbnb focuses on facilitating easy search and discovery for its users rather than automatic matching. For noncommoditized services platforms, that's the right way to go.

Matching a platform's design to its type is essential to its success. Platforms that don't get this right tend to get left behind by the competition. Within services marketplaces, TaskRabbit is a good example. TaskRabbit was one of the first big services marketplaces in the United States. It allows you to hire a "tasker" to do odd jobs, such as cleaning or home repair. However, TaskRabbit acts like a noncommoditized services platform in a commoditized industry. It initially built itself around an auction model, in which users would post tasks to the platform and contractors would seek out and bid on tasks they wanted to complete. If this sounds like an onerous process, you're right. It was. The company eventually realized it had gotten the core transaction wrong, and in July 2014, it replaced its auction model with more simple and transparent pricing. In the new model, a consumer is offered a choice of three different producers with a listing of their hourly prices and experience levels and is able to order services on demand, rather than having to wait for bids to come in. This change was a step in the right direction for TaskRabbit. But the update didn't get everything right, as it still lacked control over pricing. Commoditized services marketplaces should be responsible for setting prices to ensure its users receive the optimal price. If you look at other commoditized services platforms, such as Handy, Lyft, and Glamsquad (an Applico client), consistent and transparent pricing is a core part of their ability to deliver seamless matching. Because TaskRabbit did a poor job at facilitating its core transaction, the platform has been surpassed by upstart competitors, such as Handy. Not surprisingly, Handy puts much more structure around pricing and requesting services than TaskRabbit has. The result is a better user experience and a more seamless transaction model that has helped propel the platform to its position as the leading marketplace for in-home services in the United States.

To be clear, that a platform's core transaction is more commoditized doesn't mean that its business is at a disadvantage. (What we're talking about is different from the *business* becoming commoditized, which would be a concern.) Instead, understanding a platform's commoditization level shapes how its business model should be designed in order to optimize its core transaction. The hard part is determining how commoditized or noncommoditized a platform really is in the context of its industry and platform type. It seems obvious in retrospect for Handy to set the prices for its commoditized services, but plenty of competitors like TaskRabbit still get it wrong.

For other platform types, commoditization level plays a similar role. For example, the level of commoditization in investment platforms also dictates whether you're able to set the price and how you handle the matchmaking experience. More commoditized investment platforms like Lending Club (peer-to-peer lending) are able to set prices algorithmically. In fact, Lending Club started by letting lenders set their own interest rates before moving to setting rates itself. The platform rightly saw the opportunity to remove unnecessary friction from the transaction. However, other investment platforms such as AngelList (startup investing) require a more noncommoditized approach.

The same framework also fits social networks. On more commoditized platforms, such as Tinder, users only have a simple profile with photos and a short text description. The platform also matches you automatically with other nearby users. However, on less commoditized platforms like LinkedIn, users have much more in-depth profiles. There, connection is more about search and discovery than automatic matching. Commoditization plays a similar role in content platforms. More commoditized content platforms, such as Twitter or Instagram, typically have a large overlap between their consumers and producers, as producing content is quick and easy. However, less commoditized content platforms like YouTube have strongly differentiated producer and consumer user groups. These platforms tend to follow more of a power-law dynamic, where a small percentage of their users produce the vast majority of their content, and need to be designed accordingly.

PLATFORM DESIGN

The exchange versus maker split in platforms is not just a semantic difference. Although all platforms are focused on connecting consumers and producers, which category your platform falls under fundamentally alters the core value you will try to deliver. As we show in chapters 5 and 6, this choice translates into very different core transaction paradigms and dictates how you design your platform.

The core transaction is just one example of why the exchange/maker distinction matters for platform design. Your platform's category also influences how you design and deliver on its four core functions. For example, each core transaction paradigm requires radically different matchmaking strategies or rules and standards. Which category your platform falls under also influences your audience-building strategy. Exchange platforms, such as Uber and Alibaba, need to focus on building liquid marketplaces that have sufficient overlap of supply and demand. Maker platforms, such as Android and YouTube, are more focused on organically building "stars" who, because of their high matching intention, can act as powerful nodes in these networks. Many maker platforms want existing celebrities to join and bring their fans with them; however, when the platform can create its *own* celebrities due to the network effects within its network, you know it's reached critical mass. YouTube's PewDiePie, Instagram's Dan Bilzerian, and Vine's Nash Grier are all examples of normal producers who rose to fame by building huge organic followings on their respective platforms.

As you can see, understanding whether a platform is a maker or exchange platform has a big impact on how you design its core transaction and four functions. Figuring out which platform type a business fits into should always be one of the first steps in designing a platform.

2

HAYEK VERSUS THE MACHINE, OR WHY EVERYTHING YOU THINK YOU KNOW ABOUT THE TWENTIETH CENTURY IS WRONG

Every now and then a trigger has to be pulled. Or not pulled. It's hard to know which in your pajamas.

—James Bond, *Skyfall*

Technology is a funny thing. On one hand, the advances in the past twenty years or so are miraculous—few people a decade ago could ever have imagined what we do routinely today. Yet technology is also strangely easy to take for granted. Many people view a computer or a smartphone as simply a means to an end, as tools that allow them to do the things they want to do—call a loved one, play Candy Crush, order a pizza. But describing technology as just a tool belies the impact it has on the world we live in. Technology is never just a means to an end. It shapes our reality—and our economy—in profound ways.

Consider the creation of the steam locomotive in 1804. This new mode of transportation enabled people and products to travel farther and faster than ever before. It expanded the definition of "local," and the world suddenly appeared smaller. The automobile continued this trend. Each of these new technologies gave rise to new kinds of communities and social structures. And, of course, new kinds of businesses.

This sort of societal change happens all the time. As the saying goes, change is the only constant. But it's easy to miss the role that technology plays in this process, partly because technological change is gradual. We think of and talk about the Industrial Revolution as a singular event, but in reality, it spanned decades. It wasn't really a revolution but a gradual evolution with revolutionary implications.

It often takes a long time for these implications to play out. In the early stages of the Industrial Revolution, the economy was powered by steam and water. As a result, factories had to be built near rivers. The mass availability of electricity did away with that need. But nevertheless, decades later, companies still built their factories next to water. The full potential of electricity had not yet sunk in.[1]

The idea that technology is simply a tool is especially common in the world of business strategy. Although the body of thought behind how and why businesses succeed has changed some over the years, for much of the twentieth century, the core ideas behind business strategy were treated as immutable laws.

Today many organizations carry on with business as usual, even though the world has changed around them. And it is changing, quickly. Take the way that the Internet and smartphones have changed the relationship between companies and consumers. Consumers today have more power than ever before. For example, the rise of "showrooming"— the practice of visiting a store to examine a product before buying it online at a lower price—allows consumers to identify better, cheaper products. Consumers can also recommend products to thousands of "friends" and publicly express their dissatisfaction when something goes wrong. As a result, consumers add value to the purchasing process in ways that were impossible before. Consumers are no longer limited to the products and information that local stores put in front of them. Information no longer flows in one direction. This simple change has huge ramifications for how businesses operate. And technology is the primary reason this change has occurred. Whenever a "tool" wields that kind of power, it warrants special attention.

We live in a unique period in history when a new business model—the platform—is rapidly eclipsing the old. The full potential of the Internet era has not yet sunk in. We're just starting to scratch the surface. After all, only in the last decade or so have platforms have started to take over our economy.

Many people believe that platform businesses are only tech companies, but this is a myth. The business model itself is not new nor, historically, has it been limited to the tech industry. In truth, platforms are as old as human society itself. Examples include a Roman marketplace, an ancient auction house, a bazaar, or, more recently, the Yellow Pages, classified ads, or a shopping mall. However, the reason that platforms matter today has everything to do with technology.

To be clear, we're not advocating technological determinism, which assumes that technology determines the development of social structures, economic activities, and cultural values. This idea is the essence of Marshall McLuhan's famous phrase, "The medium is the message"—that the technology used to achieve something has more meaning than what you do with it. Although this notion certainly carries a grain of truth, it ignores the role that human actions and desires play in shaping how technologies develop and are used. Technology is not just a neutral tool. While technology shapes our perception of reality, we in turn influence its development.

The rise of platforms invites us to carefully examine the intricate interaction among technology, the economy, and society, particularly how assumptions about technology underpin some of what are usually thought of as basic laws of economics and business strategy. What we've seen over the last half century is that changes in technology—and just as important, changes in how people use technology—can fundamentally alter the basic tenets of economic reality.

In this chapter, we examine the technological changes and impacts that have led to the shift from the linear businesses of the twentieth century to the platform businesses of today. Along the way, we challenge fundamental ideas about how our economic system works and invalidate some of the allegedly immutable laws of twentieth-century business strategy.

CENTRAL PLANNING AND
THE MAN IN THE PAJAMAS

Our story starts with an age-old problem: What's the best way to organize an economy? Should economies be centrally organized, or decentralized and orchestrated through market activity? In many ways, the twentieth century was a giant war over this question. Governments and businesses alike fought to validate their view of economic and social reality. The collapse of the Soviet Union in the 1990s appeared to deliver the decisive blow in the argument, but for a long time the answer was not so clear.

The core argument in favor of markets was always that they were more efficient than central planning. In the United States, we take that as gospel, but is it actually true? Under the right conditions, markets can be perfectly efficient in organizing economic activity. However, economists also had to make a number of major assumptions for the argument to work. Chief among these assumptions was the idea of "perfect information." This notion assumed that every participant had complete knowledge of all relevant factors in the market at all times. Producers understood all of the same production techniques as other producers, and both buyers and sellers knew all the prices being charged by other sellers. There could be no "information asymmetries" wherein one individual possessed market information that others did not.

If this idea doesn't sound remotely realistic, that's because it isn't. In the real economy, imperfect information is the norm. More surprisingly, it turns out that under the conditions of perfect information, there is no difference between the efficiency of markets and of central planning. In fact, in 1975, Soviet professor Leonid Kantorovich was awarded the Nobel Prize in Economic Sciences in part because his work, *The Best Use of Resources,* proved the functional equivalency of perfect markets and perfect planning.[2] In an economy with perfect information, a central planner can allocate resources just as efficiently as a market can. Intuitively, this makes sense: If you know everything about an economy, you can figure out how to allocate resources efficiently. An omniscient central planner would just have to take into account all existing information and determine how to allocate resources in the best way possible—exactly what many economists argued that only markets could do.

Kantorovich wasn't the first person to notice something wrong with the idea of perfect information. Austrian economist Friedrich Hayek posed this same question decades earlier. Hayek was most influential in the mid-twentieth century, but he remains popular today with many political libertarians and conservatives. He is best known for his 1944 book *The Road to Serfdom,* which warned of the dangers of government control of economic decision making through central planning.

As you would expect, Hayek was a strong proponent of free markets. However, he also recognized that the conventional argument for "perfect markets" was flawed. In his essay titled "The Meaning of Competition," he lampooned the idea of perfect competition that was championed by most economists at the time. He understood that the argument for perfect markets was essentially a tautology. As Hayek put it, the problem was that the idea of perfect competition "confines itself to defining conditions in which its conclusions are already implicitly contained and which may conceivably exist but of which it does not tell us how they can ever be brought about."[3] In other words, the theory of perfect competition assumed the conditions under which markets would be perfectly efficient and then used this framework to prove that markets were perfectly efficient and worked better than central planning. Hayek knew that this was not a very convincing or logical argument. It left unanswered the question of how to best coordinate economic activity in the real world. In his essay "The Use of Knowledge in Society," Hayek emphasized this fallacy. "This view disregards the fact that the method by which such knowledge can be made as widely available as possible is precisely the problem to which we have to find an answer," he said.[4] The perfect markets argument assumes away the very problem it alleges that markets can solve.

However, in this same essay, Hayek made an alternative case for why markets are a better economic system than central planning. In reality, it was impossible for a centralized authority to coordinate the activities of a decentralized economy effectively. The problem, as Hayek identified it, was precisely that we don't live in a world of perfect information. An individual couldn't collect all the information necessary to effectively coordinate an economy. Hayek explained, "The knowledge of the circumstances of which we must make use never exists in concentrated or integrated form but solely as the dispersed bits of incomplete and frequently contradictory knowledge which all the separate individuals possess." Rather than operating under perfect information, we live in a world of highly fragmented and decentralized information. This concept is called "local knowledge," or, as Hayek puts it, "the knowledge of the particular circumstances of time and place."

For Hayek, the implications of this insight were profound. Since a central planner couldn't have knowledge of the particular circumstances at a given time and place, "the central planner will have to find some way or other in which the decisions depending on them can be left to the 'man on the spot.'" Additionally, even if one person could know all of the necessary information to coordinate an economy, he wouldn't be able to process all of it to direct an economy because circumstances constantly change. In essence, what was needed was some form of decentralization so that local knowledge could be "promptly used" in economic activity.

This philosophy is shared by superspy James Bond. In the film *Sky-fall*, when Bond first meets Q (Bond's technology guru), Q jokes that he could "do more damage on my laptop sitting in my pajamas before my first cup of Earl Grey than you can do in a year in the field."

"Oh, so why do you need me?" Bond asks. "Every now and then a trigger has to be pulled," Q says. "Or not pulled. It's hard to know which in your pajamas," Bond says. Bond, the consummate individualist, knows that you need knowledge of the time and circumstances on the ground in order to make a good decision.[5] For both Bond and Hayek, central planning didn't work because you couldn't get accurate and timely information if you're not actually in the field.

So, Hayek argued that centralized coordination of large-scale economic activity wasn't practical. What was needed instead was a mechanism for decentralization that could effectively aggregate and react to all of the local knowledge that each individual in the economy possessed. Hayek's solution was the price system, which he described as "a kind of machinery for registering change." This machine "enables individual producers to watch merely the movement of a few pointers" in order to understand what is happening in the economy at large. In essence, Hayek suggested that the price system was a primitive calculator of information and that prices were a metric, or key performance indicator, that producers could use to understand economic activity, even far away from where they lived. Since every individual acted on his own local knowledge, the market would aggregate all of this information and adjust to it in real time. This argument actually accounted for reality: Information isn't perfect and freely available. Markets solve this problem by exposing the sum total of everyone's private information in the form of prices.

History has largely proved Hayek right. Centralized coordination eventually lost out to decentralized markets, and market economies based on the price system have since become the default of most modern societies.

THE THEORY OF THE FIRM

Though Hayek was able to make a persuasive case for markets over central planning, there are other important objections to the efficient markets theory to consider. This brings us to another influential economist, Ronald Coase, whom we encountered briefly in chapter 1. Coase recognized another big hole in the concept of efficient markets. If markets could coordinate economic activity efficiently, why did companies exist? What value did companies add if markets themselves were perfectly efficient? This was a problem for pro-market economists, because, as Coase noted in his Nobel Prize acceptance speech, "most resources in a modern economic system are employed within firms, with how these resources are used dependent on administrative decisions and not directly on the operation of a market. Consequently, the efficiency of the economic system depends to a very considerable extent on how these organizations conduct their affairs, particularly, of course, the modern corporation."[6] If companies played such a big role in our economy, why couldn't the dominant economic theory explain their existence? Coase resolved this dilemma by suggesting that there were actually costs to participating in market activity, which he called *transaction costs*. We covered this concept briefly in chapter 1.

Coase's theory suggested that it was too complicated or costly for a company to search for and find the right worker at the right time for any given task or to search for supplies and negotiate prices. Each of these costs of completing a transaction in the marketplace was a kind of transaction cost. If there were no such costs, any individual could contract any good he or she needed from the market immediately. There would be no reason to form traditional organizations to produce goods or services. Using this idea of transaction costs, Coase created a "theory of the firm" that described how transaction costs shaped the boundaries of organizations in market economies. According to this theory, organizations came into existence in order to minimize the transaction costs and informational deficiencies that resulted from coordinating economic activity through decentralized market exchanges. A company would internalize activities that it could organize more efficiently than the market and externalize those it could not. A company was, in effect, a small, centrally planned economy that operated within a larger market system (see Figure 2.1).

Coase's theory had important implications for business strategy. It suggested that as an organization grew, it would be able to minimize information and transaction costs by internalizing actions it could handle more efficiently and by externalizing those it could not. This dynamic led to tremendous economies of scale, a concept made famous by Boston Consulting Group founder Bruce Henderson. Henderson took an idea from military strategy—concentrating mass to overwhelm the enemy—and applied it to business. His observation was fairly simple: The more of something you produce, the better you get at it. But Henderson's idea of economies of scale and the "experience curve" enabled managers to conceptualize the relationship between size and efficiency (see Figure 2.2).

According to Henderson, a company's efficiency per unit produced increased by as much as 25 percent every time it doubled its production volume.[7] Henderson applied this logic as a way for businesses to achieve a competitive advantage. His concept suggests that the company with

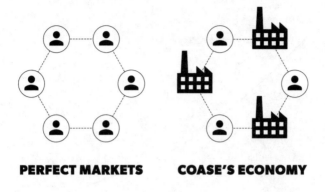

PERFECT MARKETS   COASE'S ECONOMY

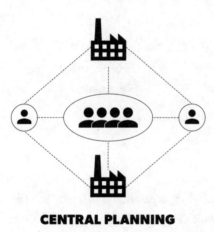

CENTRAL PLANNING

Figure 2.1.   The three different theories for how economic activity is organized.

the largest market share would also have a big cost advantage compared to its competitors.

A few years later, Harvard professor Michael Porter added another important idea to Henderson's observations—the notion of the value chain. Porter basically agreed with Henderson's ideas, but he qualified them by noting that businesses were not monolithic entities. An organization was made up of multiple components, and it was advantaged in some areas and disadvantaged in others. The combination of these

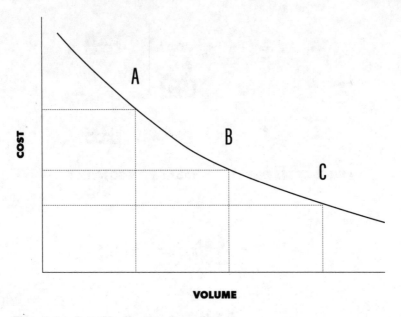

Figure 2.2.   Bruce Henderson's scale curves.

different components created what Porter called the value chain. Introduced in his book *Competitive Advantage*, the value chain was a tool intended to be used for competitive analysis. The value chain enabled a business to systematically break its organization down into a set of core activities and to understand how they fit together into one coherent system that took inputs and created more valuable outputs (see Figure 2.3). This idea fit nicely into Coase's theory of how businesses work. The purpose of value chain analysis was to design the optimal combination of links in the value chain so that you got the most value for the least cost. Ultimately, transaction costs were what held together the entire value chain. Businesses combined the different activities in the value chain because the transaction costs of handling them externally meant that it was more efficient to integrate these activities internally. By creating the optimal combination of activities, you would create a coherent system— a value chain—that would allow you to create and sustain a competitive advantage against your industry rivals.

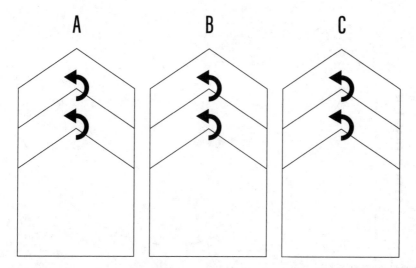

Figure 2.3. Value chains defined how a business was organized.

Porter's value chain and Henderson's economies of scale have been the core tenets of business strategy for the last thirty years. Together, they became the strategic foundation of the large, vertically integrated organizations of the late twentieth century.

However, even in these large organizations, Hayek's local knowledge problem reared its head. The coordination problems related to local knowledge that Hayek described are a primary reason why Henderson's economies-of-scale graph is U-shaped (see Figure 2.4). Because of rising coordination costs, once an organization reaches a certain size and continues to grow, it starts to experience *diseconomies* of scale, where information and transactions costs rise rather than decline when the business produces more.

As a result, most large companies facing competitive pressures (i.e., those that were not granted government-sponsored monopolies) cap out at a size well below total control of their respective markets. Beyond a certain point, growth costs more than it's worth. This fact fits neatly into Hayek's concept of why markets were effective. On a small scale, you could coordinate economic activity effectively. But if a company

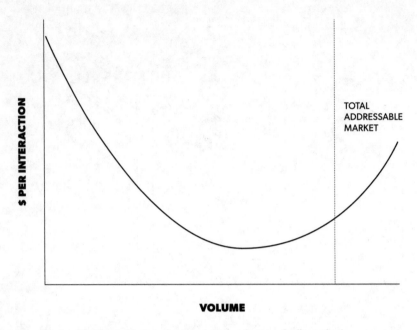

Figure 2.4.   The classic U-shaped economies-of-scale curve for linear businesses.

grew too big, it wouldn't be able to collect and react to all the information it needed to make accurate decisions. As a result, costs would rise, and the company would not be able to expand further in a competitive market. The U-shaped economy-of-scale curve that businesses experienced was a demonstration in microcosm of why central planning didn't work for an entire economy.

Much like Henderson's economies of scale, Porter's value chain was also limited and defined by transaction costs. As Coase's theory suggested, the goal of minimizing transaction costs was what held each component of the value chain together and made them into one coherent whole. If transaction costs changed significantly, value chains could break up or be reorganized in radically different ways.

For a long time, the large organizations built on the bedrock of twentieth-century business strategy ruled the economy. Large, linear companies like GM, Ford, ExxonMobil, U.S. Steel, and General Electric sat at the top of the Fortune 500 for decades. However, as new technologies emerged, the bonds that held together the traditional organization started to fray.

THE COMPUTER AND THE MARKET

In 1965, the little-known Polish economist Oskar Lange penned a rejoinder to Hayek's essay. Titled "The Computer and the Market," Lange's essay suggested that while Hayek's problem may have held true in 1945, times had changed. The advent of computers meant that there now were devices that could quickly solve complex, simultaneous equations. Remember that Hayek himself had imagined the price system as a kind of decentralized calculating mechanism that replaced the impossible work of a central planner. Lange used a similar metaphor, calling markets "a computing device of the pre-electronic age."[8] But Lange didn't mean it as a compliment. He saw the market mechanism as "old fashioned" and claimed that Hayek's price system could be replaced in its coordinating capacity by a series of calculations run on a computer.

The computer had "the undoubted advantage of much greater speed," Lange said, while the market was "cumbersome and slow working." If Lange was correct, the trade-off between centralization and decentralization that Hayek suggested was not an immutable economic law. Rather, it was an artifact of the state of technology. As technology changed, so too would the shape of the economy. Lange's essay suggested that computers could lead to the creation of a much more centralized, but no less efficient, economy.

There were two remaining challenges to Lange's thesis in 1965. Most obviously, the primitive computers of the day weren't up to the task. They usually took up entire rooms and were able to perform only limited calculations. However, in the same year that Lange wrote his essay, Gordon Moore, one of the founders of Intel, formulated what has come to be known as Moore's Law: that the computing power per chip size would double approximately every eighteen months. Put another way, every eighteen months, you can get same the processing power that your computer had before but from a chip that was half the size. For the last fifty years, this "law" has held remarkably constant.

Over time, these incremental but constant improvements in processing power had a big impact on computing technology. Exponential growth starts slow, but as it compounds, it starts to increase rapidly. Over a few decades, computer chips became very small and very fast compared to their predecessors in 1965. These chips also got much cheaper to produce. To put this in context, your smartphone today is about 1 million times cheaper, 1,000 times more powerful, and about 100,000 times smaller than the one computer at MIT in 1965.

Why were these changes so important? Information processing and storage costs are important parts of transaction costs. When these costs decline, the potential size of organizations increases. Intuitively this makes sense. With faster information processing and more information storage, you *can* manage a larger amount of information. But when processing costs fall, transaction costs also decline. Remember that transaction costs were the glue that held together a company's value chain and determined what activities an organization internalized. As processing speeds radically increased and transaction costs fell at the end of the twentieth century, some value chains began to break up. With lower transaction costs, there was less need for vertically integrated organizations. Smaller, more agile competitors started to outmaneuver their larger, older rivals. A smaller competitor could attack one piece of an incumbent company's value chain and disintermediate it or provide the same quality offering at a much lower price (see Figure 2.5).

This is exactly what happened to the encyclopedia industry. In the days of large, leather-bound books, the encyclopedia business was dependent on large sales forces in order to sell its product. A big chunk of the price of an encyclopedia went to paying the salesman's commission. When personal computers became widespread, new technologies made it much easier and cheaper to hold all of that information in one place. You no longer needed a large sales force to go door-to-door lugging around and selling large sets of books. You could just send your customer a CD in the mail. This meant that Microsoft could sell its *Encyclopedia Encarta* on CD-ROM for $50, while Britannica's big set of books cost between $1,500 and $2,000.[9] Britannica eventually introduced its own CD-ROM, but its large sales force, once an essential asset and a core part of the company's value chain, was suddenly a massive liability.

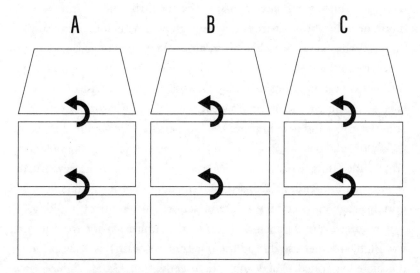

Figure 2.5. As transaction costs fell, value chains broke up, and smaller competitors could attack one component of your business.

DOT-COM DISAPPOINTMENT

However, even with all of this processing power, computers alone still couldn't deliver on Lange's promise of a more centralized economy. Although computers had the potential to solve one of the problems Hayek posed—storing and processing large amounts of information simultaneously—they still didn't address the issue of how to gather and transmit all the necessary data in the first place.

The Internet started to change all of this. In the 1990s, the Internet and the World Wide Web ushered in a new era of connectivity and networked, decentralized communication. This was a fundamental shift from the informational paradigm of the rest of the twentieth century, which was dominated by centralized, hierarchical, and top-down institutions with similarly centralized, hierarchical, and top-down flows of information. The decentralized Web gave individuals unprecedented access to information and ushered in a new wave of businesses inspired by what seemed like limitless opportunity.

However, this new informational paradigm required a new business model, which many entrepreneurs and investors didn't understand at the time. The business environment after the arrival of the Internet was fundamentally different from anything that came before. Yet many of these new businesses simply used traditional business models and set up a website as the distribution mechanism, with the expectation that the Internet would make business models work at scale because of "network effects"—even though it wasn't clear what those network effects were or how they would help improve the business's cost structure. Pets.com, which we talked about in chapter 1, is the most infamous example. But others, including Kozmo.com, Webvan, and Garden.com, eventually went under for similar reasons. The tremendous crash that followed the initial rush of enthusiasm was a testament to this failure of thinking.

Timing also was an issue. Although enthusiasm for the Internet was high, Internet use during the dot-com era wasn't as widespread as the hype suggested. Many took these early, high-profile failures as a sign that the Internet was overhyped and destined to fall short of its world-changing expectations. For example, in 1998 Nobel Prize winner and *New York Times* columnist Paul Krugman famously suggested that the Internet would have no bigger impact on the economy than the fax machine did. "The growth of the Internet will slow drastically," Krugman wrote, as it "becomes apparent [that] most people have nothing to say to each other! By 2005 or so, it will become clear that the Internet's impact on the economy has been no greater than the fax machine's."[10] Given the spectacular economic crash that followed Krugman's prediction, his skepticism at the time was warranted. But despite the sudden and dispiriting end to the dot-com euphoria, the seeds had been planted for an economic and social revolution.

THE CONNECTED REVOLUTION

It was only a few years later that the Internet really made the leap into mainstream culture. By the mid-2000s, the Internet was ubiquitous, as omnipresent as air (or advertising). The spread of broadband from the workplace to the home got the ball rolling, but the real driving force behind this shift was the mobile Internet.

Mobile phones put the Internet directly into everyone's pocket. Back in the dot-com era, the Internet consisted of only about 30 million people connecting via a dial-up modem. Despite its huge impact, the Web of the 1990s was small and slow relative to the Internet of today. Mobile tech acted like rocket fuel for the Internet. In just five years, the number of people with Internet access exploded from millions to billions (see Figure 2.6). In the United States, the Internet went from a novelty to a fully integrated part of everyday life.

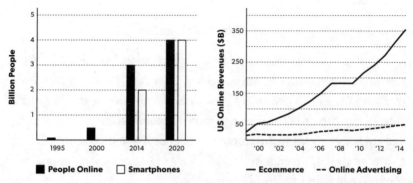

Figure 2.6. Market size is for real this time. Source: *Andreessen Horowitz, "Mobile: It Changes Everything," http://a16z.com/2015/06/19/mobile-it-changes-everything/.*

As the mobile Internet exploded in the late 2000s, four key changes flipped the world of business strategy on its head: the democratization of processing power, the declining cost of communication, the rise of ubiquitous connectivity and sensors, and growing returns to scale on data analysis. Together, these four changes have created a Connected Revolution, an economic and social transformation wherein the dynamics that drove the organizations of the twentieth century no longer apply. Let's take a closer look at why.

The Democratization of Processing Power and Computer Storage

Advances in technology have made computing a commodity. Computers are now cheap and widely available. Members of previous generations could have counted the number of computing devices they owned on one hand, but by the time today's kids reach adulthood, they won't be able to keep track. From factories to toys or food, computers are fast becoming essential to almost everything we do, make, and consume. Technological progress has even led to what's being called the Race to Zero in cloud computing, where technological advances and increasing competition are driving down cloud processing and storage prices at an unprecedented rate.

The Declining Cost of Communication

The cost of transmitting and storing information has tumbled. As a result, barriers to entry in business have fallen, and the one-way broadcast paradigm exhibited by TV and radio companies of the Industrial Revolution has given way to networked communication. Discovering and transmitting information became frictionless and cheap. Activities that typically happened within the bounds of one organization can now take place in a decentralized manner through networks.

The Rise of Ubiquitous Connectivity and Sensors

With the advent of the smartphone, almost everyone now carries over half a dozen tiny sensors wherever they go. The result has been the ability to collect more and more kinds of data than ever before. Most of that new data is collected by these sensors and transmitted by connected technology. The ease with which this information is collected and distributed would have been unthinkable only a decade ago. And the rate at which we're producing this new data is only increasing each year.

The Growing Returns to Scale on Data Analysis

With breakthroughs in data analytics—so-called big data—this new wealth of information has led to huge returns to scale on data analysis. It's now possible to make sense of and act on previously unimaginably large amounts of data, all in real time.

* * *

Let's take a second to unpack why all of these changes have been so important. First, thanks to the rapid advances in computer processing, individuals now have access to processing power and technologies that were once available only to large organizations. The result has been widespread access to cheap, easy-to-use professional tools. This change has empowered individuals to become producers of value on a whole new scale.

Second, the declining cost of communication has made it much easier to share all of that value with other people. The falling cost and rising speed of data transmission have meant that individuals who have never met before can now cost-effectively communicate with each other well enough to accomplish complex tasks. They also can develop the trust needed to collaborate or facilitate exchanges.

Contrary to what Krugman suggested during the dot-com era, it turned out that, given the opportunity, people wanted to talk to each other—a lot. Connected technology quickly migrated from the enterprise to the home, and the Internet became a central part of how we experience the world and communicate with each other. At the same time, growth exploded for YouTube, Facebook, and Twitter, which led to the rise of social media and user-generated content. *TIME* magazine even named "You" the person of the year in 2006, a reference to all of the people who created content on social networking and content platforms online. Mobile tech accelerated these trends even further by moving the Internet from an isolated activity that happened at home to something you brought with you and engaged with everywhere.

Suddenly, there was a big shift in where value was made in our economy. Businesses were no longer the sole source of value creation. *Consumers* were creating value and sharing it with each other. The quintessential example of this change was Wikipedia. Remember the earlier example of how increases in processing power enabled the shift from the hard-copy *Encyclopaedia Britannica* to the cheaper, more efficient CD-ROMs? This change happened because as processing power increased and storage prices declined, the costs of distribution greatly decreased. The Internet continued this trend, making distribution even cheaper. However, Wikipedia took this shift one step further. Rather than just lowering the cost of distribution, Wikipedia also substituted user-generated content for professionally created content and radically changed the cost of production. It turned out that, given access to new tools and the ability to communicate effectively, a community of individuals could do just as good of a job (with some qualifications about the benefits of breadth versus depth) as a vertically oriented business could at creating an encyclopedia. And they could do it at a much lower cost.

As Wikipedia showed, loosely organized communities of individuals could substitute for entire businesses. After 244 years, the *Encyclopaedia Britannica* finally ended its print edition in 2012, while Microsoft

Wikipedia—content platform

closed *Encarta* completely in 2009. Decentralized networks of autonomous individuals who existed outside the bounds of any single organization have taken over many productive activities that used to occur within a single, hierarchically organized company. In effect, individuals became competitors to many large linear businesses rather than just their customers. For example, YouTube and other online video-streaming platforms that depended on user-generated content started to compete for advertising dollars with professionally created content broadcast by television networks and cable companies.

This shift had a profound effect on business strategy. Transactions costs were now low enough that the bonds holding many traditional organizations together started to disintegrate. Economies of scale in many traditional businesses, such as the newspaper and encyclopedia industries, collapsed completely. Value chains didn't just break up into separate components, as they did during the early computer era. Pieces of the value chain actually started to fragment or fall apart (see Figure 2.7). Individuals acting in decentralized networks could now substitute for entire organizations.

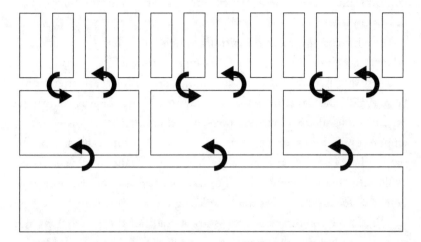

Figure 2.7.   The value chain becomes fragmented as individuals take over for organizations.

In the past, companies were effective because they vastly improved how we organized work. This idea is the crux of Coase's theory of the firm. Companies could coordinate the usage of employees and materials to create products and services more efficiently than the market could. In certain industries, such as the production of heavy machinery, these assumptions still hold true (though this could change quickly with the consumerization of new technologies, such as three-dimensional, or 3D, printing). But in many industries today, the most important resources often are not the ones that reside within any one organization but rather those that exist outside of it.

In this new environment, Henderson's and Porter's theories no longer apply. The aggregator and creator of business value is no longer a company's supply chain or value chain but rather a network's *ecosystem*. Value has moved from creating products and services to facilitating connections between external producers and consumers. The firm has collapsed as a center of production and instead has become the center of exchange. The areas where businesses could create and add economic value have shifted away from production and toward the curation and management of networks. That's where platform businesses come in.

As it turns out, these decentralized networks don't form and grow all by themselves. It usually takes an organization acting as the primary node in that network to grow and coordinate all of that activity on a large scale. These platform businesses don't operate the way traditional organizations did. Rather than investing in internal resources—such as employees, factories, or warehouses—platforms create value by coordinating these large external networks of consumers and producers. As we explain further in chapters 5 and 6, the core activities of platform businesses all focus on growing and managing these networks.

Platforms combine characteristics of traditional organizations and markets. A platform is essentially a synthesis of Coase's firm and Hayek's market. The firm no longer invests in production but rather in building the infrastructure and tools to support and grow a networked marketplace or community. What these platforms are creating are, in essence, centrally planned markets. That many would think of this as a contradiction is mostly a result of historical ideology rather than present-day fact. For example, consider the product marketplaces created by eBay or a company like Alibaba, or the content networks created by Facebook, Twitter, and YouTube, or the information and software marketplaces created by Google and Apple. All of these networks enable millions of individuals and companies to interact, but they are built and coordinated by a central entity.

The simultaneous rise of big data and ubiquitous connectivity and sensors, our third and fourth changes, come in here. Hayek lived in a world of siloed information. The cost of communication and processing power limited the amount of information that could be collected and distributed over long distances. It simply wasn't possible to collect enough information to coordinate a large economy effectively, certainly not with any useful speed. In Hayek's world, his "man on the ground" was an information island unto himself, separated from and unable to relay his local knowledge to any central planner. Besides, even if he could transmit such knowledge, there wasn't enough processing power available to make sense of it all. But today you can easily collect and distribute an almost limitless amount and variety of information all over the world.

Your smartphone is a data-creating and-transmitting machine. That's basically all that your phone is (plus a battery that lets it run for a while without having to be plugged in). These sensors are what enable you to track your runs, find directions on a map, take photos, or scan your fingerprint. The result has been a proverbial flood of information. The magnitude of this change can't be overstated. IBM estimated in 2013 that 90 percent of the world's information was less than two years old.[11] Most of this information was created and consumed online. Contrary to how people lived throughout most of human history, today siloed information has become the exception rather than the norm. However, the change is only just beginning. Market research firm IDC estimates that the world's data will grow by as much as *forty* times its 2015 level by 2020.[12]

But now, thanks to so-called big data analysis, businesses can start to make sense of all of this new information. In the past, data was something you had to go out and gather. You had to create distinct processes to measure and collect information on a business. In each case, typically you'd have a population that was well defined and a straightforward question you were trying to answer, and the data you collected would fit nicely into a spreadsheet. Today, data is no longer something you go out and get. "Data is collected automatically as a by-product of the business itself," according to Alibaba's chief strategy officer, Ming Zeng.[13] With this change has come the shift from the simple, structured data of the industrial age to an abundance of more complex unstructured data in the Internet era. Spreadsheets are no longer enough. Big data analysis allows businesses to make sense of large, chaotic data sets in real time. Businesses also can understand entirely new types of data, including audio files, photos, and videos, as well as unstructured data such as text documents, behavioral patterns, and natural language.

This ability to organize and make sense of large amounts of data in real time has dissolved Hayek's final objections to centralization. In the long run, Oskar Lange was right. Algorithms run on computers and trained on previously unmanageable amounts of data can now coordinate large amounts of economic activity, just as Lange predicted. The ability to coordinate economic activity efficiently has scaled beyond the boundaries of the traditional firm. Remember, price itself was a data point used to coordinate economic activity—it just happened to be the easiest data point to collect. Today, technology enables businesses to collect and track much more granular data about far more kinds of activity than ever before. As a result, platforms can now create and manage networks that facilitate entirely new categories of economic and social activities. For instance, on August 27, 2015, Facebook served an unprecedented 1 billion users *in a single day*.[14] Similarly, between March 2014 and March 2015, Alibaba's marketplaces facilitated a previously unfathomable amount of economic activity in China by coordinating 350 million consumers and nearly 10 million merchants.[15] Only recently did these kinds of businesses become economically and technologically feasible.

LENIN LOVES GOOGLE

The Connected Revolution has blown apart the key assumptions underlying Bruce Henderson's concept economies of scale and Michael Porter's value chain. Beyond the realm of business strategy, these changes also have fundamentally altered the way our economy works. Taken together, they have invalidated Hayek's assertion that a central planner can't organize large-scale economic activity. Today, that's precisely what's happening to increasingly large sections of our economy. The only difference is that the central planner is not a government bureaucrat. Rather it's a set of algorithms and software tools operated by a platform in order to manage and grow a decentralized network.

In truth, the core ideas underlying how we thought about business strategy and the economy were based on deeply embedded assumptions about transaction costs and the state of technology. As technology has changed, so too has the economy, in ways that most people don't yet realize. Rather than being immutable laws, the concepts that were the foundation of twentieth-century business strategy and economic theory turned out to be (like most economic "laws") a loose set of theories built on assumptions that became outdated as technology changed.

One reason this shift hasn't garnered more attention is that these new companies don't match our perception of how businesses create value. When looking at traditional companies, we usually measure the hard assets and things that the business can more or less directly control. These factors won't measure the true value of platforms. With Uber, for example, practically all of the value it creates comes from transactions it facilitates between people who exist outside the company. Its network is what makes the company valuable. The same is true for all platforms. By creating and orchestrating these large networks, platforms are unlocking new, untapped economic and social value. These markets and communities wouldn't exist or spring into existence in a vacuum—the platform had to build and manage them. In essence, platforms are correcting for market failures. This isn't a new phenomenon. In the financial sector, economic exchanges, such as the New York Stock Exchange, have served in this capacity for centuries. What's new is that platforms are now extending into more and more areas of our existence, and at a scale that was previously unthinkable.

As a result, today's most valuable businesses have become what Hayek once deemed impossible: centralized organizations that can understand and react in real time to what's happening throughout a large, decentralized economy. Local knowledge is local no more. What is Google Search, for instance, but an enormous, centrally planned economy of content and information? In a manner of speaking, Google is now creating the socialist utopia that all the might of Soviet Russia could not. That you don't think of Google in this way is basically just a matter of marketing and ideology. Google makes you feel empowered, even though it's telling you what you want. Uber makes you happy, even though its selects your car for you and picks the route your driver should take to your destination. All of this economic activity is being centrally planned and orchestrated by computers running algorithms—and it seems to bother no one. Nor should it. It turns out that people don't have any problem with central planning in principle—they just don't like *bad* central planning. Today's technology enables platform businesses to step in and create these centrally orchestrated markets where the "free market" failed to do so. As a result, they create entirely new markets or greatly expand old ones.

Now, Google isn't perfect by any means—what it "recommends" isn't always right—nor does it encompass the whole economy. Lange's vision of a perfectly centralized economy isn't yet a reality. But the pendulum has swung significantly from decentralization toward large organizations—platforms—that create what are, in effect, large, centrally planned markets. As this trend continues, we will see more and more of the economy orchestrated through decentralized, but centrally created and managed, networks.

CAPITALISM ≠ COMPETITION

Today, the success of these platforms proves that capitalism is, in fact, compatible with centralization. Yet few people realize this. The resistance is largely a relic of Cold War–era thinking and outdated ideologies. PayPal founder and former CEO Peter Thiel describes the phenomenon in his 2014 book, *Zero to One: Notes on Startups, or How to Build the Future.* "Americans mythologize competition and credit it with saving us from socialist breadlines," Thiel said. "More than anything else, competition is an ideology—the ideology—that pervades our society and distorts our thinking."[16] In reality, he said, "capitalism and competition are opposites." The companies that are driving our economy today and that will be in the future are the kind of "monopolies" that Thiel described in his book. In fact, most of the companies he described—including Google, Twitter, and PayPal—are platform companies. These monopolies "give customers more choices by adding entirely new categories of abundance to the world," Thiel said.

This is precisely what platforms do. Linear businesses can still create value, but today platforms create more. They create entirely new networks of economic and social activity where it wouldn't exist otherwise. As a result, they centrally orchestrate large amounts of new economic activity. Social networks existed informally before Facebook came along. But Facebook centralized all of these networks into one platform in order to facilitate more connections and interactions between people. In essence, Facebook built a marketplace for social interaction. As a result, billions of people today are connected who wouldn't be otherwise. Although some people may not like how Facebook handles its users' data, the company undoubtedly has created an enormous amount of economic and social value beyond what it earns as profit.

The impact of platform companies will be felt even more strongly in countries with less established economic infrastructure. For example, Alibaba has helped create a significant amount of China's growing digital economy. By one estimate, its marketplaces are responsible for as much as 70 percent of the shipping activity within China. Additionally, Alibaba's payments platform, Alipay, is responsible for half of all online transactions in China. It processes more than $500 billion in transactions annually, which is twenty times more than the amount handled by China UnionPay, the state-owned company with a government-granted monopoly over China's bank-card authorization system.[17] Alibaba e-commerce marketplaces and payments platform have allowed shoppers, even in China's most remote regions, to gain access to goods long before stores can build chains of brick-and-mortar outlets.

The way we think about businesses and the economy today is outdated. Much of the twentieth-century wisdom is no longer relevant. Concepts like the value chain and economies of scale provided incremental improvements on the old, linear model. But the shift from linear businesses to platforms that we're seeing today is not incremental. Rather, it's massive and immediate.

Despite all the controversy around Uber and the so-called sharing economy, the magnitude of change that platforms have brought to our society has gone largely unnoticed. In fact, this shift is much larger than the sharing economy, as platforms encompass many more areas of economic activity. And it will only continue in the future when connected technology is adopted by more and more industries. The rest of this book will help you understand how and why these businesses work and, just as important, when they won't. Because if you want to understand the economy today and in the future, you have to start with platforms.

3

THE ZERO-MARGINAL-COST COMPANY

Software alone is a commodity.

—Fred Wilson, venture capitalist and
founder of Union Square Ventures

Fred Wilson, founder of Union Square Ventures (USV), is a renowned investor and venture capitalist. His firm has invested in many platform companies, including Twitter, Etsy, Lending Club, Tumblr, Foursquare, SoundCloud, and Kickstarter. To explain his company's investment thesis, he has told what he called the "dentist office software story." The story, "a modern day fable about defensibility in the software business,"[1] begins with an entrepreneur who's tired of having long waits at the dentist's office. So, in typical entrepreneur fashion, this person decides to build management software for dentists' offices. He brings it to market and sells it at a price of $25,000 per year for each office. Even though the software is expensive, "dentists realize significant cost savings after deploying the system. The company, Dentasoft, grows quickly into a $10mm annual revenue business, goes public, and trades up to a billion dollar valuation."[2]

But the story doesn't end there. Next, two young entrepreneurs go to startup accelerator Y Combinator and create a low-cost version of Dentasoft. Their product, Dent.io, includes more modern software and a mobile app that allow dentists to manage their offices remotely. Dent.io gets to market quickly at a price point of $5,000 per year. Many dentists switch to the newer, cheaper entrant. Dentasoft misses its quarterly forecast, and its stock crashes. Meanwhile, "Dent.io does a growth round from Sequoia and hires a CEO." Next, an open-source software project called DentOps springs to life. A hosted version of this project called DentHub becomes popular. Dentasoft files for bankruptcy. Dent.io struggles, and the company fires its CEO.

The point of this story, Wilson explained, is that "software alone is a commodity. There is nothing stopping anyone from copying the feature set, making it better, cheaper, and faster." This is where USV's investment thesis comes in. USV realized it did not want to invest in commodity software, so Wilson and his partners asked, "What will provide defensibility?" The answer: "Networks of users, transactions, or data," Wilson explained. "That led us to social media, to Delicious, Tumblr, and Twitter. And marketplaces like Etsy, Lending Club, and Kickstarter."

One of USV's partners, Albert Wenger, has created an alternative ending for this story. In his version, a dentist named Hoff Reidman "decides that he wants to network with other dentists." He creates a site called Dentistry.com. He hustles to get initial traction, and the site takes off. USV does a small seed round of $1 million. The founder creates a product roadmap that "allows patients to have profiles on Dentistry.com where they can keep their dental records, book appointments, and keep track of their dental health. It also includes mobile apps for patients to remind them to floss and brush at least twice a day." The platform is free to use for anyone and monetizes through a combination of advertising and taking a cut of the transactions it facilitates. As a result, "Dentistry.com ultimately grows into a $1bn revenue company and goes public [and] trades at a market cap of $7.5bn. Wall Street analysts love the company citing its market power and defensible network effects."

THE EVOLUTION OF ENTERPRISE SOFTWARE

Although Fred's story is fictional, it actually tracks pretty well with the broader history of the enterprise IT and software industries. Customer relationship management software is a great example. Oracle and SAP built their businesses selling large, expensive enterprise software installations to companies. Yet years later, in the early 2000s, along came Salesforce.com, which undercut these companies by distributing its software over the Internet. At the time, Salesforce CEO Marc Benioff called this "the end of software." What he really meant was that it was the end of traditional, expensive software and the beginning of software as a service (SaaS)—essentially cloud software that can be accessed cheaply over the Internet. But over time, Salesforce's larger competitors started to create SaaS offerings, and Salesforce needed to continue to differentiate itself. What was Benioff's answer? Build a development platform. Salesforce created its Force.com development platform and AppExchange app store, which it launched in 2006. The company heavily invested in creating a third-party software ecosystem around its core applications. Today, its app store has millions of app downloads and is an important part of Salesforce's value proposition. Other cloud software industries have evolved in a similar manner, such as cloud data storage and so-called infrastructure-as-a-service (IaaS) companies. Both Google App Engine and Amazon Web Services have robust development platforms with thousands of available apps and integrations.

Healthcare software is another great example of this trend. The first wave of new healthcare software came during the dot-com era. Like Wilson's Dentasoft and most enterprise software at the time, these products were sold for large, up-front fees. Companies that emerged at this time included Epic Systems Corp., athenahealth, and eClinicalWorks. As eClinicalWorks cofounder and CEO Girish Navani said in a 2014 interview, "Healthcare in 1999 was not automated. It was archaic."[3] These backend software companies sold systems that started to digitize much of the communication and paperwork that went through a doctor's office, such as medical records. One of the enterprise software products that eClincalWorks sold to doctors was an electronic medical record (EMR) system. "If you eliminate paper from any industry, the efficiency has to improve," Navani said. But at the time, that's as far as this digitization went. Patients were still left out of the loop. As the technology and industry grew, the next generation of this software moved to the cloud. The software become cheaper and more accessible. Today the industry has matured significantly—about five major players dominate the market while market penetration for EMR systems is approaching 80 percent.[4] Most doctors' offices now run backend software systems for tracking medical records and many other office processes. The next step in this evolution was to bring the patient into the loop.

Signs of this shift toward consumer-facing platforms are everywhere. The most prominent category is telemedicine, which has gotten nearly $500 million in venture capital funding in recent years and is still expanding.[5] Leading platforms in this space as of the end of 2015 include American Well ($128 million raised), Doctor on Demand ($87 million), Teladoc ($249 million), and MDLIVE ($73 million). Google has even experimented with telemedicine.[6] "Companies that are focusing on using cloud and this idea of tying consumers to suppliers and suppliers to other suppliers and breaking the mold of this traditional payer-based system of healthcare will create a big, dynamic difference," according to Navani. These companies aren't just connecting doctors with patients but also doctors with other doctors. They're making routine healthcare more available, efficient, and affordable for patients. However, telemedicine is just the low-hanging fruit for healthcare platforms. Expect to see even more changes in the years ahead as digital technology becomes a fixture of modern healthcare. Does this mean healthcare is poised to undergo an Uber-like transformation? "It'll happen a little bit slower than it happened in the cab industry because there were fewer regulations," Navani said. "But I think it'll happen in two or three years."

YOU'RE GOING TO NEED A BIGGER MOAT

It seems Wilson was correct that software alone *is* a commodity. In the language of legendary investor Warren Buffet, pure software companies don't have an effective "moat" to defend their business; it's easy for competitors to storm the barricades and overwhelm them. Since most software industries have relatively low barriers to entry—especially today, when startup costs are lower than ever—it's practically guaranteed that a competitor will come along and offer customers similar software that's either better or cheaper. That's where network effects come in.

Put very simply, a network effect is present when the behavior of one user has a direct impact on the value that other users will get out of the same service. Network effects make a platform more useful and more valuable as more people use it. We discuss network effects in more detail in chapter 4, but their presence means that when competing with a successful platform, you aren't competing simply on the strength of your product and its features. You also are competing with the platform's ability to support an entire community of consumers and producers as well as all the value they exchange. This community is a core part of a platform's value that isolated products don't provide.

Networks are much harder to duplicate than features are. As we saw when Nokia and BlackBerry lost out to Apple and Google, any features that their phones could offer were far less valuable than the value a consumer received from a large community of app developers. Network effects are "the strongest economic moat of all," Bill Gurley, of venture capital firm Benchmark, has said.[7] Talking heads have been speculating about Facebook's decline for years, especially with the rise of new social media companies like Twitter and Snapchat and the shift on smartphones from social networks to messaging platforms. Yet as of this writing, Facebook has beaten Wall Street projections in eleven of the last twelve quarters, and its Facebook Messenger platform has taken off, acquiring more than 500 million users within a couple years' time. Its big acquisitions, WhatsApp and Instagram, have also continued to grow significantly since joining Facebook.[8] Apparently having a network with 1.5 billion active users is a hell of a moat.

INVESTORS LOVE PLATFORMS

As Fred Wilson's story suggests, investors love platforms. Successful platforms have strong moats in the form of their networks and operate at a scale that positions them to dominate their industries.

It's no wonder, then, that platforms are worth more than linear businesses. According to our research, investors value platforms more highly than their linear equivalents. Looking at the S&P 500, pure platform businesses or businesses for which a platform is a significant part of their business have an average revenue multiple of 8.9. In contrast, linear businesses are valued between two to four times revenue on average, depending on their business model.[9] Other research has found a similar valuation gap between platforms and linear businesses.[10]

This gap is actually widening over time, and there's a good reason. Platforms perform better over both the short and the long term along key financial dimensions. For example, they deliver faster growth, better return on capital, and larger profit margins. As a result, since the early 2000s, platforms have quickly overtaken other business models at the top of the economy. According to current trends, platforms will make up about 5 percent of the overall S&P 500 by 2020. They're also on track to make up the majority of the top valuations in the S&P 500 within the next five to ten years.

Potential public platform companies that could join the S&P 500 over the next few years include LinkedIn, Twitter, Zillow, and Grub-Hub. Additionally, Uber, Snapchat, Airbnb, Dropbox, and Pinterest could be future candidates once they go public, as their current valuations already exceed S&P 500 market cap requirements. (See Figure 3.1.) Many existing enterprises also will build or acquire platforms in order to incorporate platform business models and network effects into certain parts of their value chains. Finally, platforms have created an

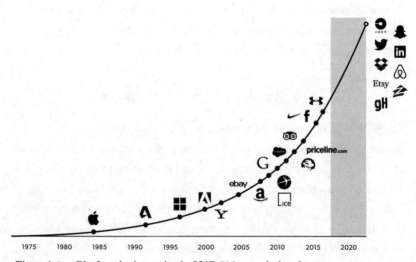

Figure 3.1.   Platform businesses in the S&P 500 over the last forty years.

Figure 3.2. In twenty-five years, 50 percent of the S&P 500's net income will come from platforms.

outsize share of income generated by the S&P 500. Projections more than a few years out are always a little fuzzy, but if current trends continue, platforms could make up 50 percent of the S&P 500's net income within twenty-five years.[11] (See Figure 3.2.)

These projections may seem outlandish, but they reflect the actual growth we've seen over the past decade. S&P 500 platform businesses have improved their net earnings on average by 330 percent in the past ten years compared to 16 percent for the overall S&P 500 (though from a much smaller base). As more platforms join the S&P, their contribution to the index's net earnings will grow very quickly.

PLANET UNICORN

Once you take a look at what's happening in the startup economy, these projections make even more sense. The next wave of large public companies is made up of far more platforms than in the past. Of the 126 "unicorn" billion-dollar private companies as of July 2015, 73 are platforms—or about 58 percent. (In tech-speak, a unicorn company is a company valued at more than $1 billion.) If you look internationally, the numbers are even more surprising. In Asia, 31 of 36 unicorns are platforms, or about 86 percent. This includes China, where 81 percent of 21 unicorns are platforms, and India, where 8 of 9 are platforms (see Figure 3.3).[12]

As this data shows, platforms are a truly global phenomenon. China is a great example of this shift. The infrastructure of commerce in China is digital, to an extent that wasn't possible in the United States, where

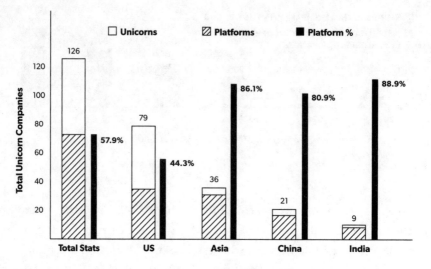

Figure 3.3.   "Unicorn" company data, July 2015.

there was already a well-established in-store commercial retail sector. As a result, the companies that have best captured the new potential brought by rapid growth are the platforms creating and growing new digital markets. These Chinese platform companies include Alibaba and Tencent as well as more recent entrants, such as Xiaomi, which built the most successful Android platform in China and is now the third largest smartphone distributor in the world behind Samsung and Apple.[13]

INVESTORS VALUE PLATFORM STARTUPS MORE

Platforms also receive higher valuations than linear startups. The average valuation for platform unicorns was $4.51 billion compared to $2.49 billion for linear unicorn companies. In other words, the average linear unicorn is valued at a little more than half of comparable platform companies. Not surprisingly, platforms also have most of the funding raised by these unicorn startups. Billion-dollar platforms have received more than twice as much funding as their linear competitors, with $46.24 billion in funding for platform unicorns compared to $21.96 billion for linear companies. To top it off, platforms also got more favorable terms from investors. Platform unicorns were valued about 12 percent higher relative to the funding they received when compared to linear platforms, indicating that investors are more confident in the upside of their platform investments.

Obviously, not all of these unicorn companies will survive. But the trends in both public and private markets show that platform businesses are quickly overtaking linear companies. In particular, the huge shift toward platforms among unicorn startups suggests that the next wave of large public companies worldwide will be mostly platforms.

THE ZERO-MARGINAL-COST COMPANY

Network effects are only a part of why platform business models are so powerful today. To see the whole picture, we need to take a deeper look at the cost and profit structures that underlie the platform business model.

Let's start with the economics of information goods, such as apps, music, or ebooks. If you create an app, it might cost $250,000 to produce the original version. But creating a copy of that app will cost next to nothing. In the language of economics, the app has close to zero marginal cost. Thanks to the Internet and connected technology, information goods today have a near-zero marginal cost of distribution. The cost to serve one additional customer is basically zero. But as we saw in chapter 2, even with this shift toward zero-marginal-cost information goods, a linear business like the *Encyclopaedia Britannica* is still constrained in terms of how large it can scale because of the high fixed costs of production. It costs a lot to gather all of that information and have it professionally written and curated into an encyclopedia.

Some of the first companies to capitalize on this shift toward the low cost of distribution over the Internet were SaaS companies. Rather than building and maintaining a physical server that the customer would have to pay for in order to host the software system, SaaS companies just distribute their software over the Internet at zero marginal cost. Still, the cost of creating the initial application is high, and if the company wants to expand its business, it needs to create additional modules to sell in order to create more inventory. In other words, it has to incur more large, up-front costs.

Platforms take this dynamic one step further. They remove the high fixed cost of creation and extend zero marginal costs to the supply side of the business. To add more entries to Wikipedia or to improve existing ones, the company doesn't hire another researcher. It just needs a user to create a page or make an edit. Although there still is an up-front cost involved in building the software product, the platform has a much more efficient business model as it grows. In fact, it becomes exponentially more efficient the larger it becomes.

The implications of this change are enormous. In the twentieth century, successfully scaling a business depended on finding channels that drastically lowered the cost of creating demand and lowering the cost of supply. The Internet itself alleviated some of the high fixed costs to launch a business as reaching large audiences became much easier and cheaper. But linear business models still face the marginal cost challenge, forcing them to economize on the cost of supply in order to compete. As we discussed in chapter 2, the whole concept of Michael Porter's value chain is built around the idea of combining activities to create the most value for the smallest cost—in other words, reducing the cost of production. This constraint was the inspiration for many of the most important business innovations of the twentieth century, including the assembly line, which improved the efficiency of production. Also included are less-heralded innovations, such as chain stores, which created economies of scale and reduced costs, and franchising, which externalized much of the up-front cost of creating a new store. The more recently created process of just-in-time production also focused on reducing waste and the dead-weight cost of holding inventory. In short, all of these innovations were focused on reducing the cost of production for linear businesses.

Linear businesses generally grow by adding staff or physical assets, or both. Because these tactics create value by controlling production, linear companies have to invest significant resources in expanding their capacity in order to sell more inventory. But physical assets and employees don't scale well. Networks do.

Platforms require much less capital expenditure to be successful at scale. They also require far fewer internal resources than linear businesses do. For example, platform companies require relatively few employees to be successful. Uber, Airbnb, and LinkedIn each run their global operations with fewer than 8,000 employees. Similarly, Alibaba had fewer than 35,000 employees at the beginning of 2015. In contrast, Walmart, which has a total sales volume similar to Alibaba, has over 2 million employees.

Platforms eliminate the marginal cost of production by just focusing on facilitating connections. The network handles production. Uber doesn't own and operate a fleet of taxis, Alibaba doesn't own factories that produce the goods it makes available online, Google doesn't create the Web pages it indexes, and YouTube doesn't create the millions of videos it hosts. Platforms are the natural business model of the Internet: They are pure zero-marginal-cost information businesses. They use data to facilitate transactions and enable networked production. The low marginal cost of production means that *expenses don't grow as fast as revenue does.*

These changes have major implications for linear companies. Platforms can scale cheaply and easily and will increasingly leave behind their linear counterparts.

Look at Hyatt, for example. Hyatt can sell room reservations online through its website and online travel sites. However, to create more inventory beyond its current capacity, the company needs to build a new hotel—no small cost. When Airbnb wants to add more rooms, it just needs someone to create a new listing on its website. This costs the platform next to nothing. Because the platform doesn't own production, it doesn't need all the resources that go into creating inventory. This networked production radically changes the cost structure of a business and alters the amount of internal resources it needs in order to create value. As a result, the marginal cost of supply drops to zero and its potential market size explodes (see Figure 3.4).

This cost structure means that platforms are capital light and provide high return on investment compared to linear businesses.[14] Thus, platforms don't require a large capital base in order to get started, and, relative to linear businesses, they require even less to expand once

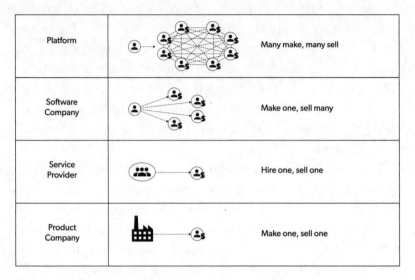

Figure 3.4.   Platform business models have lower marginal costs.

they've established their networks. Additionally, the zero marginal cost of supply means platforms can grow to a much larger size than linear businesses can. The costs of a linear business will always continue to rise as it grows, while the costs of a platform costs tend to level off logarithmically (see Figure 3.5).

The unit economics make it theoretically possible for a platform company to expand to the total size of the market—unlike linear businesses, which, as we explained in chapter 2, typically capped out well below the total market size. Being able to grow and manage a large network has become more important than having a large capital base to invest in scaling internal resources.

So why isn't everyone building a platform? Well, networked production creates unique challenges. As mentioned, Airbnb doesn't have direct control over inventory and doesn't own its most valuable assets: its users. The risks for a platform are substantial, especially when it's first starting to build its network. In order to be useful to consumers, Airbnb needed to convince external producers to make their inventory available on its platform. This issue was a particularly difficult challenge when the platform had few users. Even though members of each group of users (consumers

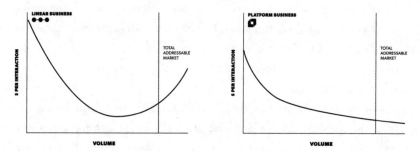

Figure 3.5.   The average cost curves for linear and platform business.

and hosts) would benefit from being on the platform, they wouldn't join Airbnb unless enough members of the other group join as well. Platforms overcome this chicken-and-egg problem when the value to new users of participating in the platform exceeds the cost of participation. The point when this occurs is called critical mass. Once a platform scales past critical mass, network effects are accretive and help the business gain a majority market share. We explore the chicken-and-egg problem in more detail in chapter 8. For now, know that growing a network is often a much more difficult problem to solve than the linear approach of scaling and improving the efficiency of a process that you own and control internally. It's much easier and simpler to tweak a supply chain than it is to orchestrate a decentralized network. However, assuming you can overcome this challenge, the potential scale for a platform business is *much* greater, since it's no longer cost constrained on the supply side after it reaches critical mass.

BETTER MARGINS AT SCALE

Although linear businesses can start generating revenue right away, platforms usually can't, owing to the chicken-and-egg problem. When a platform has few users, it doesn't deliver enough value or facilitate enough transactions to generate a lot of revenue. But as a platform's network grows, revenue begins to grow much more rapidly than costs. As this happens, the cost of user acquisition declines and the value the platform creates starts to reach the bottom line. This was the experience of OpenTable, a platform for booking restaurant reservations, as it grew its network of restaurants and diners. "The more supply you had, the easier it was to add diners," OpenTable CEO Matthew Roberts said. "And the more diners you had, the easier it was to add restaurants." As a result, "All of our cost structure goes down as we get more mature in every market," Roberts said.[15]

The ultimate impact of the network effect is that it enables more transactions. With Uber, a larger network allows the company to lower prices and wait times. Drivers can earn a similar amount of money even though prices are lower since demand from consumers is higher. With more drivers, consumers can get picked up faster and are more likely to use the platform. The end result is more transactions and more revenue.

NETWORKED VALUE: HOW HANDY OUTLASTED THE COMPETITION

Handy is an on-demand home cleaning and services platform that has a presence in thirty-five cities across the United States, United Kingdom, and Canada as of the beginning of 2016. The platform connects consumers with screened professionals who provide household services, such as home cleaning, painting, moving, and the like. Handy manages bookings and payments and offers money-back guarantees to the thousands of customers who use its site every week.

Early on, Handy set a goal of building network effects to give itself a competitive advantage. "The strategy was to continuously raise the bar for consumer expectations," according to Handy founder and CEO Oisin Hanrahan. "If your competitors are known for providing services in two days, you stand to earn a competitive advantage by reducing that lag to one day or even same day if possible. You're creating a new type of value for consumers, which will help growth and retention. But you're also pressuring the competition."

Handy—services marketplace platform

However, there was a reason none of Handy's competition had been able to accomplish this task. "When we first started, we would be able to fulfill a request within five days' time.

In order to decrease that time, each regional market needed to scale and hit bigger levels of critical mass," Oisin says. In each city it entered, the company had to create a network of home service professionals who could quickly respond to consumer demand. Building a large network with strong, positive network effects is no easy task. Handy had to figure out how it could grow both supply and demand at the same time in order to reduce wait times.

Part of overcoming this difficulty was picking the right markets. The company was meticulous about choosing which cities it would enter first. The market had to have enough producers to fill consumer demand quickly in order to make Handy's business model work. However, producer quality was just as important as quantity. There was no point in investing in serving customers quickly if they weren't going to have a good experience. "Our business model revolves around recurring purchases and we've been able to do that better than anyone else so far. Eighty percent of our over 1 million bookings have been recurring," Oisin says. When Handy successfully scaled its marketplace, it was able to bring down wait times and delight its customers. "Now that we have hit 10,000 independent pros across all our markets [in early 2015], we can usually start to fill next-day orders." By virtue of the network effect, this increased consumer demand also attracted more quality professionals.

As a result, Handy's rivals have been struggling to keep up. Its largest competitor, Homejoy, abruptly shut down in July 2015. According to sources inside the company, Homejoy wasn't able to create enough repeat business to justify its economic model. To keep up with competitors, Homejoy heavily subsidized user acquisition, so consumers were happy to book a cheap first cleaning. Many users who were drawn to the platform because of its first-time discounts had little reason to return to hiked prices. Homejoy had a classic "leaky bucket" problem that it never fixed—it had to keep bringing new users in to fill demand because its existing customers kept leaving. Its growth strategy focused on short-term goals (user acquisition, expansion) and ignored long-term issues (user retention, diminishing funds), so its gains were nothing but short-lived. Vanity growth metrics, such as revenue growth, didn't reflect the real health of the business. Homejoy was burning through money and falling behind its competition.

In contrast, Handy has done a much better job of driving repeat business and building a strong network effect between quality service professionals and consumers. *Forbes* reported that only about 15 to 20 percent of Homejoy customers booked again within a month, according to former employees.[16] Meanwhile, Handy says more than 35 percent of its customers book again within a month, with that number rising to 45 percent in some of its larger and more liquid markets. "In markets where we have hit critical mass, the key to improving quality while growing the ecosystem is maintaining that high level of satisfaction of pros and customers through the platform and continuing to exceed expectations for both sides of the equation," according to Oisin.

This type of improvement over time is the result of the *network value* that platforms create. Products or services have inherent value, where users derive value by consuming what they've purchased. The consumption value of a product can be significant, but it's static. It doesn't change much over time. Platforms add network value to this—the value that

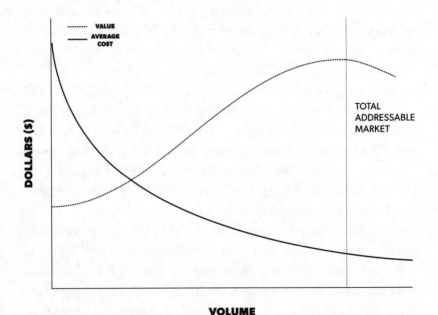

Figure 3.6. Average cost declines while value to each user increases. As a result, a platform's profit margin significantly increases as its network grows.

users derive from other people's use of the platform. As a result, value to each individual user grows naturally as the network expands. Platforms monetize by capturing a portion of the value they create, so as value grows, so too does revenue. (See Figure 3.6.) But because platforms can expand at near-zero marginal cost, their costs don't grow significantly as they expand. Therefore, profit margins improve drastically as a platform grows to dominate a market—not because a platform is raising prices or gouging suppliers the way a traditional monopoly might, but because the overall value the platform creates grows significantly.

GO BIG OR GO HOME

Since a platform doesn't own production directly, it may generate less profit than a linear business would until the platform scales well beyond the potential reach of its linear competitors. This dynamic means that there's often little point in building a small platform business. In many cases, linear businesses can serve small markets better than platforms can. The real benefits of a platform business are at very large scale.

Market size was one of the main reasons many investors were concerned over homemade goods marketplace Etsy's growth prospects when the company went public. Just how big is the market for handmade goods? Over the last few years, the platform's growth has been slowing down on the producer side, which is not a good sign for its long-term growth prospects. If Etsy's market isn't big enough, the company may not be able to build a sustainable business long term. And it may end up getting pushed out of its niche market by Amazon, which launched its Etsy competitor, Amazon Homemade, near the end of 2015.[17] Not every business will work just because it's a platform.

Picking the right market is even more important for platforms than it is for linear businesses. You usually need a large market for the business model to be sustainable. However, if you *can* dominate a large enough market, building a platform business is well worth the risk. At scale, platforms generate far better margins than linear businesses and, as Fred Wilson and Bill Gurley suggested, are much more defensible thanks to their networks and market power.

PLATFORM OR PERISH

It's not just that platforms *can* grow larger than linear businesses; they *must*. Platform businesses have to harness massive scale. Most platforms either make it big or don't succeed at all. This growth imperative for platforms is bad news for linear businesses, because as a platform reaches maturity and starts to take over the whole market, its profits both eclipse and squeeze the profits of the linear competitors still remaining in the industry.

As platforms become more common and disrupt more and more industries, platform dominance will mean that many nonplatform businesses will be left fighting for a smaller and smaller piece of the market. A nonplatform business still can succeed by capturing a slice of another platform's ecosystem (think Samsung with Android), but controlling the platform is the most sustainable—and most lucrative—way to go.

4

MODERN MONOPOLIES

Platform Capitalism and the
Winner-Take-All Economy

Exchange achieves what the medieval alchemists couldn't: it creates some-thing from nothing. It serves the proverbial free lunch. Swapping goods among people creates value.

—David S. Evans, author of *Invisible Engines* and professor
at the Law School at the University of Chicago

Because platforms' margins increase as their networks
grow, only one or two platforms will dominate an industry as the market matures. As a result, there often are fierce battles among platforms competing for dominance. "There's no openness between two competing platforms," according to Ming Zeng, who has been the chief strategy officer for Alibaba since 2002. He compared interplatform competition to a fight between warring nations.[1] Zeng is no stranger to interplatform wars. He has been a core part of Alibaba's team through the company's battle with eBay in the early 2000s and its fight with Baidu, the largest Chinese search engine, at the end of the decade.

Shortly after Alibaba launched Taobao in 2003, eBay entered the market with "an unstoppable determination to be number one in

China," according to then-eBay CEO Meg Whitman.[2] eBay invested hundreds of millions in EachNet, which at the time was China's leading online auctions site. This acquisition made eBay the dominant e-commerce platform in China. But eBay-EachNet made the mistake of introducing transaction fees for sellers right away. In an effort to generate the increased profits that Wall Street investors were demanding, eBay wanted to replicate in China its fee-based model from the United States. Alibaba CEO Jack Ma decided to go all in on the company's efforts to defeat eBay. As Ma famously said, "eBay may be a shark in the ocean, but I am a crocodile in the Yangtze River. If we fight in the ocean, we lose—but if we fight in the river, we win."[3] Alibaba promised to keep Taobao free for its first three years of operation. By allowing users to transact for free, Taobao gained a big edge in the price-sensitive Chinese market. Additionally, thanks to its free-to-transact model, Alibaba was able to build much stronger network effects in China than eBay could.

Because eBay charged a percentage fee for each completed transaction, it couldn't allow buyers and sellers on EachNet to communicate before completing a transaction. Otherwise, they might complete their transaction outside of the platform. Alibaba had no such problem. Taobao introduced its hugely successful Wangwang chat service to allow buyers and sellers to communicate before completing a transaction. In fact, on many listings, you could immediately click through to the seller and initiate a live chat.[4] This feature was a big hit in China, where users often haggle over price before agreeing to a sale. Additionally, product quality in China is more variable than it is in developed countries, so facilitating that communication between buyer and seller was a key advantage for Alibaba over eBay in China. This disparity was also why Alibaba introduced more nuanced reputation ratings; buyers could rate sellers on many more variables than they could on eBay. The Chinese company clearly understood its market better, a fact that was reflected in Taobao's superior user satisfaction scores and rapidly growing market share.

The finishing blow came when Alibaba introduced its own payments system, Alipay, in January 2005. Alipay acted as an escrow system that held the money until buyers verified that they received the products they'd ordered in satisfactory condition. Because consumer usage of credit cards is much less common in China, Alipay proved an extremely effective way to get skeptical Chinese consumers to transact online.

By the end of 2006, eBay had admitted defeat. The U.S. company all but pulled out of China and shut down its Chinese site, handing over local operations to Chinese startup TOM Online. "The competition is over," Jack Ma said. "It's time to claim the battlefield."[5]

ROUND TWO: FREE IS NOT A BUSINESS MODEL

Beating eBay left Taobao as the dominant e-commerce marketplace in China. "When eBay withdrew from the China market, it left only Alibaba Group (and its Taobao marketplace) as the lone e-commerce giant in the market," Porter Erisman says. Erisman, a former Alibaba VP, is the author of the book *Alibaba's World* and creator of the award-winning documentary *Crocodile in the Yangtze*, which details Alibaba's early rise in China as well as its battle with eBay.

Alibaba's Taobao—product marketplace

Now Taobao needed to make money. However, given Alibaba's promise to keep Taobao free, the company needed a different type of business model than eBay had. As Alibaba's many critics at the time said, "Free is not a business model." The strategy Alibaba used to defeat eBay backed the Chinese company into a corner—it needed to find a way to monetize without charging transaction fees. Ultimately, Alibaba decided on a revenue model that looks more similar to Google Adwords than it does Amazon's or eBay's e-commerce marketplaces. Instead of depending on a percentage fee from each sale, Alibaba makes most of its profit through its advertising model. Because product search is one of the most lucrative segments of search advertising, Alibaba recognized that this model had huge revenue potential.

In order to build a business model based on product advertising, Alibaba first had to deal with a serious competitive threat. Baidu, often called the Google of China, was the dominant Chinese search platform. Baidu's Web crawlers would archive Alibaba's inventory and Web pages and connect its users to Alibaba's product pages when they searched for products on Baidu. According to our sources, a double-digit percentage of Alibaba's website traffic came from Baidu at the time.

Jack Ma decided that Alibaba needed to become a leading player in China's search market when he gained operational control of Yahoo China as part of Yahoo's 2005 investment in a fledging Alibaba. But as a stand-alone search engine, Yahoo/Alibaba wasn't able to compete with Baidu. Baidu also responded to the potential threat by creating Youa (an eBay-like marketplace) to compete with Alibaba's Taobao marketplace.

Alibaba decided that it needed to be the go-to website for product searches in China, not Baidu. Alibaba initially marketed its decision to block Baidu (and Google) as a way to prevent fraud from merchants who were manipulating paid search results on external sites. The hope was that consumers would find more value going to Alibaba than to Baidu. But the decision was ultimately a strategic one. If Alibaba let Baidu crawl its marketplace websites, Baidu could act as the middleman between consumers and Alibaba. Instead, Ma wanted consumers to go to Alibaba first.

To understand the magnitude of this decision, imagine if Amazon had shut out Google ten years ago. Would you still start a search on Google when you wanted to buy something? Would Amazon have been nearly as successful as it is now? It's hard to say how such a move would have worked out in the U.S. market, but it was indisputably key to Alibaba's success in China. Alibaba needed to change user behavior for shopping searches so that consumers would *start* their e-commerce shopping on Alibaba's site, not Baidu's.

The bet has clearly paid off. After Alibaba blocked external search engines, its marketplace became the dominant destination for shopping in China's e-commerce market. It became the go-to platform for product search in China, a feat that neither Amazon nor eBay could achieve in the United States, where Google is usually the first go-to destination for shoppers. "One can imagine that, had Alibaba allowed Baidu to index Taobao's pages, shoppers would have gradually migrated to Baidu to begin their product searches," Porter Erisman says. "Rather than let that happen, Alibaba sealed a wall around Taobao by blocking Baidu. It was a once-in-a-company's-lifetime opportunity that changed e-commerce history in China."

PLATFORM CAPITALISM: WINNER TAKE ALL

As Alibaba's story suggests, platform battles are often winner-take-all. Alibaba fought fiercely with eBay and then Baidu and beat out its rivals both times. As a result, Alibaba has controlled as much as 90 percent of the Chinese e-commerce market through its Taobao and Tmall platforms. (Alibaba launched Tmall, short for Taobao Mall, in 2008 as a marketplace where global brands could sell to Chinese consumers.) When eBay lost, it didn't just settle for the second position; it pulled out of China entirely. And although Baidu has still built a valuable business around its search engine, its failure to dominate product search is a big reason why it's a much less successful business than either Alibaba or Google, Baidu's U.S. doppelgänger.

Such fierce battles between competing networks have become a hallmark of platform capitalism, and they continue today. In 2013, Alibaba suspended the use of WeChat, a megapopular communications platform owned by rival company Tencent, on all of its marketplaces. In response, Tencent blocked Alibaba's payments platform, Alipay, from WeChat. More recently, Tencent has banned Uber's accounts on WeChat as the U.S.-based company goes up against Chinese competitor Didi Kuaidi, which has received significant investment from Tencent.

The result of most of these fights is a strong winner-take-all dynamic. One example of this phenomenon is smartphone operating systems, where Android and iOS own more than 90 percent of the market. Their closest competitor, Windows Phone, has less than 3 percent market share. In Web search, Google has a similarly dominant share of the market, with 65 percent in the United States and more than 90 percent in Europe. Despite years of heavy investment, Microsoft's Bing search engine is still at about 20 percent of U.S. search traffic, and its gains have mostly come at the expense of perennial second-banana Yahoo rather than Google.

The winner-take-all nature of platform competition does have some exceptions. When users can participate in more than one platform's network at the same time, the strength of network effects on any one platform will be weaker. An industry where users can switch easily between networks often can support more platforms, even as the industry matures.

However, the best platforms tend to decrease the incentive for users to switch between competing networks by creating additional value through software tools that make transacting easier and through the use of data and personalization. An example is the reputation scores that sellers and hosts accrue on eBay, Taobao, and Airbnb. Building your reputation is an investment in a platform that increases over time with repeated use. Numerous studies have shown that higher reputation scores help producers earn more money in marketplaces, either by selling more or by being able to charge higher prices. On the consumer side, the personalization aspect of platforms, such as Amazon's recommendations feature, tends to be a key part of creating additional value. This value strengthens network effects and creates a situation where a platform becomes even more valuable the more that you engage with it. This property isn't exclusive to platforms—linear businesses like Netflix make use of data as well. But combined with the network effects of established platforms, this additional value creates the kind of lock-in that makes competing with a successful platform extremely difficult.

THE NEW TITANS OF INDUSTRY

As platforms have taken over more of our economic life, they've naturally attracted comparisons to the monopolies of old—businesses like U.S. Steel and Standard Oil. Google is the most recent platform company to attract scrutiny related to its market power, especially in the European Union. The association is obviously not a flattering one. However, other than size and market dominance, today's titans of industry have little in common with the monopolies of the nineteenth and twentieth centuries. The difference between how these old monopolies and today's platforms established their market position is illustrative.

Let's start with Standard Oil. Like most linear monopolies, it created its dominant market position by acquiring large amounts of assets, effectively buying up large portions of the productive capacity in its industry. For example, at one point Standard Oil owned more than 90 percent of the production of oil in the United States—nearly all of the country's oil refineries.[6] In other words, at Standard Oil's peak, no one else could even *make* a competitive product, let alone sell it.

This method of establishing market dominance contrasts starkly with how platforms operate today. Platform businesses grow not by acquiring more factories but by connecting more and more users within their networks. In other words, platforms become dominant not because of *what they own* but rather because of the *value they create* by connecting their users. They don't own the means of production, as industrial monopolies did. Instead, they own the *means of connection*. This fact helps explain why old monopolies were largely despised while today's platforms are not. Although every business has some detractors (we all have that one friend who refuses to use Facebook), consumers love Facebook, Alibaba, and Google.

Additionally, while these platform companies do have significant market power in their industries, they don't control their users in the same way that Standard Oil controlled its sources of production. Alibaba can't just flip a switch and change the output of its sellers. It controls its market, but it does so only indirectly by providing value to its merchants and consumers. Platform monopolies dominate an industry, but they aren't as entrenched as the industrial-era monopolies were because today's platforms succeed based on *participation*, not *ownership*. "You can't cull out something called a platform from the ecosystem itself," Alibaba CSO Ming Zeng said.[7] Today's platforms are dominant because users chose them, not because they were able to buy up all available sources of supply. It was we, collectively, who created these modern monopolies. Their dominance is the result of widespread participation and usage, not narrowly managed ownership and control.

Nowhere has this difference been clearer than in Uber's battles with lawmakers and regulators. Uber's users have been its biggest asset in these fights. The most recent example was the company's fight with New York City mayor Bill de Blasio during the summer of 2015. De Blasio wanted to introduce a temporary cap on the number of Uber drivers on the road, citing traffic complaints from the taxi industry. The goal was to hit pause on Uber's growth so the city could study the impact that platforms like Uber had on congestion. But Uber, which planned to add 10,000 new drivers during the proposed time period, wasn't about to give up easily. In response, Uber introduced a "de Blasio mode" for users located within the city. The feature showed riders the lengthy projected wait times that they could expect if de Blasio's legislation passed. The view also invited users to email the mayor and city council to demand they vote "no" on the bill. The mayor received emails from 40,000 people and Twitter messages from 20,000 as a result, according to the *Wall Street Journal*.[8] Shortly thereafter, the mayor backed down, agreeing instead to a four-month study of congestion with no cap on Uber's growth.

To be sure, Uber also employed traditional public relations tools in its political battle, such as TV ads, celebrity endorsements and lobbyists. But as a *New York Times* editorial suggested in the wake of de Blasio's concession, "the company uses its customers to do much of its political heavy lifting."[9] Uber's defeat of de Blasio wasn't the first time it had enlisted the mass support of its users either. It's been part of the company's DNA from the beginning. One of its earliest regulatory battles was in the nation's political capital, Washington, D.C. Three years earlier, during the summer of 2012, Uber was readying to launch its UberX service in the D.C. market. But days before the service was supposed to launch, the D.C. city council passed an amendment to a taxi regulation bill designed to keep Uber from operating in the city. (The amendment was literally called the "Uber Amendment.") As Uber CEO Travis Kalanick tells it, the council crammed the bill through, submitting it at 4 p.m. on a Monday and voting on it the next day at 11 a.m. Uber responded by enlisting its users to fight back. "In 18 hours, 50,000 emails were sent by riders to city council along with 37,000 tweets," Kalanick said.[10] Around noon the next day, the city council pulled the amendment.

It's hard to imagine similar popular support for old-school monopolies like Standard Oil or even for more recent monopolies such as Comcast or Time Warner Cable. Like Uber, most platforms enjoy widespread support from their users. These are not your traditional, topdown monopolies of the past. Rather they are monopolies of the willing, built from the bottom up. Uber's growth is the result of more and more users finding the platform valuable. The same can be said of Facebook, Google, Alibaba, and Airbnb. Without the support of their users, these platforms would never be able to sustain their success and take over their respective markets.

NET GAIN: PLATFORMS EXPAND MARKETS

Another reason platforms differ from old-school monopolies is that network effects operate differently from the economies of scale that drove previous generations of monopoly businesses. Linear businesses became monopolies largely because they built economies of scale on the supply side. This allowed them to decrease their costs as they grew. Platforms dominate markets because as their networks grow, they deliver more value to their users.

Monopolies are typically viewed as a result of market forces breaking down—the forces of supply and demand aren't able to keep a company's market power in check, and it finds a way to capture an unusually large share of the market. However, this view doesn't hold for networks, where greater size brings more value, more efficiency and greater convenience for users. Platform monopolies aren't the result of market forces breaking down. They're the result of markets working correctly, a phenomenon that economists call a "natural monopoly."

Because of this fact, the belief that more competition is always better doesn't hold in platform markets. As the Alibaba story shows, interplatform competition can create mutually exclusive networks until a clear winner emerges. For consumers, this fragmentation is often an inefficient outcome. In fragmented markets, the potential value that could have been created through network effects goes unrealized. A perpetual war among multiple platforms can have the same effect as the lack of trade between warring nations: less economic activity and less value. In fact, having more platform competition actually can be worse for consumers, creating both higher prices and fewer transactions.[11] The cost of excess fragmentation in platforms can be much higher than the cost of letting one or two platforms capture the market.

Additionally, by building networks and marketplaces that wouldn't have existed otherwise, platforms have an expansionary effect on economic activity, as opposed to typical monopolies, which often profit by using their dominant positions to squeeze value from an industry without stimulating new economic activity. For example, Uber has created a multibillion-dollar business not by cutting itself a large slice of the existing economic pie, as many of its critics claim, but by *growing* the size of the pie several times over. Whatever you feel about the company, Uber has unquestionably expanded the taxi market in many cities. It's been able to do this by leveraging the network effect between drivers and passengers. The platform has attracted more than 1 million drivers worldwide—most of whom have never driven for money before—along with millions of passengers, many of whom probably took taxis very rarely before.[12]

This kind of economic growth is typical of platform industries— platforms succeed by significantly growing their industries. In software development, Apple suggests that the app economy it built around its iOS platform has helped create more than 600,000 developer jobs. Airbnb has had a similarly expansive effect on economic activity. In fact, a recent study has even suggested that Airbnb's success has had a minimal impact on hotel bookings, even though Airbnb has created a marketplace with more than a million listed properties.[13] Airbnb hasn't grown at the expense of hotels but rather by creating entirely new sources of economic activity.

Although Alibaba did not invent the first e-commerce marketplace in China, it succeeded by creating the infrastructure that supported the vast majority of the world's fastest growing e-commerce market. Today Alibaba's marketplaces have nearly 10 million active sellers. As part of an annual promotion ("Singles Day"), in 2015 it facilitated $14.3 billion in transactions in one day.[14] The company has even inspired a phenomenon in China—so-called Taobao villages—where hundreds of towns that were once farming villages now orient their economic activity around selling products through Alibaba's Taobao marketplace.[15]

As Peter Thiel suggests in his book *Zero to One*, platforms "give customers more choices by adding entirely new categories of abundance to the world." In other words, platforms perform a kind of economic magic, doing what the medieval alchemists could not. By facilitating exchanges, they create something from nothing. They create the proverbial free lunch. This economic phenomenon, which economists call gains from trade, has been known for centuries. Rarely, though, has this concept been applicable to individual businesses. But it definitely is today, when platform markets can be bigger than the gross domestic product of most countries.[16]

TODAY'S MONOPOLIES ARE COMPETITIVE

Although monopolies get a bad rap, they're not always a bad thing. In the short term, modern monopolies are often a boon to consumers. They bring valuable new inventions to market, and, in the case of platforms, they build new communities and markets that would not exist otherwise. The downside comes much later, as the monopolist ages and starts to crowd out potential new competitors without delivering new value. As renowned legal expert and author Tim Wu said, monopolies "tend to be good-to-great in the short term and bad-to-terrible in the long term."[17]

However, unlike the monopolies of old, platforms today are highly competitive. This difference results from the different mechanics of platform markets compared to traditional ones. Platforms don't compete based on their assets but rather based on their networks of users. Users today can migrate much quicker than productive capacity could in the nineteenth and twentieth centuries, as they are locked in by the value the platform delivers, not the assets it owns. As a result, a platform that dominates one industry is still vulnerable to attack from platforms that have similar user bases. This process of platforms competing across industries is surprisingly common. For example, Amazon effectively created the ebook industry in the United States. Yet after Amazon proved out the market, both Google and Apple have moved from adjacent industries and become competitors. And, as noted earlier, Alibaba used its rapidly growing product marketplace to attack Baidu's dominance in product search.

Additionally, the speed of technological change today means that, absent government enforcement, modern monopolies aren't likely to last nearly as long as their predecessors. Barriers to entry in most industries are far lower than they were a century ago, while the boundaries between industries also are much more fluid than they have been in the past. Although networks today do create the strongest and most defensible moats, they don't create the same barriers to entry as past monopolies that required vast investment in physical infrastructure in order to succeed. AT&T's domination of the telephone industry lasted from the beginning of the twentieth century until its 1984 breakup. Not surprisingly, in its later years, the company delayed or killed many important innovations in an effort to keep new entrants out of the market. Yet no platform today is likely to dominate an industry for anywhere near that long. Start-up costs are at an all-time low (thanks, it should be said, in no small part to the effects of many platform businesses). And new businesses today are able to grow faster than ever before. These changes mean that even if an industry is consolidated around a single dominant platform at any given time, there is always a looming threat of entry by a new firm or displacement by another successful platform. Because of the low cost of entry, this threat is constant and credible in a way it was not a hundred years ago.

This competition between established platforms and new entrants is exactly what befell Microsoft. For much of the last two decades, there was even more worry about Microsoft as a monopoly than there is about Google today. In the early 2000s, most industry experts expected a major competition between Microsoft and Nokia over who would own the dominant smartphone operating system. Google's move to create Android was actually a response to its fear of Microsoft's dominance in mobile.[18] Today Microsoft is still the dominant platform in PC operating systems. However, it turned out that the kingdom it built was much smaller than everyone thought it would be. The dynamism of platform competition accomplished what the U.S. government's antitrust case in the late 1990s could not. Less than a decade later, Microsoft became a bit player in the mobile-phone market. Apple and Google eclipsed its dominance as new technologies evolved and expanded the market in unexpected ways.

More recently, Google has attracted increasing scrutiny from antitrust regulators due to its dominance in Web search, especially in Europe. But in just a few years' time, Google's dominance in search may seem much less important than it does today. There are signs that this shift is already happening. Although Google has long dominated digital advertising, it's increasingly competing with platforms like Facebook, Twitter, and Pinterest for advertisers' money. This competitive danger is especially strong on mobile, since the vast majority of Google's revenue comes from desktop search. Google's creation of Android as a mobile operating system was designed primarily as a defensive move to protect its search business, but the company still hasn't figured out a great business model for the mobile Web, where search doesn't monetize as well as it does on the desktop. Many analysts attribute the slowing growth of Google's search-advertising revenue to this shift from desktop to mobile. Clicks on smartphones just aren't as profitable as those on personal computers. Additionally, new entrants from China who are building on top of open-source Android could threaten Google's dominance of Android in the near future. Meanwhile, Facebook has built an enormous presence on mobile, and Google is in danger of being eclipsed by the next round of dominant platforms. If it isn't able to expand its revenue engine to mobile—where the potential advertising market ultimately will be much larger than desktop search is—it too could be relegated to secondary status within a decade. Google could always try to buy out new competitors, as Facebook did with Instagram and WhatsApp. But repeated, large acquisitions will only incentivize the creation of even more startups that will become future competitors. Google's market position may seem insurmountable today, but this very well could change as the mobile Internet expands and mobile ad revenue eclipses that of the desktop Web.

How should governments react to the rising dominance of platform monopolies? Historical perspective is important here. Enduring monopolies like Standard Oil and AT&T are what gave the term its negative reputation. However, absent government protection, no business is likely to enjoy such a prolonged period of dominance today. As we saw with Microsoft in the 2000s and may potentially see with Google in the next decade, a modern monopoly's dominance in any one industry belies the competitive threat it faces from adjacent competitors and a constant onslaught of new entrants. Governments should worry about the long term later. As the famous economist John Maynard Keynes said, "In the long run we're all dead." The right answer usually is to let consumers reap the windfall of social and economic gains that new platforms are creating today. Most of these modern monopolies won't be dominant for long enough for the downside to materialize.

To be clear, this lack of longevity does not mean that governments and regulators shouldn't worry about platform monopolies. In some areas, the incentives of users as a whole diverge from those of a platform. For example, the ways that many platforms handle users' personal data and address individual privacy concerns are areas that merit attention. However, these concerns are not unique to platforms but apply to Internet businesses as a whole, as well as any business that collects personally identifiable information on behalf of third parties. Many linear businesses have not handled user privacy any better than Facebook or Google have. Meanwhile, some platforms, such as Apple and WhatsApp, have proven themselves to be much stronger advocates for their users' privacy. The answer here is not to limit the market power of these platform businesses—a move that would likely diminish overall consumer welfare—but rather to address the behavior of these businesses in specific areas of concern.

5

DESIGNING A BILLION-DOLLAR COMPANY

How the Core Transaction Explains Tinder's Success

The trick isn't adding stuff. It's taking away.

—Mark Zuckerberg, founder
and CEO of Facebook

Now that you understand what makes a platform tick, it's time to look at how to build one.

When it comes to business model design, linear businesses have it easy. Not only is the design process much simpler, but there are established frameworks you can work within. Some entrepreneurs have found ways to shoehorn tools aimed at linear businesses into working for platforms. For example, Airbnb used storyboards to help it understand how to balance the needs of consumers and producers. "We storyboard like crazy," Airbnb founder and chief product officer Joe Gebbia said. "We embarked on an ambitious project to map the entire guest and host terrain of Airbnb, and we did it through illustration. We looked at key emotional moments of the journey and we drew them. We visualized them. It's allowed our entire company to achieve a whole new level of empathy with our customers."[1] This type of process is important. It helps you identify your consumers and producers and understand both what they value individually and how they interact with each other. This interdependency is key to figuring out how you can create value for both groups by bringing them together.

However, this process is just the start. Because most frameworks were designed with linear businesses in mind, they don't help you structure and design the processes that drive repeated transactions for platforms. Essentially, *platform entrepreneurs need a whole new toolkit* for business model design.

For instance, a key tool for understanding linear businesses is the value chain that we mentioned in chapter 2. Michael Porter created the value chain as way to visualize and understand how linear businesses created value (see Figure 5.1).

The value chain was the set of activities that a company performed in order to deliver a valuable product or service to its customers. Porter broke these actions down into two categories, which he called primary activities and support activities. Primary activities were related to the actual creation and distribution of value, while support activities were the actions required to enable the primary functions. Taken together,

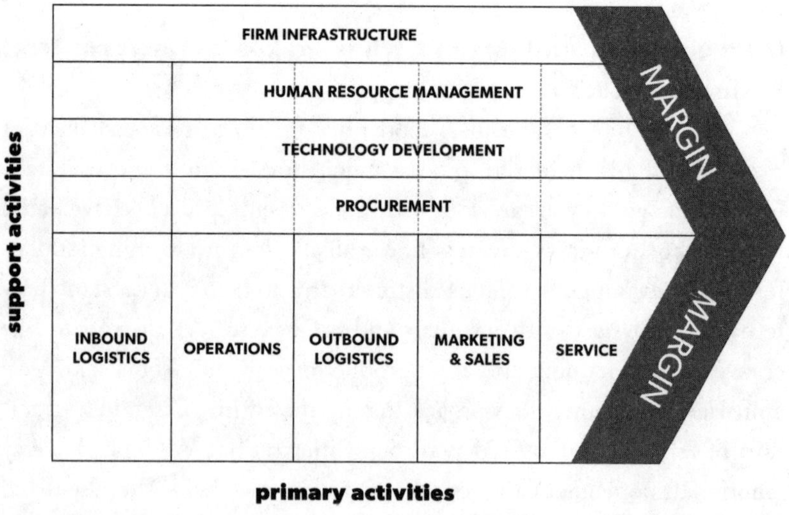

Figure 5.1.   The value chain as designed by Michael Porter.

these sets of activities comprised a chain that determined how a business acquired inputs and transformed them into its outputs, as well as how it delivered those outputs to consumers.

However, a platform business does not have simple inputs or outputs. A linear business's primary inputs are internal—it acquires resources and turns those inputs into outputs. But a platform's biggest resource is its network. A platform doesn't directly create much of the value that gets consumed. Rather, it facilitates a two-way exchange of value among its users. As a result, platforms don't have value chains in the traditional sense. And a "chain," which made sense as a visual metaphor for how value flows in a linear business, isn't a great representation of how value flows in a distributed network. So what's the platform equivalent?

Just like linear businesses, a platform has a set of primary activities that directly create value for its users as well as a set of secondary activities that serve to support that value creation. Combined, these activities form a *value ecosystem* (see Figure 5.2).

The primary activity in this ecosystem is *the core transaction*. The core transaction is the process that facilitates the exchange of value among its users. The support activities are the four core functions mentioned briefly in chapter 1. We cover those four core functions in more

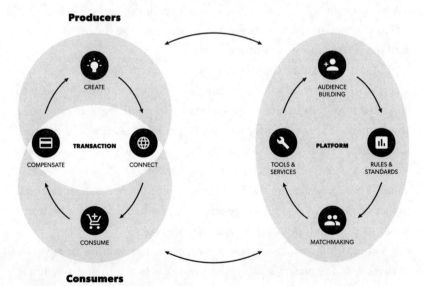

Figure 5.2.   The value ecosystem.

detail in chapter 6. The rest of this chapter focuses on the design of the core transaction.

THE MEANS OF CONNECTION

For the last couple of centuries, linear businesses created value by owning the means of production. They focused on creating value from the capital base of the company, whether it was factories, human capital, or intellectual property. They aggregated internal resources and designed processes to turn their capital base into valuable products and services for their customers. This was a linear process in which the business acquired inputs and turned them into more valuable outputs, whether that product was a Ford truck, investment advice, or tax software.

For a linear business, the means of production were the primary activity in Porter's value chain. In other words, the primary activity governed the way a linear business manufactured its product. This process started with gathering the raw material (inbound logistics), converting it into more valuable outputs (operations), and then getting it in the hands of customers (outbound logistics, sales and marketing, and services).

In contrast, a platform creates and manages large networks and facilitates the exchange of value among its users. Unlike Ford, Uber doesn't own any of the value that is being produced and consumed. Instead, Uber owns the way its users connect—not the means of production but the means of connection.

Linear businesses create value by manufacturing products or services; platforms create value by creating connections and using them to "manufacture" transactions. The core transaction is how platforms make this happen. It's how a platform takes the potential energy of its network and converts those connections into the kinetic energy of transactions. Without a core transaction, even a large network won't be able to create value. That's why getting the core transaction right is the most essential aspect of platform design. To generate and exchange value, a platform needs its users to repeat this process over and over.

What is the core transaction? *The core transaction is the set of actions consumers and producers must complete in order to exchange value.* Every platform has a core transaction. On Uber, drivers make themselves available and consumers submit requests for rides. On YouTube, producers upload videos and consumers watch, rate, and share them. On Lending Club people or small businesses request loans and others fund them. These examples of the core transaction highlight its purpose: to construct a set of simple, repeatable actions that producers and consumers take to create and consume value through a platform.

At a high level, the core transaction on every platform includes the same basic set of four actions. These actions are:

1. **Create:** A producer creates value or makes it available to be consumed through the platform.
2. **Connect:** In every transaction, one user takes an action that sparks the exchange by connecting with the other party.
3. **Consume:** Once consumers find the right match, they can consume the value created by the producer.
4. **Compensate:** Consumers create value for the producer in exchange for what they consumed.

All four actions are necessary for a platform to facilitate transactions successfully. This process is the platform's "factory," the way it repeatedly manufactures value for its customers. However, as mentioned earlier, unlike a factory, a platform doesn't create value based on what the company owns. Its most valuable assets—the people in its network—are external to the company.

Facilitating the core transaction is the way that platforms create value. The multisided nature of this transaction means that value doesn't just flow in one direction, from the producer to the consumer. Both producers and consumers create value on a platform, as we show in a moment. This ability to create value on both sides of the transaction is what incentivizes continued participation from both sets of users.

THE CORE TRANSACTION

Create

Platforms don't create their own inventory, so they need to incentivize external producers to do it for them. What producers create is the platform's inventory, the atomic unit of value in a platform. Although inventory is just one of the outputs of the production process of a linear business, it's the *starting point* for a platform. For Airbnb, for example, a host listing is the initial "raw material" that the platform converts into transactions. If hosts don't create listings on Airbnb and input their availability, travelers won't be able to book reservations. Similarly, if merchants don't list their inventory on Taobao or the Amazon Marketplace, there will be nothing for consumers to buy. And if producers don't upload videos to YouTube, there will be nothing for other users to watch.

If producers stop creating, the platform won't have any raw material to convert into completed transactions, just as a microchip factory without silicon won't be able to make its product.

Connect

You need one user to take an action that acts as a catalyst for the exchange. Which user group starts the transaction will vary depending on the platform. But each platform has one side that typically acts as the catalyst. On Kickstarter, a project's creators market their projects to consumers in order to bring attention (and contributions) to their campaigns. And on Skype and Snapchat, the producer is the one who initiates communication.

In other platforms, the consumer is the one who acts as the catalyst. On Uber, for example, the consumer enters in location information to initiate a ride request. On Amazon, shoppers search for products. And on Tinder, consumers swipe through profiles of potential matches. In each case, one user is the spark that sets the exchange in motion.

Consume

Once consumers have connected to a platform's inventory, they can extract value from the platform. This step takes on different forms depending on what the platform's inventory is. If the inventory is digital, then consumers usually can consume it directly through the platform. For example, on YouTube, this means watching a video. On Instagram and Snapchat, it's viewing a photo. On Lending Club, it's making a loan. But for platforms that include physical products or services, fulfillment happens outside the platform.

On Uber, the platform doesn't give you a ride, and on Airbnb, the platform doesn't host you in its own apartments. In the context of these marketplaces, "consumption" refers to the listings within the platform, not the product or service itself. On Etsy and Alibaba's Taobao, users consume a product listing by clicking the buy button. On Airbnb and Uber, they consume the listing by submitting a vacation or ride request.

The platform always optimizes first for the consumption of inventory *within its system*. As we show in chapter 6, platforms that have a physical product or service component that occurs outside them will also build tools and services to support the delivery of a product or the fulfillment of that service, but they don't handle that part of the interaction directly. That's why this external fulfillment is *not* part of the core transaction.

Compensate

Last, consumers create value for the producer to complete the exchange. The most obvious type of value is monetary payment. On Uber, you pay a driver for your ride. Or on Amazon, you pay when you purchase an item. But that's not the only way consumers can compensate a producer. On both Uber and Amazon, you can also rate and review the service or product. On YouTube, you can comment on a video and give it a thumbs up or thumbs down. Whether the feedback is positive or not, it is still valuable information for the producer and the platform. Additionally, the mere act of watching a video provides the uploader with a reward— a view on YouTube. As in this example, compensation can be a frictionless byproduct of consumption.

This type of nonmonetary value is an important part of how you reward and retain quality producers over time. In the context of a platform, monetary value is transitory—it passes through and out of the platform quickly. In contrast, reviews, ratings, likes, shares, comments, follows, and other types of compensation create value that's stored in the platform and can increase the producer's ability to get value out of it in the future. This stored value makes it less likely that producers will stop using the platform as it gives them the opportunity to grow their reputations and their businesses through the platform.

These nonmonetary rewards help close the loop on the transaction in order to maintain quality within the network and also serve as a way to collect data to spark subsequent transactions. As mentioned previously, many studies have shown that sellers with lots of reviews on eBay do better than those with only a few. The same is true on Airbnb. And Uber's matching algorithm favors drivers with lots of positive reviews. On other platforms, such as Handy, the number of positive reviews can affect the level of compensation that a producer is paid by the platform.

On content platforms like YouTube and Medium, likes and comments improve how content is ranked in search listings, recommendations, and leaderboards. Similarly, shares expose that content to new consumers. And a follow enables the producer to expose future content to users directly. As you can see, there are many different ways to compensate producers, and for the platform, direct monetary payment isn't always the most valuable.

THE TRANSACTION FACTORY

Create. Connect. Consume. Compensate. These are the four steps that make up the core transaction. If a platform is thought of as a transaction factory, these four steps are its assembly line. They are how a platform takes potential connections in its network and turns them into transactions. Platforms design the process of turning these potential connections into transactions and then repeat this process over and over. One of the first steps in building any platform is to design this process, the same way you would build a factory only after first designing the manufacturing process.

However, a platform's "assembly line" doesn't function quite like its linear counterpart. A platform is constantly changing and evolving, while an assembly line is a fairly static process. Also, the four steps of the core transaction don't necessarily occur one after the other as the steps in an assembly line do—often they occur asynchronously. If I upload a YouTube video today, it still can be consumed a year from now.

Yet, if any one of the steps in the core transaction is not functioning well, the flow of transactions breaks down—just as if one process in an assembly line stopped working, production would grind to a halt.

A factory is focused on how well it translates inputs into outputs. Its owners want to make this flow from raw material to product as efficient as possible. Any stoppages in this process will reduce the factory's ability to create products. Similarly, a platform aims to maximize the efficiency of its core transaction. This task isn't quite as simple as optimization of a linear business, since a platform is fine-tuning the actions of external users rather than internal resources that are fully under its control. If a platform business wants to increase its output (total completed transactions), it can't simply choose how much additional inventory it needs to create and specify the different types of products it will make. Platforms are entirely dependent on external producers for their inventory. A platform can incentivize its producers to create more inventory, or specific kinds of inventory, but it can't control these processes the way that a linear business can.

Additionally, a platform can't just optimize each step in the process by tweaking each step separately. Remember, a platform's two user groups are interdependent because of the network effect between them. What happens within one user group influences the experience of the other group. So if you change something to optimize the producer side of the business, it often has unintended effects on consumers. For example, improving efficiency in creation could lower quality in consumption. Trade-offs and knock-on effects must be considered with every change you make.

Still, the ultimate goal is the same for both linear and platform businesses: to design a repeatable process that will create value. This process also needs to encourage efficient, high-quality throughput at every step. For example, on a platform, if producers don't create the right kind of inventory—that is, if the inventory is of low quality—then you waste potential connections on bad transactions. On the other side, if you aren't connecting consumers with the right inventory, some of the value created by your producers goes to waste. The same goes for consuming and compensating. The better job that a platform does at facilitating each step of the core transaction, the more successful it will be.

THE CORE TRANSACTION:
MAKER VERSUS EXCHANGE

The details of the core transaction differ in important ways between exchange platforms and maker platforms, (which we covered in chapter 1). At a high level, the four steps of the core transaction remain the same, but the nature of the transaction changes depending on whether we're talking about an exchange platform or a maker platform.

The Core Transaction for Exchange Platforms

On an exchange platform, the paradigm for the core transaction is an exchange—an action in which two actively involved parties give and receive reciprocally. Because this is a 1:1 exchange where both parties are directly involved, the core transaction for exchange platforms is almost always *double opt-in*. Both parties have to agree to the exchange at that moment for the transaction to take place. This is as true for marketplaces like Uber, where both driver and passenger opt in to the transaction, as it is for social networks like Facebook and LinkedIn, where both parties agree to connect with each other. It's also true for a communication platform like WhatsApp, where users send and receive messages directly to and from their contacts. Some of these transactions may involve groups of people instead of just one consumer and one producer; however, in exchange platforms, a finite number of consumers and/or producers is involved in any transaction.

The Core Transaction for Maker Platforms

For a maker platform, the core transaction has a broadcast paradigm—a producer creates something and sends it out to many people. This 1:Many interaction is *single opt-in*. One party broadcasts out content and the other side consumes it. Once a producer creates value and broadcasts it, he or she doesn't have to interact directly with consumers in order for them to consume it. Once you tweet, anyone can read that tweet. Once you upload a video to YouTube, anyone can watch it. If you stream live on Periscope, anyone can view it.

This is why maker platforms with a social interaction almost all use the "follow" model. Twitter, Instagram, and YouTube are great examples. A follow interaction model is inherently single opt-in. When you follow someone, you subscribe to that user in order to see anything they tweet, upload, or post in the future. But this user doesn't have to approve you (or friend you back) in order for you to follow them. Contrast the follow model of a maker platform like Twitter with the friending model of an exchange, social networking platform like Facebook, and the difference is clear.

SWIPE RIGHT FOR GROWTH: HOW THE CORE TRANSACTION EXPLAINS TINDER'S SUCCESS

Let's look at an example of how getting the core transaction right can make a big difference. The double-opt-in interaction is the underlying principle of the core transaction for social networks, of which dating platforms are an important subset. Take Tinder, where both parties have to opt in by swiping right in order to be connected. Tinder's genius was in *correctly understanding the double-opt-in nature of dating interactions* and building a platform that made that core transaction as easy and seamless as possible. Instead of requiring custom messages to be written and read before completing a match, the mutual "swipe right" took the place of the match, leaving custom messages to be exchanged afterward.

Older dating platforms, such as OkCupid and Match.com, don't do nearly as good a job of facilitating the core transaction—two mutually interested people connecting with each other. On these platforms, users typically have to first send a *message* to the other user before they can be matched. As a result, lots of men send out many custom messages but receive no or few responses. On the other side, a smaller group of women are inundated with messages, mostly from men they have no interest in.[2] They then have to sort through that haystack to find the needle they're looking for—someone they want to reply to. These messaging interactions are effectively double opt-in—both parties have to opt in to the interaction in order to create a "match"—but the platform treats them as if they are single opt-in. Not surprisingly, these older dating platforms end up with a lot of dissatisfied users and a lot of unnecessary friction in the core exchange. Ultimately, this means the platforms facilitate fewer exchanges and generate less value. As we said earlier, getting the core transaction right is *the* most important piece of platform design.

Tinder nailed its core transaction and quickly became the most popular dating platform in the United States. Its core transaction was so successful, in fact, that an army of similar apps copied its interface.

Tinder—social networking platform

These copycat apps have become so common that there's even a term for designs that use a Tinder-style interface: Tinderfaces. You can find apps using Tinderfaces to try to build platforms in such widely divergent industries as fashion, job applications, and real estate. However, most of these clones won't be successful, as Tinder's core transaction won't fit every industry or platform type. Cloning another platform's core transaction and blindly adapting it to other contexts is a recipe for failure. Tinder's innovation wasn't just its interface but rather how well its design fit the core transaction for dating platforms.

FROM ZERO TO ONE:
FINDING PRODUCT/MARKET FIT

One of the biggest mistakes that we've seen many founders of platform startups make is to try to do too much at the same time. Tomasz Tungus, a partner at Redpoint Ventures, a venture capital firm that frequently invests in platforms, called this chasing two rabbits at once.[3] For platforms, this mistake most frequently takes the form of trying to build multiple core transactions from the start. Founders will look at successful platforms, such as LinkedIn, Uber, or Facebook, and think that they have to provide a similar experience to their users in order to be successful. But creating multiple transactions right away is usually a big mistake, as it confuses users and makes it harder to grow the network and optimize the core transaction. "If you chase two rabbits, both will escape. Pick one and seize it," Tungus said. Eventually, it makes sense to start building multiple transactions in order to expand the network. But that first transaction is always the hardest one to get right. Early-stage platforms should almost always start with just one transaction. Trying to deliver on more than one core transaction at a time is often a death sentence for such platforms.

In fact, none of the more established platforms we mentioned started out with the complex, multitiered networks that they have today. When LinkedIn launched in 2002, it started with simple profiles that allowed users to connect with other professionals.

Only after the network had grown to nearly 2 million users did LinkedIn start to build additional transactions. In January 2005, it launched LinkedIn Jobs, a marketplace for online recruiting. Not only was this a new core transaction, it also was a completely different platform type—a services marketplace built on top of a social network. Later LinkedIn built in more advanced messaging features, and after a few acquisitions, it eventually built out a content platform with the LinkedIn Publishing Platform. (Applico was an early adopter of the latter; we were invited to participate in the platform's pilot program.) However, going after multiple platform types from the start is a surefire path to failure. Building liquidity in one market is hard enough. Doing it in two at the same time is almost impossible. At best, you'll end up with a platform that has weak penetration in two markets. Multiple platform businesses with low market penetration will be much less valuable than one platform that dominates its market. "Founders should ask whether faster growth and dominance in one market segment builds a more valuable business than smaller penetration of and slower growth in two markets," Tungus said. "Most of the time, and particularly in early stage markets, a focused startup perceived to be on the path to monopolizing a market will be more valuable."

LinkedIn's progression from simple social network to a platform conglomerate with multiple platform types is typical. Uber started out just with black cabs before it expanded into so-called ride-sharing with UberX, now by far its most popular service. And only after it had established itself as the dominant taxi network in the United States, well ahead of competitor Lyft, did Uber begin to experiment with other transaction types, such as UberRUSH (courier service) and UberEATS (food delivery).

SIMPLICITY BY DESIGN

Facebook's platform followed a similar trajectory. When Facebook first started, it had only very simple profiles, and users could view only other people who went to the same school.

Users couldn't "share" links, messages or photos with friends, and users couldn't "like" anything. There were no third-party apps and no Newsfeed. There wasn't even a "wall" on friends' profiles where users could write messages to them. All of these features were developed later as the platform grew over time. At the start, Facebook was just a collection of profiles that could connect with one another through the double-opt-in interaction of "friending."

This simplicity was by design. Many of Facebook's earlier competitors had many more features. Club Nexus, created in the fall of 2001 by Orkut Büyükkükten, the future creator of Google's Orkut, was the first college-specific social network. (Facebook wasn't launched until 2004.) Launched at Stanford, where Büyükkükten was a student, Club Nexus allowed students to chat, send emails, post events and personal ads, buy and sell used goods, and post images and articles.[4] A talented programmer, Büyükkükten loaded Club Nexus with every interesting feature he could think of. However, this glut of features made the platform very difficult to use and weakened the strength of its network. Users didn't get the sense that there were many other people on the platform, as they were each dispersed over many different types of transactions. As a result, Club Nexus never really caught on. It reached 1,500 members out of a student body of 15,000 within six weeks of its launch at Stanford, but after reaching about 2,500 users, usage leveled off.[5] The platform was just too complicated, which diluted its network effects.

Another of Facebook's early competitors was houseSYSTEM, a social network created by a Harvard senior in September 2003, a few months before Facebook was founded. HouseSYSTEM allowed Harvard students to buy and sell books and review courses, among other features. It also allowed them to upload photos to what it called a "Universal Face Book." Sam Lessin, a classmate of Mark Zuckerberg's who would later go on to become head of product at Facebook, remembered using houseSYSTEM. He called it "a huge sprawling system that could do all sorts of things." A few hundred students signed up, but hous-eSYSTEM never got much traction. After Facebook launched, house-SYSTEM's creator, Aaron Greenspan, met with Zuckerberg at Harvard and invited Zuckerberg to incorporate houseSYSTEM into Facebook, but Zuckerberg declined. He said it was "too useful," according to Greenspan. "It just does too much stuff," Zuckerberg continued. "Like, it's almost overwhelming how useful it is." In contrast, Facebook "was almost obsessively minimal," Lessin said. "The only thing you could do immediately was invite more friends. It was that pureness that drove it." Zuckerberg agreed. "The trick isn't adding stuff," he said. "It's taking away."[6] Compared to its competition, Facebook focused on creating a relatively simple core transaction. Only later, once it had optimized its initial transaction—friending and viewing other people's profiles—did it begin to add new transactions and new features.

6

THE VISIBLE HAND

The Four Functions of a Platform

Well-designed networks reduce friction and help good stuff be found.
—Ev Williams, founder and CEO of Medium,
founder and former CEO of Twitter

Now that we've covered the core transaction, our next
step is to take a closer look at the four functions of a platform, which we
covered briefly in chapter 1. Economists like to talk about the invisible
hand as the magical force that guides markets to work efficiently. However, in the case of the platform, the hand is very visible. A platform's
network doesn't appear out of nothing. The platform has to create it and
enable the core transaction to turn that network into value. To do this, a
platform needs to engage in four key support activities. Think of a platform as a visible hand, with the four support activities as its fingers and
the core transaction as the thumb. Without the thumb, the other fingers
aren't very useful. But if you lose a finger, the whole hand doesn't function as well. By combining these four activities with the core transaction, the platform is able to create networks, markets, and communities
that didn't exist before and wouldn't exist otherwise.

What are these four support functions? First, a platform needs to get users to join its network. Then it needs to be able to match those users together so that they can exchange value. Finally, it needs to have the right tools and services to support its users and the right rules and standards to facilitate transactions and maintain quality in its network.

These are the four core functions of a platform:

1. **Audience building:** Build a liquid marketplace by attracting a critical mass of consumers and producers.
2. **Matchmaking:** Connect the right consumers with the right producers in order to facilitate transactions and interactions.
3. **Providing core tools and services:** Build tools and services that support the core transaction by lowering transaction costs, removing barriers to entry, and making the platform more valuable over time through data.
4. **Creating rules and standards:** Set guidelines that govern which behaviors are allowed and encouraged and which are forbidden or discouraged.

Different platforms accomplish these functions in different ways, but every successful platform accomplishes all of them. These functions are the infrastructure that supports the network and enables transactions to happen easily and efficiently. Platforms create networks that are both open and highly participatory while also being curated and governed. Producers and consumers should both be able to access the platform and complete transactions easily. But at the same time, the platform needs to prevent undesirable behavior and make sure that users can find what they want. These priorities conflict surprisingly often. Let's take a look at how successful platforms have tackled these challenges and created the very visible hand that manages their networks and makes transactions possible. We'll show you one example from Uber in each function so that you get a relatively complete picture of how one platform works. And we'll include other stories from lots of different platforms (and platform types) to provide a broader perspective.

AUDIENCE BUILDING

The first of the four core functions is *audience building*. Because a platform doesn't have direct control of its inventory, it needs to attract external producers who will create inventory within the platform. At the same time, the platform needs to attract consumers who will complete the exchange of value. Audience building is all about growing the network and creating the potential energy of connections that can then be turned into transactions. Without both consumers and producers, a platform will fail. As we show next, platforms can get pretty creative when it comes to creating growth.

Operation SLOG

In major cities around the United States, you can join a team of secret operatives that spends its days patrolling the streets. If you join one of these street teams, you will be offered a burner phone and a score of fresh credit cards in order to avoid detection. Your mission? Gather intelligence about the competition and try to convert its assets—and make sure you don't get caught.

As an operative, you are given a playbook that gives strict instructions on how to avoid detection while finding your mark. This playbook tells you how to approach an asset. You use a few opening questions to begin the conversation and build up a rapport. After assessing the asset's openness, you have several ways to work up to the topic of defecting. Finally, you have a five-point plan for converting an asset. If you succeed, you're rewarded with cold, hard cash. If you're caught, your employer will deny your existence.

No, this isn't the plot of a movie about high-stakes corporate espionage. This is Operation SLOG, Uber's covert, ethically dubious, and possibly illegal attempt at poaching drivers from rival ride-hailing service Lyft. "SLOG" stands for Supplying Long-term Operations Growth, a name that hints at why Uber goes to such great lengths to recruit drivers. Uber understands that one of its core functions is to grow its network.

Aggressive marketing is nothing new, but for a platform like Uber, the task goes beyond marketing. Uber has to attract two separate groups of users—drivers and passengers—and it has to balance the number of each in order to maintain an equilibrium between supply and demand.

When it first started in San Francisco in 2009, Uber needed to create what in finance is known as a "liquid" marketplace. A marketplace is considered liquid when there's enough overlap in supply and demand that most transactions can clear quickly. But a platform also needs to maintain a balance between both sides. For Uber, getting this balance right is essential. If too many drivers join, some will sit idle and wait for passengers. When drivers sit, they lose money. And if they're losing money, they're going to leave the platform. Conversely, if there aren't enough drivers on the road, passengers will face long wait times before they can get a ride, or will not get one at all. Consumers who can't rely on Uber for a ride are much less likely to use it in the future.

Many of Uber's more controversial practices are aimed at addressing this challenge. For example, Uber's "surge pricing"—dynamic pricing that rises in response to high demand—is a direct attempt to balance supply and demand. Surge pricing is designed to increase the number of drivers available on Uber, even as it reduces the number of passengers who can afford the service. Rather than keeping the price constant and facing the prospect of high wait times and unfilled rides for customers, Uber raises prices in order to better balance the number of drivers with the number of people looking for rides. Many consumers have bristled at this practice, but dynamic pricing can be very helpful in creating the balanced growth a platform needs.

Uber—services marketplace platform

In this light, Uber's win-at-all-costs approach to acquiring drivers also makes more sense. The company has had a lot of success at increasing demand for its service, but drivers are much harder to come by. Based on leaked financial data, the ratio of drivers/riders in major cities is usually about 1/10.[1] This is a pretty common producer/consumer ratio for services marketplaces, which is why producers are often the user group that companies compete over the most. If Uber can't attract more drivers, it won't be able to support a growing number of consumers who want to use the service. Attracting more drivers is key to Uber's long-term growth, which is why the company has been so aggressive about securing additional drivers.

Hacking Networks for Growth: How Airbnb Built Its Platform Off of Craigslist and the Democratic National Convention

Although Uber has gotten most of the negative PR, it isn't the only platform that has gotten its hands dirty in order to grow its network. Airbnb, a marketplace for short-term home rental, has a much cleaner reputation than Uber does. Airbnb built its brand around the idea of "belonging," no matter where you are. As of 2015, its website claims that Airbnb creates "a sense of belonging anywhere in the world," and the text at the top of its homepage reads "Welcome Home." But to get where it is today—with a valuation of $25.5 billion and nearly $2.4 billion raised—the company didn't play nice.

Back in 2010, Airbnb was a tiny startup that had just raised its Series A, a company's first round of significant funding. It was still a small player in the online short-term rentals industry, especially compared to the leader in that market, Craigslist. Craigslist had more traffic and more listings than Airbnb did, but Airbnb's site provided higher-quality listings and better customer support. In an effort to grow its network, Airbnb created an unofficial "integration" with Craigslist.

The feature was called "Post to Craigslist" and it allowed any host to post their listing on Airbnb to the relevant section of Craigslist with a few clicks. But rather than lettings viewers respond to the listing through Craigslist, the Craigslist posting would send them back to Airbnb to book a reservation. The end result was that Airbnb was able to divert a lot of consumers from Craigslist to booking reservations on Airbnb.

At the same time Airbnb was taking traffic from Craigslist, the upstart company was also tapping into Craigslist's network of hosts. It allegedly used multiple Gmail accounts to spam Craigslist posters. The emails didn't appear to come from Airbnb itself but from an individual who simply wanted to inform the poster about another vacation rental site they should "check out."

Except for naming the city where the listing was located, the text from each of these emails was almost exactly the same. LakePlace.com CEO Dave Gooden, who investigated Airbnb's growth tactics, received four nearly identical emails when he posted vacation rental listings on Craiglist over a period of three weeks. Each email read roughly like this:

> Hey,
> I am emailing you because you have one of the nicest listings on Craigslist in [location], and I want to recommend you feature it (for free) on one of the largest [location] housing sites on the web, Airbnb. The site already has 3,000,000 page views a month. Check it out here to list now.

Airbnb later blamed the actions on a "rogue" external sales team it contracted to acquire listings through person-to-person sales.[2] Although these tactics weren't illegal, they did violate Craigslist's rules. Despite having a relatively small social media presence and just-okay search engine optimization, Airbnb was able to tap into Craigslist's existing network to build liquidity in its own marketplace. Like Uber, Airbnb knew that without liquidity, nothing else mattered, so the company was willing to play dirty to get its platform started. However, this strategy wasn't the only reason for Airbnb's spectacular early growth.

When the 2008 Democratic National Convention announced it was going to Denver, Airbnb cofounder and CEO Brian Chesky saw an opportunity. The Democratic Party made the last-minute decision to move presidential hopeful Barack Obama's speech from the Pepsi Center (capacity 18,007) to the larger outdoor venue of Invesco Field, since renamed Sports Authority Field (capacity 76,125). But the city wasn't ready to host 80,000 out-of-town attendees. Only 28,000 hotel rooms were available. The problem was obvious. And no one was doing anything about it. By then, Chesky knew what to look for. "We looked for high profile events and said, 'We're going to solve a high-profile solution to a high-profile problem,'" Chesky said.[3] His startup had been launched unintentionally in 2007 when an international design conference went to San Francisco and there weren't enough rooms available for attendees. Struggling to make ends meet, Brian and his roommate, cofounder Joe

Gebbia, decided to offer up three air mattresses along with a complimentary breakfast in the loft of their apartment. They set up a simple website, and three conference attendees took them up on their offer for $80 per night. Airbnb was born. And the rent got paid.

When the convention went to Denver, Airbnb was ready to capitalize on the opportunity. "In the summer of 2008, all anyone was talking about was Barack Obama. And the Democratic National Convention was coming up and they had moved him from the 20,000-seat Pepsi Center to the 80,000-seat football stadium where the Denver Broncos play," Chesky said. "Suddenly, all these mainstream media outlets are saying, 'Where are we going to stay?' And we're like—light bulb goes off—'they're going to stay at Airbnb! Obama supporters can host other Obama supporters all over the world. This is going to be a huge story.'" The hustle paid off, as Airbnb received national news coverage for its novel solution to the lodging crisis.

As we show in chapter 8, finding other networks to tap into, whether they're digital or exist in the real world, is a key strategy for audience building. In the wake of the DNC event, Airbnb started to gain traction. Just two years later, in 2010, the platform had booked approximately 125,000 guest nights.

PayPal's Charity Robot

Long before Airbnb had figured out how to tap into Craigslist's network, PayPal had a similar challenge. In 1999, PayPal faced intense competition from better-funded rivals like X.com and dotBank. Who would win the market for online payments was anyone's guess. After failing with its initial idea of a peer-to-peer payments system for PalmPilots, a handheld PC device (also called a PDA) popular in the late 1990s and early 2000s, PayPal pivoted to facilitating payments for online auctions. This strategy meant going after sellers on eBay, the leading auction-based product marketplace on the Web. Luke Nosek, a cofounder of PayPal who served as its VP of marketing and strategy, had an idea. "What we need to do is go out and start buying

Paypal—payments platform

stuff on eBay and insist on using PayPal to pay for it," he suggested. "We don't need to buy every auction. Many sellers list multiples items at a time. All we need to do to introduce them to PayPal is just purchase one."[4] However, he still needed a way to convince the sellers to want to accept PayPal. The answer was PayPal's "charity robot."

PayPal built a bot, a computer script that would automatically scan eBay auctions. Before bidding, the bot would identify itself to sellers by sending an email that said it was collecting goods that would be donated. But, the bot would say, it could only pay with PayPal. If the seller agreed, the bot would automatically place a bid. However, even if the bot didn't win the auction, at least the seller would have been introduced to PayPal.[5] This charity robot became PayPal's "secret weapon," according to former PayPal marketing executive Eric M. Jackson. The company even secured the participation of the Red Cross, which would accept the goods that PayPal's charity robot bought. PayPal's marketing team started sending out pitches to sellers using the email address charity robot@paypal.com. Not surprisingly, the vast majority of the people the robot contacted were happy to accept PayPal.

Do or Die

In addition to these controversial tactics, many platforms also use more traditional marketing channels. A key part of eBay's success against auction-based offerings from competitors like Amazon and Yahoo! was a traffic-buying deal it struck with a then-dominant AOL.

Whether a platform dabbles in black-hat tactics or uses less controversial methods, the point is that for platforms, building liquidity is a do-or-die proposition. This is especially true in a platform's early stages, when the network hasn't yet achieved a baseline level of liquidity and the positive feedback loop of network effects hasn't yet kicked in. Without a large network, a platform doesn't provide much value. There are no bonus points for being nice.

MATCHMAKING

Once you get lots of users onto a platform, you need to figure out how you're going to connect them. That's where matchmaking comes in. You need to be able to connect the right producers with the right consumers in order to facilitate exchanges. This is easy to do when you only have a few hundred or a few thousands users. But as your network grows, the task becomes exponentially more complex. Without a scalable system for matchmaking, a platform won't be able to connect consumers and producers effectively. The more efficiently a platform can match its users, the stronger its network effects will be and the more transactions it will enable—which, of course, translates directly into more value and more profit.

Typically, building a matchmaking system involves using data to identify the key product characteristics that will matter to each user group. Then you have to build the right matching system that captures and uses this data to connect your users as efficiently as possible. As we show next, doing this includes everything from building automatic, algorithmic matching to designing user-friendly search and discovery capabilities.

The Traveling Salesman

Although a lot of ink has been spilled over Uber's controversial marketing tactics and surge pricing, the real magic at the heart of its platform has been overlooked. This bit of pixie dust is Uber's automatic matching algorithm.

There's a good reason this key part of the platform hasn't gotten much attention. To both drivers and riders, it's mostly invisible. As a consumer, you simply hit a button and within seconds you're informed that your driver is on the way. If you're a driver, the process is similarly automatic. You're sent a ride request, and once you accept it, you're off to pick up a passenger. What Uber does behind the scenes doesn't matter much to the users on either side of the transaction, yet it's the key to the kingdom. This is a common sign of effective matchmaking. If it works well, users will take it for granted. It's low friction and doesn't require much thought on either user's part.

How does Uber do it? First it's helpful to consider a related problem. Imagine a paper with 10,000 dots scattered across its surface. If you drew a line that passed through every dot, what would be the shortest possible path to connect all of them? This is the traveling salesman problem, one of the most-studied optimization problems in mathematics, and one with a wide range of applications. But in the context of a transportation network, Uber founder and CEO Travis Kalanick identified its usefulness early on. "We have 100 cars out there and riders sprinkled all around the city," Kalanick said. "Each car has its own traveling-salesman problem."[6] Uber's algorithm uses location tracking to try to pick the most efficient driver to send.

This is an age-old problem for the cab industry. Dispatchers are tasked with trying to get the most efficient use out of the cab company's limited resources. But for Uber, the issue is even more urgent. If a cab company doesn't use its resources optimally, it might lose out on a few extra rides and a little additional revenue, but its cab drivers aren't likely to quit over suboptimal routes. If Uber, however, doesn't match its drivers with passengers efficiently, that doesn't just mean less money for Uber—it means those drivers are more likely to leave the platform, possibly for a rival network.

Uber's scale only magnifies this issue. A taxi dispatcher who operates inefficiently will have a limited impact. But if you're trying to manage thousands or even millions of transactions simultaneously across hundreds of cities, being a little less efficient at matching drivers and riders can mean the difference between completely dominating a market and going out of business.

Collaborative Filtering

Uber isn't alone in having a difficult matchmaking challenge. Amazon faced a similarly thorny problem: how to match users with the products they might want to purchase out of hundreds of thousands of items. This problem is even more difficult because of the Amazon Marketplace, a platform that allows third-party merchants to sell items on Amazon. These third-party merchants create listings for their items, meaning Amazon can't predefine related items based on its own inventory. Instead, Amazon chose to use collaborative filtering, a process that looks at the individual behavior of large groups of people to identify common patterns. This process is the source of Amazon's famous "Customers Who Bought This Item Also Bought" feature. The algorithm behind this feature uses data on items customers often purchase together (like two books by the same author, or batteries along with a remote control device) in order to create a list of related items.

Both Amazon's related items feature and Uber's automatic matching use data to make sure the right consumers can find the right producers. Both platforms have a huge number of users, meaning they've succeeded at building liquidity. But all the liquidity in the world won't matter if you can't match the right consumers with the right producers. Without matchmaking, your users will be left looking for a needle in a giant haystack. Part of the platform's job is to make sure customers can easily find that needle. Doing this at scale requires the smart use of data.

Why YouTube Changed How It Measures Success

For YouTube, March 2012 will go down as one of the most traumatic months in its history. Just as Google Search was an empire built on links, YouTube was built on clicks. For a long time, YouTube used clicks ("view count") above all else as a proxy for popularity and quality. Likewise, YouTubers didn't see clicks as just a vanity metric. Since views were used to determine advertising rates, clicks were currency. But on March 15, 2012, YouTube's view count plunged by 20 percent in one day—on purpose.

YouTube—content platform

What happened? Well, YouTube decided to change how it measured success. Clicks were out, and engagement was in.

For YouTube, how best to match viewers with videos is an important question. Every minute, users upload more than 300 hours of video to YouTube.[7] The platform hosts billions of videos. Its content includes everything from cat videos and song parodies to entire college courses, political debates, or (most important) the latest Justin Bieber videos. There's more content on YouTube than you could ever watch in your lifetime, but only some of it is relevant. "We believe that for every human being on earth, there's 100 hours of YouTube that they would love to watch," said Cristos Goodrow, YouTube's director of engineering for search and discover. "The trick is helping you find it."[8]

Prior to the change, YouTube's matching algorithms were optimized to get you to click more. "Our video discovery features were previously designed to drive *views*," read a post on the company's official blog. "This rewarded videos that were successful at attracting clicks, rather than the videos that actually kept viewers engaged. (Cleavage thumbnails, anyone?)" This system often resulted in users clicking through several videos before they found what they were looking for. Users frequently hopped from one video to the next without watching any to completion. According to Goodrow, clicks just weren't a good measure for the quality of a match. "We realized that if we made the viewer click that many times, it didn't seem to be a good estimate of how much value they were deriving from YouTube." So YouTube decided to make the switch to prioritizing viewing time over clicks. According to the company, the goal was to "increase the amount of time that the viewer will spend watching videos on YouTube, not only on the next view, but also successive views thereafter."[9]

So on March 15, 2012, YouTube flipped the switch. Watch time—not just views—was now the determining factor for its matching system. Not surprisingly, the move upset many content creators, who were used to optimizing their videos to take advantage of the old system, where they would get paid based on clicks even if users didn't stick around for long. This system led many content creators to use tricks, such as setting their video's thumbnail to an image of an event that users were likely to search for (say, a recent sporting event). But then when users clicked through to the video, it would be someone talking about the event rather than footage of the event itself. As frequent users of YouTube in its early days, we can attest to how frustrating this experience was. Luckily, YouTube agreed. In the new system, these misleading videos would get buried in search results, as users usually didn't watch them for long. Ultimately, the experience was better for viewers, and content creators were encouraged to upload better content.

Creating Rules and Standards

Twitter is a famously noisy place. With over 300 million active users and hundreds of millions more who view tweets each month, it's impossible for any one person to keep up with everything that's happening on the platform. There's a good reason for that: Twitter wants to be the real-time pulse of the world's information. As its home page declares, you go to Twitter to "see what's happening right now."

As of November 2015, more than 600 million tweets were sent out each day.[10] That's close to 10,000 a second. And that number is growing every day. In the time it takes you to read this

Twitter—content platform

sentence, tens of thousands of new tweets will be posted. Twitter's raw data feed is sometimes (aptly) called a firehouse of information. No one can keep up with all of that activity. But if you're Twitter, you *have* to. Like any platform, Twitter has to govern the behavior of its users. But how do you control the behavior of hundreds of millions of people, the vast majority of whom you will never meet in person? Well, you can't. But you can set rules and standards, and most users will comply voluntarily. You can also create the detection systems and penalties to deter those who don't. These rules and standards are an essential part of how platforms can manage large and essentially ungovernable communities of users.

Some of these standards are laid out by the company, like Twitter's suggestions on tweeting best practices, which include guidelines on how to use its @reply functionality and the right way to follow other users. Other standards are more implicit and community enforced, such as not loading your tweets with hashtags or the idea that you should post tweets that benefit your audience, not just yourself.

Many of these rules also are explicit and hard-coded into software, including Twitter's famous 140-character limit on the length of tweets. This constraint originated from the 160 maximum character length of SMS text messages, which were how you created tweets when Twitter started in 2006. However, even when the platform's technology evolved beyond those limitations, Twitter chose to keep the 140-character limit. Why? Because the short messages had become a part of the platform's identity. Tweets were easy to write and even easier to consume, and the shorter message length helped differentiate Twitter from other micro-blogging platforms. If you had something longer to say, you could do that elsewhere. Twitter's users didn't have time for that. Twitter was for what's happening *right now*.

Enforcing this character limitation on tweets was a key part of how the company built and delivered on its value proposition. True, the limit has relaxed a bit over time. The characters in HTTP links no longer count against the 140-character total, and the platform has added other features, such as the ability to quote other tweets without using up precious characters. You can also add all kinds of rich media to tweets now that you couldn't when the company first started. But despite all these changes, the underlying principle has stayed the same. Tweets should be short and to the point. They should show you what's happening right now.

The Mayor of Twitter

In order to manage this massive community, a host of other rules govern everything from obvious issues, such as spam, to more unusual ones, such as username squatting (the practice of holding for ransom a potentially popular user name) or impersonation. Identity is a big issue on Twitter. In a platform that's all about what people have to say, what you can say and who can say what are important issues for Twitter to consider.

As Twitter's own guidelines acknowledge, these rules aren't all set in stone. They change and evolve over time, just as the platform does. One area where this change has had a big impact is on Twitter's developer community. Developers have long had an uneasy relationship with Twitter—though, to be fair, you can say the same for its rival, Facebook. Still, Twitter has had a lot of success in growing its developer community. Today Twitter handles millions of requests from external apps every day through its API. These API calls pull information from Twitter that another app's users have granted it access to, including login information, contact lists, and tweets.

Handling all these API calls for free costs Twitter money, so the company needs to be sure that these external applications are acting in a way that isn't detrimental to the platform. Creating the rules and standards for this community was a unique task, as Ryan Sarver well knows. Sarver, now a partner at venture capital firm Redpoint Ventures, was formerly the platform director at Twitter, where he managed its rapidly growing development community. "On Twitter, there were three or four million different websites we were working with and maybe a million different developers," Sarver says. "It's huge ecosystems where you're only going to meet a very small fraction of the people. So our job was to create policy that lets people know where the guardrails are and what behaviors are expected out of them."

Sarver worked at Twitter between 2009 and 2013, a key period in the company's growth. He was there just as Twitter started to go mainstream and until just before the company went public. "The way I used to talk about it to our team at Twitter is that we're the mayor of a town," Sarver says. "Our job is to create incentives and disincentives to produce the best behavior, the best outcome, from a bunch of people you'll never meet." In effect, he was creating public policy for Twitter's developer community.

This attitude is surprisingly common among those who have spent time leading platforms. In fact, it was a key reason that Mark Zuckerberg hired Sheryl Sandberg as Facebook's chief operating officer. "We spent a lot of time talking about her experience in government," Zuckerberg said. "In a lot of ways, Facebook is more like a government than a traditional company. We have this large community of people, and more than other technology companies, we're really setting policies."[11]

Sarver agrees. "I went into the job having never done any real policy work before, and I never realized how important policy was going to be. It ended up being a huge part of our time." Sarver's job was effectively to be the mayor of Twitter's development community. But as in any town, the mayor's mandate can shift as the town changes and grows.

How Twitter Became a Business

The Twitter that handles millions of API calls today is not the same platform that Twitter was in its early years. For years, Twitter didn't even have an official mobile app, so third-party apps played an important part in Twitter's early success. "The development platform was something that allowed people to develop clients for mobile and for desktop and for Linux. They created different web versions and the myriad other ways that people could then connect to Twitter," Sarver explains. "It allowed Twitter to stay stickier in users' lives, because Twitter was now available wherever they were. So, if mobile was taking off and Twitter didn't have the resources to go build a mobile client, other third-party developers built out these mobile clients. And if Twitter didn't have some kind of mobile presence at the time, I think we would've lost a lot of those users in the early days."

In Twitter's early days, the company took a let-a-thousand-flowers-bloom stance toward its developer community. These developers could provide many features that Twitter itself just didn't have the resources to build. However, as the platform grew and the company's resources expanded, there was an obvious downside to this approach: Twitter had little control over how its users experienced the platform. When Sarver started at Twitter, as far as most users were concerned, the development community *was* Twitter. "If you remember the early days of the Twitter platform, it was mostly about third-party clients," Sarver says. "Twitter was just a website and SMS, and it could barely stay up each day." But as the platform evolved, Twitter started to exert more control over its development community, particularly on unofficial Twitter clients. These were apps that connected you to Twitter but that weren't made by the platform.

Effectively, early Twitter mostly provided the underlying technology that other developers were building user experiences on top of. As Twitter investor and prominent venture capitalist Fred Wilson put it, "Much of the early work on the Twitter Platform has been filling holes in the Twitter product."[12] Rather than building new, complementary businesses on top of Twitter, these developers were simply plugging holes in the core experience that Twitter hadn't yet filled. Although this dynamic helped Twitter grow, it also prevented the company from developing into a real business.

Developers who built on top of Twitter's API made money by selling software—popular Twitter clients typically sold for a couple of dollars on the App Store. But Twitter itself was still free. It didn't charge developers for access to its API, and it didn't charge users for posting or viewing tweets.

Without controlling the core Twitter experience, the company could do little to improve the platform and even less to monetize it. It also faced threats from companies that were trying to take over the core Twitter experience, like Bill Gross's UberMedia. Gross bought up a number of the top Twitter clients and consolidated them under one roof, at one point controlling as much as 20 percent of daily tweets.[13] Faced with the prospect of losing control of its network and needing to make money, Twitter clamped down on third-party Twitter clients. First it bought Tweetie, one of the most popular Twitter clients at the time, in 2010 and reintroduced it as Twitter for iPhone. It also released a Twitter for BlackBerry app. Twitter was no longer just a simple website—the platform now had its first official mobile apps.

Shortly thereafter, Twitter tightened the screws on its developer community. Posting on Twitter's developer forums in March 2011, Sarver was particularly blunt about Twitter's new direction. "Developers have told us that they'd like more guidance from us about the best opportunities to build on Twitter," he said. "More specifically, developers ask us if they should build client apps that mimic or reproduce the mainstream Twitter consumer client experience. The answer is no."[14] This pronouncement followed an episode a month earlier where several Twitter clients owned by UberMedia had temporarily stopped working. Why? Because Twitter shut off their access to the Twitter API. The message to the developer community was clear: Thanks for your help, but we'll take it from here.

Developers were still welcome to build on Twitter's API, but only if they built businesses that complemented Twitter's core experience. As Twitter's then-CEO Dick Costolo put it, "What you'll see us do more and more as a platform is allow third parties to build *into Twitter* [emphasis added]."[15] Rather than trying to build client applications that would effectively *be* Twitter and own the core experience, developers would be allowed only to add value to the platform by creating new, and nonessential, experiences. Thus, Twitter made it clear that it alone was going to own the core transaction on its platform, and it set the rules and standards around its user experience.

The Future of Twitter

These were tough decisions for Twitter, but they were necessary to help scale and monetize the platform. Balancing the interests of producers, consumers, and the platform is always a tough task. Sometimes the platform needs to make decisions that will be unpopular with some of its users. In fact, Twitter found itself in a similar place in 2015. Despite growing revenue numbers, Twitter's network has stalled out at about 300 million monthly users. Many have started to question Twitter's value, and the company has taken a beating on Wall Street. Although Twitter has long catered to its hardcore users, the platform is very hard to understand for most users.

Twitter can be a cold place. Spam overpopulates timelines and buries the good stuff. You can tweet influencers, but they're likely to never respond because they're inundated. You can get followed only to be unfollowed moments later, just because someone is fishing for followers. Many people will say that they just don't "get" Twitter. "Why would I tweet?" most new users ask. It's not uncommon for a user to test out Twitter, not immediately understand the experience, and never return. Not surprisingly, Twitter has had trouble with user retention. According to a *Wall Street Journal* report in May 2014, less than 11 percent of users who had signed up in 2012 were still using the platform. The numbers haven't gotten any better since then; Twitter's overall user numbers are at best flat or possibly even declining, depending on how you measure active users.[16]

Part of this confusion stems from an identity crisis that Twitter itself didn't resolve until recently. Some of Twitter's founders, recently rehired CEO Jack Dorsey chief among them, saw Twitter as a way to connect with friends. In this view, like Facebook, Twitter was fundamentally a social network.[17] Ev Williams, also a founder and now a former CEO, had a different idea: Twitter was for finding out what was happening right now. According to tech journalist Nick Bilton, whose book *Hatching Twitter* details the company's origins and meteoric ascent, Dorsey saw Twitter as "a way to talk about what was happening to *him*." But Williams saw it as "a view into what was happening in the world."

It took a long time for Twitter to resolve this conflict, with the platform eventually defining itself around the latter vision. Twitter isn't a social network like Facebook. It's a content platform. Bill Gurley, partner at top venture capital firm Benchmark, agreed. "Facebook is a few-to-few communication network designed for sharing information and life events with friends. Twitter, on the other hand, is a one-to-many information broadcast network. The only way magic happens on Facebook is through reciprocity: I friend you and you friend me back—then information flows. But on Twitter, I can get something out of following Shaquille O'Neal, who has no social obligation to follow me back."[18] Additionally, if Twitter is for finding out what's happening now, you don't need to tweet to use it. "The power of this discovery platform is much more about the tweets themselves, and not simply about every single user having the ability to tweet," Gurley said. In other words, Twitter is more like Twitch or YouTube than Facebook. You go there to consume content rather than to communicate with or check on friends. That everyone doesn't tweet is just fine.

Not surprisingly, Twitter also shares the same problem regarding user comments that neither YouTube nor Twitch has solved. On all three platforms, spam and harassment are rampant. Twitter's CEO Dick Costolo even admitted as much in June 2015 before he stepped down. "We suck at dealing with abuse and trolls on the platform and we've sucked at it for years. It's no secret and the rest of the world talks about it every day," Costolo wrote in a leaked internal memo. "We lose core user after core user by not addressing simple trolling issues that they face every day."[19]

However, rampant abuse isn't Twitter's only problem. Until recently, very little effort had been made to improve engagement and discovery on Twitter for new users. Recent product enhancements, such as Moments, While You Were Away, native video, and group Direct Messages, are all good steps, but Twitter's flawed interaction model remains. This model serves only a small but highly active subset of all potential users who actively curate who they follow and even create "lists" for specific topics.

With all of the negative attention the company's been getting from Wall Street, Twitter may seem to be in dire straits. There's reason to hope the company will turn itself around, but to do so, Twitter will have to do a much better job of setting rules for its community going forward.

Preventing Unintended Consequences

As Twitter's issues with harassment and user engagement suggest, governing large numbers of users is no easy task. Platforms that stall out once they've started to grow—think Friendster and MySpace, which we'll cover in more detail in chapter 7—typically have done a poor job of governing their communities. As a result, quality diminishes as the network grows. Every platform has to face this challenge, and setting the right rules and standards is an important part of overcoming it.

Some of this abuse can be dealt with by algorithms that detect abusive behavior, but often these methods aren't accurate enough on their own. Similarly, centralized editorial control can help resolve governance challenges. Twitter has experimented with this in its new Moments feature, but many platforms used this type of curation much earlier. For example, Instagram's first hire was community manager Josh Riedel.[20] However, editorial control doesn't scale well as a network grows, As a result, many platforms also use user-powered rating systems to help solve this problem. These rating and reputation systems are especially common in Airbnb, eBay, and Uber. Getting consumers to help curate the quality of producers (and vice versa) can significantly reduce the difficulty of community governance. Uber, for example, uses driver ratings to determine which producers get the best fares and even which producers are allowed to participate in the network. Drivers with less than a 4.6 rating out of 5 are kicked off of the platform.

However, just as algorithmic and editorial curation don't solve the problem, reputation systems aren't a panacea. Platforms need to be careful about providing users with explicit metrics for quality, as often this leads to people gaming the system. For example, Alibaba has had trouble with merchants creating counterfeit transactions (where no goods are actually exchanged) to generate fake positive reputation ratings. This concern also is a big reason why both Google and Facebook keep their Page Rank and Newsfeed algorithms secret. If content creators knew exactly how they were being ranked, it would be very easy to cheat.

Additionally, digital reputation scores are limited in their effectiveness. Because they can account for only a limited amount of information, they are more blunt instruments than fine tools. Reputations are very context dependent. Although many have criticized Uber and Airbnb because they don't let you export your reputation data to other networks, these platforms have good reason for protecting their data, beyond the obvious competitive concerns. Taken out of context, these ratings have little to no meaning. What does a 4.8 rating on Uber say about your ability to be a good host on Airbnb? Or to sell T-shirts on Amazon? What does the number of subscribers you have on YouTube tell me about your ability to fix a toilet on Handy? Like identity, reputation isn't monolithic. It's contextual. Allowing you to export your rating to other sites would provide you with little real benefit while potentially harming the originating platform. Enabling you to import your reputation scores from other sources would be even worse, as it would pollute the platform's reputation data with irrelevant information. Uber already arguably doesn't give passengers enough context on what driver reputation scores mean. (What deserves a four-star or five-star rating from a passenger? Uber doesn't tell you. Passengers have to make up their own rubric.) Adding even more data that's not contextually relevant would make the situation even worse.

Finally, reputation systems are largely reactive. They tell you about something that's already happened. It's more important to be proactive and to take time to create the rules and standards to motivate your users to take the specific actions you want them to take. This will encourage good behavior and discourage the bad. "My advice here to anyone trying to grow a platform would be to think through what you want the desired outcome to be," Sarver says. "Try to find the most explicit way to write the policy to produce that behavior. If you become lazy or take broad strokes with your policy, you create a lot of unintended consequences, usually in a negative way where you disincentivize certain behaviors that could have been really positive for your platform."

The best platforms use a balance of algorithmic, editorial, and user-powered curation to enforce the rules and monitor user behavior. However, it's important to be mindful of the strengths and weaknesses of each method when designing a platform's governance structure. Ultimately, the goal should be to get both consumers and producers to have a high degree of trust in the platform. If a platform's rules and standards work well enough, users won't have to worry about trusting the person they're transacting with. They know and trust the platform the other person is using, and that should be enough. For anyone building a platform business, the level of trust users have in your platform is usually a good litmus test for how effectively you're governing your network. If a platform does a poor job setting rules for its network, as Twitter has done recently, this second-order trust in the platform won't materialize. This lack of trust is always a bad sign. The ability to replace individual trust with trust in the platform is an important part of removing friction from the core transaction.

PROVIDING CORE TOOLS AND SERVICES

Last, but certainly not least, a platform has to provide the tools and services that support the core transaction.

The distinction between tools and services has to do with what a platform chooses to centralize. Tools are self-service and decentralized. Anyone can use them, and they don't require ongoing involvement or assistance from the platform. Tools typically include much of the technology and software products that will help users create value connect with each other. Examples include the tool for uploading videos to YouTube, the filters that Instagram provides for editing photos, the scheduling tool that Airbnb provides to hosts, and the navigational tools Uber provides to drivers. Most tools are meant to be "plug and play," so that consumers and producers can transact with each other easily.

In contrast, services are centralized, and require continued involvement from the platform. Customer support is the most common example, as it's a service that most platforms have to offer. Services can play an important part in customer satisfaction, as they provide a buffer between your users when something goes wrong. For example, Airbnb's customer safety team plays an important role in helping the platform keep its users happy.

Each tool or service that a platform provides should be directed at a particular step in the core transaction. Instagram's filters are focused on enabling creation, for example, while Airbnb's customer safety team focuses on enabling consumption. Tools or services that don't line up with one of the four steps in the core transaction are often unnecessary. Platform entrepreneurs often make the common mistake of trying from the start to add every tool that they think users might want. But remember Mark Zuckerberg's advice from chapter 5: "It's not what you add, it's what you take away." Especially early on, a platform should stay laser-focused on building tools that enable the core transaction rather than on creating tools that provide new kinds of value. You don't want to create a platform that is "too useful," as Zuckerberg said in regard to houseSYSTEM. Simplicity and efficiency are key.

How Instacart Went from Startup to $2 Billion Powerhouse in Just Three Years

As new Uber-for-X companies continue to join the on-demand economy, it seems impossible to stand out. But Instacart, founded in July 2012, has done just that. The on-demand grocery delivery platform has raised nearly $300 million in funding at a valuation of over $2 billion—all in just three years. A key part of Instacart's success has been its effectiveness in helping its producers complete transactions efficiently. Instacart knows its shoppers are critical, because they are the ones who create value—without these shoppers, Instacart would have nothing to sell to consumers, just as Uber wouldn't have anything to sell without its drivers. But it's the extent to which Instacart has worked to perfect its dedicated shopper mobile app that has really allowed its business to grow.

Instacart—product marketplace

"Our software—and the capabilities we build in to our shopper app—is designed to best help shoppers through every step of the shopping process, so we can optimize accuracy and efficiency," Instacart founder and CEO Apoorva Mehta says. He isn't just guessing here, nor is his team. "I go shopping weekly to experience it for myself," Mehta says. "And our engineering team regularly spends time in the stores with shoppers to go through the process and verify how the app will be the most effective."

What's perhaps most unbelievable about Instacart's growth is that just three years ago, the company had only one shopper: Mehta himself. "When I started Instacart, I began writing code for the first version of the app and, when it was ready, placed the first order. Then, I went to the grocery store, picked up my groceries and delivered them to myself," he recalls. "So, technically, we started with one shopper in the summer of 2012 and have about 7,000 across the nation today."

To improve its shoppers' efficiency, Instacart has implemented several innovative features in its shopper app. One such feature is aisle navigation, which allows shoppers to know exactly where specific items are located within a store. Another feature allows shoppers to adjust quickly when a specific product isn't available. "We've integrated replacement options into the app—from naming actual products to designating characteristics that would best match the original request. The shoppers can access over four million catalog items in real time and add custom replacement items," Mehta explains.

As for its consumers, Instacart created tools to close the gap between their locations and the in-store shopping experience. The company arms its shoppers with the right information and tools so that they can make decisions as if the customers were in the store themselves. The app allows for this smart shopping with features like in-app chatting that allow shoppers to communicate easily with customers. This way customers will know right away if there are any changes or issues and can provide feedback if necessary. The app even has a few advanced features that let shoppers ensure they're picking the right products. "We've integrated barcode scanning technology into the app so that [shoppers] can immediately verify that the item picked is the exact item requested," Mehta says.

According to Mehta, building out these tools hasn't been easy. "There's no one doing what we're doing—the challenges that we are solving for, and the scale at which we're doing so, have never been done before. As a result, we've had to invent the technology from scratch." Mehta credits the app's improvement to the team's speed and flexibility. "Our team is really nimble in trying new things and adjusting the way we are currently operating." And the Instacart team, from the engineers to the executives, is constantly looking for more ways to improve the shopper app and deliver a better customer experience.

Now Instacart is looking past the app and into the store to optimize shopping efficiency. It's currently pairing the shopper app with in-store technologies, and the company even has its own staging and operating areas in some stores, complete with storage, refrigeration, and printers as well as a checkout line just for Instacart shoppers. "These stores were not originally designed with our services in mind, but through our partnerships with retailers, we've been able to work with retailers to retrofit them to meet our needs," Mehta explains.

In Case of Emergency

For most platforms, automated tools can support the core transaction more or less on their own while the platform's rules and standards police and prevent most harmful behavior. The platform needs to step in only in rare instances where obvious abuses occur. Collectively, these tools and standards act like traffic lights. They make coordination easy and simple, as long as everyone follows the same rules.

However, for some networks, transactions involve a lot of risk. This means that the platform has to play a more active role. One example is platforms that involve high-value assets—most obviously, money. PayPal struggled with fraud detection early on, with one case costing the company $5.7 million over a four-month period in mid-2000.[21] But PayPal isn't alone. Struggles with transaction risk are common for early-stage platforms, especially platforms that enable in-person interactions that take place outside of the platform. For example, once you've ordered an Uber, you have to get into a stranger's car. You need to trust that the driver (a) won't abduct you or kill you and (b) won't crash, among many other potential worries. Similarly, when you order a cleaning professional from Handy, you have to trust that person enough to let them into your home. And when you book an apartment on Airbnb, you usually have to meet the host to get a key, if nothing else. Even if you don't, you're still staying in another person's home and have to trust that they don't have bed bugs, or, for example, that the heater isn't broken and won't explode when you try to turn it on. That's a little hyperbolic, but you can see the point.

The transaction risk is usually high when it includes the potential for personal harm. On YouTube or Facebook, someone might leave a nasty comment on one of your videos that cuts a little too close to the bone. While cyber bullying is a real and growing concern, especially among children, the likelihood of experiencing physical harm while using these platforms is low. However, when in-person interactions are involved, the risk of physical injury or worse is a legitimate concern. "With Airbnb, people are sleeping in other people's homes and other people's beds," Airbnb CEO Brian Chesky said. "So there's a level of trust necessary to participate that's different from an eBay or Facebook."[22]

As we mentioned in chapter 5, these in-person interactions fall outside of the core transaction. The core transaction contains only the exchange of value that happens inside the platform. Luckily, most platforms are able to cover the whole exchange in the core transaction. However, when they can't (as is the case for many services marketplaces), these external interactions still have a material impact on how both consumers and producers will experience the platform. If customers have a bad experience with a cleaner on Handy, they're going to blame Handy, not just the individual who (e.g.,) accidentally dyed their favorite sweater pink. In these cases, the platform needs to provide additional services that fill this online-to-offline gap.

The best way to make sure users are safe is to make sure bad actors don't get onto the platform in the first place. The most common way to tackle this challenge is to collect personal information that will help screen unwanted users. For example, on-demand massage platform Zeel requires new consumers to input the last four digits of their social security number. It then uses ID verification service Experian to confirm that the person is real before it confirms the appointment and sends a massage therapist into the home. (The goal is to ensure its producers' safety.) Most platforms don't go this far with consumers—usually they'll ask for a credit card, for example, which allows them to gather minimal personal information and at least confirm that you're able to pay and have a bank account—but on the producer side, this kind of verification is very common. (So common, in fact, that a business built around

Airbnb—services
marketplace platform

providing background-check services—aptly named Checkr—raised $30 million at a valuation of $250 in October 2015.[23]) All Uber drivers undergo what the company calls a "rigorous background check," and in 2014 Airbnb started its Verified ID program to confirm the identities of hosts through a combination of their social media accounts and government-issued identification. Similarly, Handy puts all of its cleaners through a background check and, once they've passed that, an in-person screening.

However, when you're dealing with hundreds of thousands of producers, these prescreening services aren't going to catch everyone. Nor will customer feedback or ratings systems, which we covered earlier. The occasional bad actor will still slip through, as many of these services marketplaces have found out the hard way.[24] Uber has had its share of high-profile mishaps, such as one incident where an incensed driver struck a passenger in the head with a ball-peen hammer. In April 2014, Uber added a $1 "Safe Rides Fee" to every UberX ride to fund improvements in its safety procedures. Part of this fee goes toward paying for background checks as well as the commercial liability coverage that Uber offers to drivers. After adding the safety fee, Uber upped its driver coverage to $1 million when you're driving a passenger and up to $100,000 if you have the app open but aren't with a passenger. It's also working with insurance companies to provide more comprehensive but affordable coverage designed specifically for Uber drivers. These services won't stop all incidents from happening, but they'll go a long way toward providing coverage for users when they do.

Airbnb too has had its fair share of problems. The first well-publicized case happened in June 2011, when a host's home was vandalized and robbed by a guest. Airbnb appeared slow to respond until the host's blog posts on the incident went viral (thanks to the Twitter hashtag #RansackGate) and became national news. Airbnb scrambled to make up for its mistake and decided to invest heavily in customer safety.

In the wake of the incident, Airbnb upped its Host Guarantee coverage to up to $1 million in damages. Some users try to abuse the system—one customer safety employee noted that she was very familiar with Google Image Search results for pictures of trashed houses.[25] But the company also hired Phil Cardenas and Anna Steel, a former military intelligence officer and a former government investigator, respectively, to run its expanded trust and safety team. The goal was to better prevent another #RansackGate and to respond better and faster if it did happen. This team became a key part of Airbnb—it now includes more than 100 of the 300 people based out of its customer service center in Dublin, Ireland. The customer safety team has helped cut down on the cases of fraud and damages significantly, for both hosts and travelers. It's also worked to improve the company's system for handling customer disputes. A year after #RansackGate, Airbnb's Steel noted that only about 400 out of 3 million Airbnb stays became Host Guarantee cases.[26] Airbnb's safety procedures are still a target for criticism, especially from the strictly regulated hotel industry, but the company has come a long way.

It's Alive!

Now that we've covered each piece of the value ecosystem, you should have a good understanding of what makes platform businesses tick. Just as the value chain did for linear businesses, the value ecosystem gives a holistic snapshot of a platform and how well it's functioning. It also can be used as a rubric to assess competitive advantage by comparing how well certain platforms handle each part of their ecosystems. As we mentioned in chapter 5, Tinder's breakthrough in the core transaction for dating platforms was a key factor in its explosive growth. Older platforms that use a less efficient core transaction model are falling behind, although the smartest ones have started to copy Tinder and introduce similar swipe-based, double-opt-in matching features. Likewise, Uber's success in audience building and matchmaking are key factors driving its big lead over rival platform Lyft. Additionally, when you're looking to build a platform business—or if you're trying to defend your existing business against a platform disruptor—the value ecosystem provides a tool for you to highlight your competitors' weaknesses and focus your thinking on where you should differentiate or where you can attack.

However, once you've used the value ecosystem to design or map out your business, it's not a set-and-forget tool. Unlike an assembly line or a factory, a value ecosystem is not something you design once and then ignore until you're ready to do a major overhaul. We chose the word "ecosystem" deliberately. The ecological metaphor fits very well. Like an ecosystem in nature, a platform is constantly evolving along with its constituents. Because most of a platform's key activities involve external participants, it doesn't control its key assets the way a linear business does. A platform has to constantly keep its ear to the ground and adapt to its network, which is as alive as the people that are a part of it. For these reasons, designing a platform is less about industrial process design and more about sociological insight and continuous behavior design.

For example, the design of a platform's core transaction will change over time. As its network grows and the strength of its network effects increase, it can start to introduce secondary transactions. Uber started with Uber BLACK (private, black-car service) before expanding to add UberX, which today is by far its most popular service. However, the company didn't stop there. On the back of UberX's success and the strength of its massive network, it added UberPOOL, a carpooling service that enables drivers to pick up multiple passengers along the same route while also allowing passengers to get cheaper rides and see their fare price up front. (UberX riders see their fare only once the trip is complete.) More recently, Uber's started expanding into delivery services, such as UberRUSH (courier service) and UberEATS (food delivery). Although these newer services haven't found anywhere near as much success as the company's core UberX service, they demonstrate how platforms can use the success of their core transaction and growing network to extend into new tiers of service and new transaction types.

In fact, adding secondary transactions is a primary way that platforms scale. Almost all successful platforms start with one, simple core transaction. But like Uber, most expand into many secondary transactions over time. For example, as we mentioned in chapter 5, Facebook started as a simple social network that allowed people to connect with classmates and friends. There were no wall posts and no Newsfeed. Over time, Facebook added these features to support its core double-opt-in friending model. However, once it got enough people to join, it also was able to expand into new transactions. With Facebook Pages, and now Instant Articles, it didn't just add a new transaction. It also expanded into an entirely new platform type: a content platform. The transaction model for Pages and Instant Articles was different from the core friending interaction, and it included new kinds of participants in Facebook's network, namely businesses, news organizations, musicians, and celebrities. By adding these new transactions (and, later, building advertising features on top of them), Facebook was able to greatly expand the reach of its platform. Facebook's later move to add software developers into the mix had a similar effect and was a key driver of its impressive growth leading up to its IPO in 2012, as we will cover in the conclusion.

Most successful platforms follow a similar trajectory. Twitter started as a way to share simple text messages before adding support for links, videos, photos, and even one-click shopping. Similarly, Google started with Google Search and Adwords before adding Android and then Google Play into the mix, while Amazon started its Marketplace with a focus on books before expanding its platform into fashion, food, home supplies, electronics, digital content, apps, and more. Finally, in China, Tencent's QQ and WeChat each started as a simple messaging platform before expanding (as we cover in the conclusion) into pretty much everything.

Like the core transaction, the four functions evolve as a platform expands. Most obviously, all four need to adapt to account for new transactions and platform types that are integrated into the platform's ecosystem. But each function also needs to change as the network grows, user behaviors change, and competitive priorities shift.

Reputation and user-led curation mechanisms may break down as the platform adds more users. Tools designed to work on a small scale might need to be redesigned to handle a network that's an order of magnitude larger. Matchmaking needs to improve and add ever-more sophisticated filters and personalization methods to help users find the right needle within a larger and rapidly growing haystack. Rules that effectively govern a community of thousands must be redesigned to orchestrate a network of millions.

Because networked value increases as a platform expands, growth also alters the tension between the conflicting priorities of open access and effective governance. When the platform is small and offers little value, it usually makes more sense to enable easy access. Audience building takes precedence over setting robust rules. But as a platform grows, it can be much more selective about who it allows to join and how it allows users to interact. Twitter could clearly improve in this area. What worked for orchestrating an insular community of venture capitalists and techies in Twitter's early days clearly isn't working now, as evidenced by the platform's well-documented issues with abusive behavior and trolling. Twitter's struggles aren't uncommon. For example, Facebook and LinkedIn grappled with privacy issues as they grew, and Uber and Airbnb have battled issues with customer safety. In China, Alibaba has struggled significantly in its battle against counterfeit products on its marketplaces. What's uncommon is that Twitter has yet to evolve its platform to adapt to its new reality—the network has changed, but Twitter hasn't. Whether it is able to do so will be an important factor in determining the company's long-term prospects.

Finally, although the need for constant evolution represents a real challenge, overall it should be viewed as a strength of platform business models, not a weakness. Platforms are constantly changing, and they also have the data that allows them to see in real time what's happening in their networks and adapt. This real-time intelligence is a huge competitive advantage, as it enables platforms to externalize innovation and let user behavior indicate where new features or transactions are possible. Often users will take matters into their own hands, as they did with Twitter.

Two of Twitter's defining features are the @ symbol for user names (e.g., the authors' Twitter handles are @AlexMoazed and @NLJ_1, respectively) and the hashtag (#), which is used to connect related posts and highlight interesting topics or trends. Yet neither of these ideas came from Twitter or its employees. Use of the @ symbol for replies originated with Apple designer Robert Andersen, who first used it on November 2, 2006, when he replied to a tweet from his brother by placing an @ symbol before his name.[27] The @ symbol was commonly used by engineers, who use it to talk to other people on a server. So it was a natural fit for Twitter's tech-savvy early users. Shortly after Andersen introduced the @ sign on Twitter, it became a permanent fixture of tweet-based communication. Similarly, the first use of a hashtag came from another Twitter user, Chris Messina. At the time, the hashtag was already commonly used on photo-sharing platform Flickr to group similar or related images. Once Messina used the hashtag on Twitter, it quickly caught on there. Before long, both the @ sign and the hashtag became official Twitter features. Today they're used so often that they're almost synonymous with the platform.

Platform Modeling

This sort of user-led innovation is common for platform businesses. For example, both iOS and Android closely monitor app trends to decide which features to incorporate into future updates, whether that involves incorporating existing apps into its core feature set or adding support for features that will help third-party developers build new kinds of apps. Airbnb's evolution took a similar path. Its founders originally envisioned it as a way for travelers to stay *with* people who had spare room in their apartment. However, after they talked to a number of their early hosts, they discovered that a more common use was to rent out a property when the host *wasn't* there. This type of activity quickly became very popular on Airbnb, and today it makes up the bulk of its bookings. We could mention countless other examples, but you get the idea.

The importance of user-led innovation for platform businesses means that the traditional software company approach of building a complex, fully featured product before going to market doesn't make much sense. It's usually a better idea to model the core transaction and potential network value early on to get a sense of how the platform will work (and whether it will at all) in the real world. Both Handy and Glamsquad are successful platform businesses that started by going through this process. This kind of testing is easier for some platform types than others—for example, development platforms tend to be more complex and harder to prototype—but most platforms should start with the simplest possible system and build from there.

Everyone's trained to think that you need to build software to start a tech company. However, in many cases, this is no longer true. In fact, it's possible to launch platform startups with *zero* custom software. You can easily cobble together a number of free (or very cheap) plug-and-play tools that will allow you to test out your idea. If you're spending much more than a few weeks' time validating your initial platform startup idea, you're wasting precious resources. We've gone through this validation process with many of our early-stage platform clients through our Platform Modeling service.[28] The goal is to create a lightweight model for the business as quickly as possible and to use it to validate the idea and gather feedback. Once you've figured out what works and what doesn't, you can worry about building out the fully featured, scalable software that you'll need to run the platform long term. Our advice to potential platform entrepreneurs is to validate your idea quickly before you start building software. Let your users lead the way.

7

LET THE NETWORK DO THE WORK

Sequencing markets correctly is underrated.

—Peter Thiel, founder and former
CEO of PayPal

"Nothing can really prepare you for the latest online phenomenon." That was how the *New York Times'* Nick Bilton began a February 2010 article on the brief Internet phenomenon that was Chatroulette.[1] The lead was accompanied by a photo of a man in a full-body cheetah costume. That same month, *New York* magazine featured an article whose tagline asked "Is Chatroulette the future of the Internet?" The article dubbed Chatroulette "the anti-Facebook."[2] Bilton's article ended with the suggestion that the platform might be the beginning of "a new kind of category online."

What was Chatroulette? The idea was astoundingly simple. It was a rudimentary website that generated a live connection via webcam between users and random strangers on the platform. No special software or registration was required to use it. The service was completely anonymous. Every time a user clicked "next," he or she was connected with a new stranger, potentially on the other side of the globe. It was the only place on the Web where users could "chat about sports, watch a guy play live guitar, and join a house party in the United Kingdom—all within five minutes," as Michelle Kessler wrote in *USA Today*.[3] While it lasted, the experience was exhilarating. "Entering Chatroulette is akin to speed-dating tens of thousands of perfect strangers," Bilton wrote. Created by a 17-year-old Russian named Andrey Ternovskiy only a few months earlier, Chatroulette quickly went viral and became a pop-culture meme. Jon Stewart made fun of it on the *Daily Show*. *South Park* parodied it. It was a big hit in the tech world too. The site's young founder enlisted Napster creator Shawn Fanning as an advisor. Ternovskiy was even flown out to Silicon Valley and wooed by future Uber and Airbnb investor Shervin Pishevar. At the time, another potential investor cited Chatroulette's "unlimited" potential as a future destination for online dating.[4]

The site's traffic grew 400 percent by the end of February, reaching 4 million users worldwide, with nearly 1 million coming from the United States.[5] At its peak, hundreds of thousands of users were online at the same time. It became a particularly big hit among college students, who made up about 40 percent of its overall users. But just a few months later, Chatroulette was all but dead. Traffic dried up, and the spotlight faded.

THE CHATROULETTE RULE OF THE INTERNET

What happened to Chatroulette? Although its explosive growth seemed great on the surface, the quality of its network wasn't pretty if you looked too closely. And if you used Chatroulette after it went viral, you probably regretted looking too closely. The problem was that not all users are created equal. And as the site grew, the quality of its users greatly decreased. What was initially a cool way to be surprised and meet someone new quickly lost its luster. After a few months, many users were using the site to indecently expose themselves, or worse. Unsurprisingly, this lewd activity scared away most other users, and Chatroulette quickly developed a bad reputation. The platform's users skewed overwhelmingly male—as much as 89 percent by one estimate. And about 15 percent of those users were "R-rated or worse." These users, which the study labeled "perverts," were generally naked and engaged in "lewd acts." Not surprisingly, fewer than 10 percent of these kinds of users were female.[6]

The site tried to implement a feature that could quickly scan the video feed and detect nudity, but by then most of its users had fled. The feature eventually became a monetization strategy, as it started referring users engaged in inappropriate activities to adult websites. As one journalist for *Salon* wrote, "All that's left of a once great civilization is dead air and a bunch of guys sitting around with their pants off."[7]

Because Chatroulette was anonymous and required no registration, it was difficult to police its users. The very low barrier to entry turned from a positive to a negative as it was easy for the wrong kinds of users to join. This leads us to *the Chatroulette rule of the Internet:* When left unchecked, a network of sufficient size will naturally deteriorate in its quality of users and usage (e.g., naked men sitting in front of a camera).

HOW TO KILL A BILLION-DOLLAR IDEA

Chatroulette wasn't the first social platform that had struggled to manage its growth. Years earlier, Friendster had been the first large-scale, successful social network. The social network launched in 2002 and grew quickly. Its founder, Jonathan Abrams, thought online dating was "too anonymous and creepy."[8] He developed Friendster so that users could connect to their friends and see second-degree connections (friends of friends). "We're trying to make the process more accountable," Abrams said.[9] By the fall of 2003, the site had 3 million users.[10]

However, since Friendster was open to anyone, the platform struggled to scale its technology to keep up with its growth. Every time a page loaded, Friendster's servers would calculate a single user's connection to other users within four degrees of separation. This calculation could include hundreds of thousands of users.[11] And because the network was constantly changing as new users joined and connected with each other, these calculations had to happen continuously. As the social network grew, buying enough servers to keep up with growth was a challenge. The load on its servers became so bad that its website could take as long as 40 seconds to load one page.[12]

Another problem was that Friendster didn't have a good way to validate its users' identities. Fake profiles quickly became popular. "Fakesters," as these profiles were called, included pages for "famous people, fictional characters, objects, places and locations, identity markers, concepts, animals, and communities."[13] Friendster realized that these fake profiles would hurt the quality of its network. While many participants enjoyed these profiles, the Fakesters annoyed users who wanted to use the platform for serious networking. Fakesters also caused additional server strain when their profiles occasionally went viral and attracted lots of temporary traffic. Given that the company was already struggling to serve its core users, the extra strain was not something it could afford. Friendster decided to purge fake users, and the platform's growth slowed significantly as a result.

This wasn't the end of Friendster's problems, however. The platform had a little-known third problem that it was too late to address. In early 2004, Friendster's director of engineering, Chris Lunt, noticed that the platform's traffic would mysteriously spike at 2 a.m. Looking at the data, he realized that all of these users were coming from the Philippines. Unbeknownst to its owners, the platform had gone viral in Southeast Asia. For Friendster's business, which was hoping to attract U.S. advertisers, this revelation was devastating.[14] However, the result was even worse for its network. Because they had few natural connections in the Philippines, most of the platform's early adopters in the United States weren't interested in networking with people on the other side of the world. Worse yet, these foreign users were even more likely to create fake profiles than U.S. users were. All of these international users also put additional strain on the company's struggling servers without adding much value to the core business, from either a network effects or a monetization standpoint. By the end of 2004, with the platform's core technology failing and its network effects weakening, Friendster's early U.S. adopters had mostly abandoned the service as similar alternatives sprang up.

IT'S 11 O'CLOCK. DO YOU KNOW WHAT WEBSITE YOUR CHILDREN ARE ON?

Friendster's biggest successor was Myspace, a company that was founded in September 2003 just as Friendster was faltering. Myspace was built as part of a conglomerate called eUniverse, which had two primary lines of business. The first was a linear ecommerce business that sold goods of dubious quality, such as "scooters and Iraqi trading cards" as well as diet pills and remote-controlled helicopters. The company's return rates from customers were reportedly very high.[15] But eUniverse's unscrupulous activities didn't end there. Its second line of business was to secretly install spyware on users' computers and use it to serve them advertisements. Remember all of those random pop-ups that you used to get while surfing the Web? That's how eUniverse made money before Myspace.

Myspace started out as a social network for musicians to connect with their fans. Its two cofounders, Chris DeWolfe and Thomas Anderson (the infamous "Myspace Tom"), used to prowl clubs in Los Angeles in order to recruit musicians to use the platform as a marketing tool.[16] But not surprisingly, given its parent company's origins, the cofounders took a very laid-back approach to regulating user behavior. They quickly expanded beyond their initial user group to add anyone and everyone they could. With the backlash Friendster faced for cracking down on Fakesters, Myspace tried to position itself as the anti-Friendster. It allowed users to sign up with user names or fake names and to pose as anyone they wanted to be. Myspace also had a much laxer attitude toward the types of things users could do on the platform.

To improve server performance, Myspace did away with the networking code that Friendster used to calculate degrees of friendship. Instead, Myspace just made Tom everybody's first friend. This meant that when a new user signed up, Tom already connected that user to everyone else on the network. As a result, Myspace was wide open—anyone could view anyone else or add them as a "friend." In April 2004, Myspace even dropped the requirement that users be logged in to view users' profiles, photos, and other content. Page views spiked, as voyeurism became a core part of the Myspace experience.

This laissez-faire environment attracted many popular Friendster users, including Tila Tequila, one of the Internet era's first e-celebrities, who had been banned from Friendster several times for posting provocative photos. She went on to become Myspace's most popular user.

However, this hands-off approach had real downsides. As Myspace learned, not all growth was good growth. Myspace became littered with spam since users could add custom code to their profiles. This feature enabled users to directly embed junk advertisements into their profile pages. Prominent users also started to spam their many "friends" with posts from paid advertisers. Additionally, because it did not require its users to provide reliable personal information, Myspace attracted both child sex predators as well as minors who lied about their ages. Once again, MySpace's hands-off approach invited the Chatroulette dilemma to rear its naked, balding head.

Not surprisingly, this problem attracted a lot of negative attention. In February 2006, Connecticut attorney general Richard Blumenthal announced that he was launching an investigation into minors' exposure to pornography on Myspace.[17] Blumenthal's announcement set off investigations in other states and attracted a wave of negative media attention. "If you have a teenager at home, odds are they've visited the blog site myspace.com," *CBS News* warned its viewers in 2006. "And there are fears that this popular social networking website, and others like it, have become places where sexual predators easily prey on children."[18] Myspace's bad reputation started to scare away its users, just as Chatroulette's reputation did a few years later. The site peaked at 75 million users by the end of 2008, but all of that growth turned out to be short-lived. By 2011, the platform had fewer than 35 million users, after hemorrhaging an average of a million users a month for more than two years.[19]

FACEBOOK TAKES OVER THE WORLD

Another social networking platform, started in February 2004, took a very different approach from either Friendster or Myspace. Unlike these platforms, which let anyone join, thefacebook was very specific about what—and who—it was for. Its initial homepage told users that they could "Search for people at your school; Find out who are in your classes; Look up your friends' friends; See a visualization of your social network." And thefacebook, more widely known now as Facebook, was very careful about whom it allowed to join.

The platform launched at the beginning of the spring semester at Harvard. It was open only to students with a Harvard.edu email address, and you had to use your real name. The timing was deliberate. Harvard students were in the middle of "shopping week," a period when students can try out different classes and easily add or drop them before they settle on their final course schedules. The previous semester, Facebook's founder, Mark Zuckerberg, had created a piece of software called Course Match, which helped students pick classes based on who was taking them. You could see who had signed up for a class or see all the courses that a specific person was taking. Zuckerberg included a similar feature in Facebook, which made the social network immediately useful to students. By the end of the week, about half of Harvard undergrads had signed up for the platform, and by the end of February, nearly 75 percent of them had joined.

Facebook was very deliberate about its growth. Zuckerberg had seen the troubles of Friendster as it expanded and was turned off by the Wild West that was Myspace. By requiring an .edu email address and mandating that users sign up under their real names, Facebook took a very different approach to building a network: one that prioritized the quality of its users and usage over sheer numbers. The platform's restrictions on who could sign up made it almost the po- 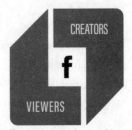 lar opposite of its competitors, where just about anyone could join.

Facebook—social networking platform

Facebook expanded next to other Ivy League schools, including Columbia, MIT, Princeton, and Stanford. Those schools were where the real-world social networks of Harvard users already existed, which was a key reason for the choice. Harvard users could connect to their friends from high school who had gone to other "elite" universities. However, adding users from other networks created a problem because, at the time, Facebook limited your friend network just to other students at your same school. Users wanted a way to link with their friends cross-campus. Zuckerberg decided that these links could be created by mutual agreement between both people—thus the double-opt-in "friending" feature was born. These cross-campus links proved to be important drivers of Facebook's growth, as users would invite their friends from other campuses whom they wanted to connect with online.

Leveraging these cross-campus linkages become a core part of Facebook's strategy. The way the social network handled its growth was nothing short of genius. Facebook was not the first social network targeted at college students, nor was it the only one that was growingly quickly at the time. So rather than take these other networks head-on, Facebook used what it called a "surround strategy." If a competitor had already established a foothold in a certain school, Facebook would open not only at that school but on as many nearby campuses as possible. The goal was to use the network effects from other campuses to create pressure on its targeted campus. As a result, students from the target campus who were friends with users from neighboring schools would tend to choose Facebook over its competitors. This strategy worked spectacularly and helped Facebook overtake already established social networking platforms in different parts of the country.

As Facebook expanded to more campuses, students at schools that were left out were clamoring for access. Zuckerberg resisted pressure from advertisers, who wanted the platform to expand to larger schools right away. Instead, he stayed focused on schools where many students were asking Facebook for access. But even with new users pounding at the gates, Facebook didn't just let all of them in. Zuckerberg waited until the number of students on the waitlist for a given school passed about 20 percent of the student body before opening access. This strategy guaranteed that Facebook wouldn't lack initial users when it opened up at a new school, and it could use students from other schools to build demand at adjacent schools. As a result, whenever Facebook opened the gates for a new college, usage typically exploded.

Using this methodical approach, Facebook blanketed the college market. By the end of 2005, the company had captured approximately 85 percent of all college students in the United States, with 60 percent of them using the site daily.[20]

The natural next step was opening the platform to high school students. However, adding high schools posed a problem. Most high school students didn't have .edu email addresses, so the platform couldn't validate those users the same way it did college students. Facebook's approach to identity had become a core part of the platform, so it had to figure out how to open itself up to new kinds of users without compromising quality. Once again, the answer was to build on top of users' existing social networks. Facebook decided to let college students invite friends who were still in high school. Only users who got an invite could sign up. Then those users could invite their own friends. Initially, high school users couldn't see the profiles of college users, meaning the high school Facebook was sequestered from the main network. This strategy meant that growth in new high schools would be slower. But it wouldn't compromise Facebook's commitment to using real identities, and it protected the quality of the network. Once it made sure it could add high school users without compromising its network, Facebook abandoned the divide between the college and high school networks. Users could now friend and message anyone regardless of what school they went to.

By April 2006, the platform passed 1 million high school users, and from there its growth took off even more quickly. On September 26, 2006, Facebook opened itself to anyone age 13 or older with a valid email address.[21] By the end of the year, it had 12 million active users. On November 6, 2007, a little more than a year later, Facebook officially opened itself to businesses when it launched Facebook Pages along with a new advertising system.[22] And by the end of 2008, the platform had 150 million users.[23] Today, less than a decade later, it has 1.54 billion. But, as Mark Zuckerberg has repeatedly acknowledged, none of that success would have been possible without the platform's very meticulous launch and growth strategy early on.[24] By carefully sequencing and planning its early growth, Facebook succeeded where Friendster and Myspace (and later Chatroulette) failed: It found a way to maintain the quality of its network even while its user base grew by orders of magnitude in a few years' time.

LESSONS FROM THE SOCIAL NETWORKING WARS: WHY THE CONVENTIONAL WISDOM ABOUT NETWORKS IS WRONG

In chapter 3, we gave a simple definition of a network effect. We defined a network effect as a benefit that makes a platform more useful and more valuable as more people use it. Something has a network effect when the behavior of other users has a direct impact on the value that you will get out of the same service.

The classic example of this kind of effect is a telephone network that gets more valuable to each individual user as more people join its network (see Figure 7.1). Metcalfe's Law, named after one of the inventors of Ethernet, Robert Metcalfe, suggested that the value of a network is proportional to the square of the number of connected users in a system (network value = n^2).

As more users join a network, the number of possible unique connections within the network grows according to the function: $(n^2 - n)/2$, where n represents the number of users. As the number of possible connections gets very large, this mathematical function approaches a limit of n^2, hence the mathematical definition of Metcalfe's Law.

Platforms have a similar dynamic. The more people there are on one side of the network, the more valuable the platform is to the other side. For example, the more app developers there are making apps for Apple's iOS platform, the more valuable the platform is to consumers. This relationship goes both ways, so that the more consumers there are on a platform, the more valuable that platform is to producers (the app developers).

This type of network effect is called an indirect network effect or cross-side network effect, where the value delivered to each user in one user group (say, consumers) increases as the number of users in another, interdependent user group (producers) grows. (See Figure 7.2.) Thus,

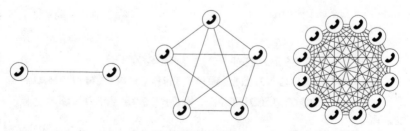

Figure 7.1.   Network effects in a telephone network: Value grows as the number of connections increases.

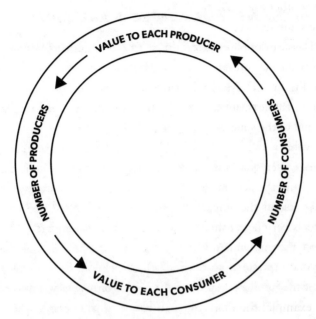

Figure 7.2.   *How indirect network effects create value for platform businesses.*

there's a network effect across two separate user groups. This effect creates a positive feedback loop between both sides of the network. The more producers a platform has, the more valuable that platform becomes to each consumer, and vice versa. As a result, once a network reaches sufficient size, network effects make it much easier for a platform to attract new users of each type and grow the number of transactions. Growth leads to even more growth.

However, according to these conventional definitions, building a strong network is simply a numbers game. The more users that join a network, the more valuable that network will be. Note, for example, that the result of the equation for Metcalfe's Law cannot be negative. Any new user is as good as any other. This definition of network effects assumes that all growth is equally valuable and has a positive impact on other users. But the stories of Chatroulette, Friendster, and Myspace suggest otherwise.

MOST NETWORK EFFECTS ARE LOCAL

Why is the traditional understanding of network effects wrong? Well, not every potential connection in a network is a relevant one. This may seem obvious, but inherent in the Metcalfe's Law view of networks is the idea that all network effects are global—everyone values being able to connect with everyone else in the network. In this view, every individual who joins a network is equally valuable, no matter how closely connected to you they are. Look at the classic telephone-network example depicted in Figure 7.1. Any user who joins the network is assumed to provide the same potential value as any other, no matter where they are located. In reality, this view doesn't make much sense. Some users are more valuable to you than others. And at a certain point, the marginal value of an additional user starts to decline. On Facebook, for example, most people are interested in communicating with only a very small fraction of the platform's 1.5 billion users. In practice, you benefit when more members of your immediate social network join the platform, but you get no direct benefit when strangers join with whom you have no desire to communicate. Although the network's overall value will continue to grow, for you the chances are pretty good that you will get the same value out of the platform whether it has 1.4 billion or 1.5 billion users. A hundred million users is a lot, but most of them are not likely to be closely connected to you.

Some connections are more valuable to you than others based on their proximity to you in the network. The farther away from you a new user is in the network, the less valuable the ability to connect with them is. The value to you of a new user joining isn't *zero*, but at a certain point, the marginal value of each new user becomes negligible. Uber may grow its global network from its current 1 million drivers,[25] but if all of those additional drivers are located in a city you never visit, the value of the network doesn't change much for you. In other words, most network effects are *local*, not global.

For platforms like Uber, where location is an important factor, the term "local" can be taken literally. As a consumer, you value potential drivers who are in close geographical proximity to you. But local network effects don't refer just to literal distance or location. Rather, we are referring to metaphorical distance within a network. What really determines proximity in a network is the frequency and density of interactions between users.

Still, the term "local" intuitively expresses what we mean: Within the network, how closely connected you are or are not with another user matters. Each user typically values adoption by a distinct subset, or cluster, of other users, hence each user has a "local network" that matters to them. The variables that are most relevant to proximity in a network will vary by platform type. For Facebook, geographic proximity isn't always a good indicator of the strength of a connection. Users who are closely connected may live in different cities or even different countries. On many other networks, geographic location may have little to no relevance. Most people don't particularly care if you're located in Des Moines, Iowa, when you upload the latest video of your cat to YouTube. Nor do they need to be located near you to enjoy reading your latest tweet. In both of these cases, the subject matter is much more important than the location.

The local nature of network effects helps us understand why network density matters just as much as network size for platforms. The denser a network is, the more overlapping local networks there will be. This means that more of the potential connections in the network will become actual transactions, as these users are more likely to interact with each other. Transactions, not potential connections, are where platforms create real value. As a result, a small but dense and highly active network is usually much more valuable and useful than a larger but more dispersed network. The smaller network will create more transactions and more value.

To achieve higher-density network effects, most platforms initially target a smaller niche with a very simple use case before expanding to a broader audience. For example, this is why most services marketplaces, like Uber, start in one city, usually New York or San Francisco. (Uber initially launched in San Francisco.) They focus on building up a dense network in one city before moving to a new one, where they will have to build the network all over again. But this strategy isn't limited to marketplaces. Yelp started in San Francisco and built up its network of reviewers before expanding to other cities. Similarly, Q&A platform

Quora, founded by two former Facebook employees, started with a focus on venture capital, technology, and startups. By limiting its early users (Quora started as invite only) to people who could answer questions on these niche topics, Quora grew the core network cluster that would seed its later expansion into other topics and industries.

This framework helps us understand Facebook's success. It also explains Myspace's eventual demise and why Google's multiple attempts at building social networks have been doomed to fail. Facebook started as a niche social network for college students. College is when people's social networks are densest and the time when people are more actively social than at any other period in their lives. One of Facebook's cofounders, Dustin Moskovitz, did a study for a class he was taking using early data from the platform. He found that, on average, any student was within two degrees of separation from any other student on a given campus. "That's why thefacebook grew so well in college," Moskovitz said.[26] Facebook was built on top of a dense network of already existing real-world relationships. The platform simply extended those relationships to the Web. Facebook had a very specific use for a specific subset of people. It was laser focused on creating the tools that enabled those students to interact online. And its rules intentionally limited what information you could see based on what school you went to and who you were connected to.

Similarly, Myspace started by building its initial network around the connections between musicians and their fans. However, as the platform grew, Myspace quickly opened itself to many other kinds of users, without much focus on how they would use the platform. This attitude was reflected in Myspace's haphazard approach to feature development. Cofounder Tom Anderson routinely scoured the Internet looking for interesting features on other websites, then told Myspace developers to copy those features. One example was a feature that allowed users to rank each other's photos based on attractiveness on a scale of 1 to 10, a blatant rip-off of the Internet sensation Hot or Not. Not surprisingly, the fact that Myspace basically cloned Hot or Not's site angered the latter company's CEO, prompting him to demand that Myspace change the feature, which it eventually did. Blogging site Xanga also sued Myspace after it copied many of its popular features. Myspace eventually settled the case for $40,000 and agreed to stop using Xanga's trademarked feature names.[27]

While this strategy helped Myspace grow very quickly, it also introduced a lot of noise into its network. This growth helped increased vanity metrics, such as the number of users, but it didn't create a sustainable network. Many of the new users didn't particularly value a lot of the other users—they had little in common and no coherent framework for how they should connect and interact on the platform. Increasingly, Myspace became a place to connect with people you didn't know. "Myspace had the right idea, where a band would have 900,000 friends," according to Kent Lindstrom, the former CEO of Friendster. "That's what became Twitter."[28] However, as Myspace expanded, it moved away from its core network and diluted the value it provided to users. Eventually, it ended up as a place with many users but little valuable interaction between them—in other words, a large network without localized network effects.

Myspace isn't the only platform that ended up creating a large ghost town. Google is intimately familiar with this problem. Its first attempt at building a social networking platform was Orkut. The platform was named for one of Google's engineers, Orkut Büyükkökten, who had created Club Nexus, a failed social network he built while he was at Stanford. (We covered Club Nexus's failure briefly in chapter 5.) Google launched Orkut in January 2004, just two weeks before Facebook opened at Harvard. Orkut initially thrived in the United States and for a time was considered a potential competitor to Myspace, which was then growing rapidly. But by the end of 2004, Orkut had become much more popular in Brazil than in the United States. A grassroots campaign in Brazil (not promoted by Google) had taken off with the goal of making the platform more popular there than it was in the United States. The campaign succeeded, and the platform took on a distinctly Brazilian and Portuguese-speaking identity. Not surprisingly, many U.S. users—most of whom were not particularly interested in connecting on a social network with users speaking another language—started to leave the platform.[29] Orkut went on to become the largest social networking platform in Brazil, and in 2008 Google even moved the platform's headquarters to that country.[30] However, the platform never took off in the

United States, and, within a few years, Google had largely abandoned its efforts to grow the network. Google's next big effort to create a social network (not counting the abortive Google Buzz or Wave) was Google+ (pronounced "Google Plus"), which launched in June 2011. Google+ positioned itself as the anti-Facebook. It allowed users much tighter control of their privacy settings than its rival did. Google+ also easily attracted millions of users, because Google connected Google+ to many of its existing platforms, like Gmail and YouTube, to jump-start the network. However, without a clearly defined purpose, Google+ never got users to interact. "It was clear if you looked at the per user metrics, people weren't posting, weren't returning and weren't really engaging with the product," according to one former employee. "Six months in, there started to be a feeling that this isn't really working."[31] The running joke in the tech press was that the only people who used Google+ were Google employees. It was clear why Google needed Google+ to exist—it was afraid of the competitive threat from Facebook—but because Google+ was never able to find a core use case and user group, it became a ghost town with a nominally large number of users, just like Myspace.

REVERSE NETWORK EFFECTS AND THE
DEATH OF FIRST-MOVER ADVANTAGE

There's another big problem with the Moore's Law conception of network effects. Not all network effects are positive. Some users can act in ways that affect others negatively. Or, to put it more bluntly, some users harm others. These "bad" users create network effects that work in reverse—the more of this harmful activity there is, the *less* value a user can get out of a network. Consider what happened to Chatroulette. Most users came to Chatroulette wanting to experience talking to a random stranger. What most of them *didn't* want to find was an intimate, up-close view of a hirsute naked man. The more often you had this unsavory experience, the less likely you were to keep using Chatroulette. Another example is "trolling" on Internet message and comment boards, where one user deliberately tries to anger or offend others. Other instances include the Fakesters who took over Friendster and the spammers and predators who gave Myspace a negative reputation. These are all examples of reverse network effects.[32] Rather than benefiting the network by creating value for other users, these bad users harm or impose costs on other users. Left unchecked, these bad users can take over a network and drive away other users. Much like the "lemons" problem in other consumer markets, bad-quality users can chase out the good. As more of these bad users join, they create a reverse network effect that motivates other users to leave. So although every platform spends a lot of resources trying to grow as quickly as possible, sometimes you should be careful what you wish for.

This concept of reverse network effects is an important one, as it greatly changes our understanding of how you should go about building a network. The idea of network effects and their articulation through Metcalfe's Law first became popular in the 1990s, as the Internet's popularity was growing. Backed by a simplistic notion of how networks created value, the common view of network effects viewed competition between platforms as a simple matter of getting the biggest the fastest. This concept also was known as first-mover advantage. The idea of first-mover advantage was so powerful that, according to technology columnist Kevin Maney at *USA Today*, "it could instantly win a startup millions of dollars in financing, boatloads of publicity and board members who seemed, for a moment anyway, important."[33] Be the first to take over any new business category on the Web and it was yours, or so the thinking went. The idea of first-mover advantage took a hit after the dot-com bubble burst, but it still lives on today. Steve Blank, a serial entrepreneur and one of the founders of the Lean Startup movement, called first-mover advantage "an idea that just won't die."[34] In the past, part of the problem was that this concept was applied to businesses that didn't have any real network effects and very little sustainable advantage, even if they were to succeed. Pets.com and Kozmo.com are both examples from the dot-com era. But another problem with the emphasis on first-mover advantage is that it gives you the wrong ideas on how you should go about scaling a network. The growth-at-any-cost mind-set is a big reason why platforms that get initial traction often fail to reach scale. Both Friendster and Myspace got big fast. But they did so largely by ignoring the effect this growth had on the quality of their platforms. In Friendster's case, it failed to create a robust system for establishing real identity at the start. As a result, much of its growth came from fake profiles that irritated many core users. When Friendster tried to crack down on these fake users, many of them left, and its growth evaporated. Myspace had a similar problem. Given its more libertine origins, Myspace's lack of focus on the quality of its user base is less surprising. A company that made its money by installing spyware on your computer isn't likely to take seriously issues like community governance or user quality. Myspace intentionally created a very limited governance system and began to impose some controls only after receiving negative media attention and government pressure.[35] For example, part of the company's early growth plan was a seventeen-city tour of nightclub parties, where it would feature scantily clad women as a ploy to attract new users. Not surprisingly, Myspace subsequently had a big problem with pornographic images popping up on user profiles.[36] In both of these cases, the company prioritized growth over all else, and at one point it was the largest social network in the world. But because of reverse network effects, this growth was short-lived.

Fake users helped Friendster grow quickly, but its success was ephemeral. Its network collapsed just as fast as it grew. Similarly, as Myspace grew, so did its notoriety. Its user experience deteriorated as well, as many user profiles became filled with the sort of spam and advertisements you'd usually see in your junk-mail folder. This lack of quality drove away many of Myspace's core users and effectively prevented any future growth by scaring off new users. As both of these examples show, being a first mover with big numbers isn't everything. A large network isn't a good moat if it's too polluted.

In a more nuanced analysis of network effects, the importance of first-mover advantage largely disappears. Yes, growth is very important, especially when multiple platforms are battling for control. Because of competitive pressure, most platforms feel a strong pressure to amass users as quickly as possible. This urgency is appropriate. However, growth is not an end in itself. A large, incumbent network has an advantage over new entrants and smaller competitors, but that advantage matters only if it's sustainable.

Not all growth is good growth. Growth is useful when it creates more value to your users. Growth also is what enables a platform to make enough money to build a sustainable and defensible business. But to realize these advantages, it has to be *sustainable* growth. Otherwise, your network may dissipate as suddenly as it disappeared. As we covered in chapter 3, home-services platform Homejoy is the most recent victim of this mistake. The company chased growth without paying attention to the quality of its supply. As a result, it had very poor user retention compared to its competitors and burned through money to acquire users who didn't stick around. The company folded in July 2015. Clearly, racing to acquire any and all users can be a mistake. Choose wisely.

YOUR USERS DEFINE YOUR PLATFORM

Many early-stage platform startups think of themselves as software companies. This is a mistake. Software companies are more likely to focus strictly on the features they're creating and less on the community that's using those features. The thinking is often that if you create a bunch of killer features, users will materialize, and growth and success will follow. If you just tweak this feature and move that button, suddenly you'll get growth. This view isn't wrong, per se. Optimization *is* important for any software business. But for a platform, even one built with software, the ultimate killer feature is its network value. In fact, the more successful a platform is, the less its feature set matters. As your platform grows, you give up a lot of control in exchange for better economics and more value. But you have to pay careful attention to whom you're getting to join. Once your network has established an identity, reshaping it is very difficult.

In 2012, the Chinese platform Momo learned this lesson the hard way. Momo was a location-based instant messaging platform that enabled users to find and message strangers nearby. You can probably guess where this is going. Despite its owners' best efforts, Momo developed a reputation as a hookup app. One viral video described it as "a magical tool to get laid."[37] The company spent millions of dollars on marketing trying to reverse course, but to no avail. More recently, Tinder, Momo's U.S. equivalent, had a similar problem after it developed a reputation as *the* hookup app in the United States. In September 2015,

Vanity Fair even put out a feature titled "Tinder and the Dawn of the 'Dating Apocalypse,'" which profiled the app as a central component of so-called hookup culture.[38] Tinder responded on Twitter with the social media equivalent of a public relations meltdown,[39] but the company has long protested that its platform isn't just for short-term hookups. Tinder does so for good reason: If it's just a hookup app, it has a much smaller addressable market. But its efforts have done little to change public perception.

If this reputational issue was just a short-term one, it wouldn't be such a problem for platforms like Momo and Tinder. But growth in networks isn't random. It's *path dependent*. What does this mean? It means that the types of users your network will attract in the future depends on the composition and behavior of your network's existing users. A network's future growth depends on the path it has taken to get there. In other words, users aren't making a decision at random about joining a platform. Potential new users are driven by their attraction to (or distaste for) your existing user base. Once a platform has attracted a critical mass of a certain type of users, more users of the same type will favor it. Dating platforms provide an unusually simple example. Users typically have a strong preference for either short-term or long-term relationships. If the platform attracts many users who are looking for hookups, it inevitably will be viewed as a platform for finding hookups. After a platform develops a reputation as having users of one type, it becomes almost impossible for it to position itself to attract the other type, no matter how it markets itself or what feature set it provides.

This path-dependent nature of networks makes platform design especially crucial early on. Who uses a platform at the start can have a big effect on its growth trajectory. You have the most leverage to shape your community and its culture when your network is still forming. As we described earlier, Facebook's early founders were especially conscientious about how it built its network. Unlike its competitors, Facebook thought very carefully about what it wanted its community to be. The platform adopted strict rules to prevent bad behavior even though it was initially targeted to (and started by) college kids. When he speaks about Facebook's early days, Mark Zuckerberg talks a lot about how important establishing its community's culture was. Facebook was very intentional about creating "a culture of real identity," Zuckerberg said. He and Facebook cofounder Dustin Moskovitz had a "really long debate about what quality meant for us and the community we wanted to establish, and the culture of it."[40]

Facebook's founders also had a very clear vision about what the platform was meant to do—even if this meant striking out on a very different path from its most successful competitor. "Myspace was a much better service early on for meeting people," Zuckerberg said. "Facebook was never primarily about meeting new people. It was about staying connected with the people you knew and mapping out the real relationships that existed." In practice, this meant that people were required to use their real identities on Facebook and could sign up only through their school-issued .edu email address. This way, Facebook prevented the spread of fake profiles (schools typically issued only one email address to each student) and established the precedent that users acted as themselves on the platform. According to Zuckerberg, "most of the way people interacted online was anonymous. The idea at the time was that it was pretty scary to put your name and real identity online without the right privacy controls and community infrastructure. That's a lot of what we built—a framework where people would be comfortable sharing in that way." Unlike Friendster, which failed to create a community built around its users' real identities, Facebook focused its efforts early on building the tools and infrastructure to enable and grow this culture of real identity.

Additionally, the .edu email restriction intentionally limited Facebook's growth to colleges. The slower pace was deliberate, Zuckerberg said. Facebook wanted to make sure it was ready to scale before it expanded its network. "Friendster was the service that had massive scaling problems. They grew quickly and it was very hard for them to scale. That we could go college by college and optimize the service, make it more efficient and offer new features but make sure they worked, I think it was really key." Although it might have been easier to grow in the short term without these constraints, this focus on community culture set the tone for Facebook's eventual explosive growth once it expanded beyond schools. "Once we got to a few million people and the culture was established, it was able to bootstrap into something much bigger that kept that culture even though most people in the world don't have emails issued by some institution that vouches for their identity."

Even with 1.5 billion users, Facebook's culture of real identity remains a core part of the platform today. In 2008, Facebook employees even disabled an account owned by actress Lindsay Lohan after discovering that she was on the site under an alias.[41] This culture of real identity was also a major reason why Facebook was able to surpass Myspace—a feat that was anything but a foregone conclusion in 2005. Myspace's anything-goes attitude turned off many users. In contrast, Facebook "set this tone where there's a lot of clean data on Facebook," Zuckerberg said. "You can rely on it." Because networks are path dependent, this effect compounded over time. In one study, Microsoft researcher danah boyd (who spells her name without capital letters) even compared Myspace's demise to the phenomenon of white flight in U.S. cities.[42] boyd suggested that Myspace developed a reputation as a "digital ghetto," which drove away users, many of them into Facebook's waiting arms. In contrast, Facebook's exclusivity, Ivy League pedigree, and cleaner reputation helped drive its early growth with the college audience. "MySpace was like a big party, and then the party moved on," according to Michael J. Wolf, the former president of Viacom's MTV Networks. "Facebook has become much more of a utility and communications vehicle."[43]

NETWORKS AND USER SEQUENCING:
NOT ALL USERS ARE CREATED EQUAL

There's another big problem with the traditional accounting of network effects. Not only does it assume all network effects are global, it also assumes that all of its users are equally valuable to the whole network. However, in practice this doesn't hold true. Some users are more valuable to a platform than others. This is especially obvious on content platforms like YouTube or Twitter, where celebrity users have many more subscribers or followers than the average user. Not surprisingly, both of these platforms go out of their way to attract these celebrities, creating special features and marketing initiatives that are aimed at retaining their most valuable users. Sina Weibo and Youku Tudou, China's answers to Twitter and YouTube, respectively, followed similar strategies to attract celebrities. However, the importance of marquee users isn't unique to specific platform types. The top services marketplaces, including Uber, Lyft, and Handy, all have programs that incentivize their producers to take more jobs on the platform. For these platforms, high-quality, full-time producers are especially valuable, as they help to improve both liquidity and quality.

Combine this insight with the path-dependent nature of networks, and it's clear that the order in which you attract users can have a big impact on a network's growth. For platforms, not just the number of users but the sequence in which it acquires user groups is key. This is a big reason why development platforms like the Xbox spend heavily to secure exclusive, marquee games at launch. Microsoft spent a reported $1 billion to secure fifteen exclusive titles for its latest gaming system, the Xbox One.[44] The goal was to attract a few hit games early on, with the idea that this would attract lots of consumers, which would in turn attract more high-quality developers to create games for the Xbox One.

A common way for new platforms to accomplish this goal is by limiting participation to a high-value subset of users at the start. As we noted earlier, Quora started as an invite-only network that targeted prominent tech entrepreneurs and venture capitalists. By connecting this small, dense, and exclusive network of experts, Quora was able to build a repository of high-quality content. After it had this initial group of high-value users, Quora found it easy to attract a broader audience. Many new users would want to gain access to the insights of those early users, so they would have a strong incentive to join Quora. Eventually the platform opened up to allow anyone to join and answer questions. More recently, Medium, a popular blogging platform started by former Twitter founder and CEO Ev Williams, launched as an invite-only network limited to journalists, successful entrepreneurs, and other thought leaders before it opened up to anyone. "Our philosophy is that quality begets quality, so we will grow Medium smartly," Williams said at the time.[45] Starting with these high-quality users helped seed the platform with a lot of quality content, which then attracted a lot of readers and other producers who wanted to reach them. Pinterest, a photo-sharing content platform now valued at more than $10 billion, used a similar strategy. Pinterest started as an invite-only network that targeted influential design bloggers. Anyone could view "pins" and browse existing "pin boards," but before you could create and curate pins of your own, you had to request an invitation. This strategy helped to build up demand, as anyone who followed bloggers on the platform could view their pins. But if they wanted to post their own, they needed to seek out an invite. Pinterest gave more invites to bloggers who attracted the most users, giving its early producers a strong incentive to create content and attract consumers.[46] These marquee users acted as magnets and gatekeepers for the network—a position that gave them a nice ego and status boost—and as a result, they were happy to bring their readers to Pinterest.

THE NETWORK EFFECTS LADDER:
A FRAMEWORK FOR GROWING QUALITY NETWORKS

Now that we have a more nuanced view of how networks work, it's time to talk about building network effects. Clearly, creating a network is more complicated than just aggregating many users, but until now, there hasn't been an alternative framework for understanding how to grow quality systematically as a network expands. Now there is: The network effects ladder (see Figure 7.3).

Five "steps" on the ladder dictate the quality of a platform's network: Connection, Communication, Collaboration, Curation, and

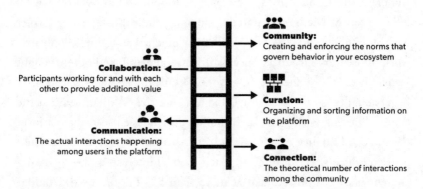

Figure 7.3.   The network effects ladder.

Community.[47] The goal for any network should be to increase quality and community involvement as the platform matures by climbing from one step to the next over time.

Connection

Connection is the most basic step in building a network. You need to attract consumers and producers to increase the theoretical number of interaction pairs in the community. As each participant, or node, is added to the connections graph, the theoretical number of connections doubles. The emphasis here is on theoretical connections, as connections alone do not translate to actual interactions. Unfortunately, as we saw with Metcalfe's Law, connection is also where most people's understanding of network effects begins and ends.

Communication

Communication is how you the turn potential energy of connections into kinetic energy by encouraging real transactions among a platform's users. Great platforms like Facebook and Kickstarter provide a spectrum of engagement opportunities, not just aggregated presence. Similarly, in chapter 3 we saw how enabling communication between its users was key to the success of Alibaba's Taobao marketplace. The goal here is to focus on facilitating better interactions among your users so that they actually can exchange value. Without this step, the theoretical value of a network will remain just that: theoretical. Creating interactions between users is how the magic starts to happen. As we saw with the core transaction, a platform needs to motivate its users to create and consume value. For example, as noted earlier, Myspace still has 300 million user profiles, with a gazillion potential connections, yet it sits like a giant empty amusement park. There's nothing worse than a party with a DJ and nobody dancing. Move your users.

Curation

Most platforms build some element of curation into the compensation step of the core transaction. Rating and reputation systems are the most common example. For example, when using Uber, you're required to rate your driver after you complete a transaction before you can submit another request. But that's not all: Drivers also rate passengers in the same fashion. When you request a ride on Uber, drivers can see your passenger rating, and once they accept, the platform shows you their rating. These reputation systems encourage good-quality transactions from both consumers and producers. By inviting users to provide value through feedback, the platform involves them in the process of maintaining the quality of its network. However, a platform can go even further by inviting users to create additional value through rearranging others' work. Allowing this meta-creativity to be shared creates new segment of producers in the network, ostensibly filling all the value gaps left open by the original producers. Many content platforms use this type of curation to enable additional types of production. For example, a retweet both provides feedback on that tweet and broadcasts it to a new audience (your followers). Similarly, music-streaming app Spotify allows for individual expression around content you didn't create, through playlists. In creating a playlist, a list of others' songs, you're creating new kind of inventory for the platform. Other users can then follow or copy a playlist to listen to your curated collection of music. This kind of creativity via curation enables users to create another layer of personalization within the platform and encourages the creation and discovery of high-quality inventory.

Collaboration

Curation involves getting users to contribute to the network by acting individually. Collaboration takes your users' involvement to the next level by inviting them to work with and for each other. As its network grew, AngelList, an investment platform that makes it easy to invest in early-stage startups, built collaboration into the core of its platform. The idea for AngelList came in early 2010 when its founders, Naval Ravikant and Babak Nivi, posted a list of angel investors on a popular venture capital blog as a resource for founders who were looking for early-stage funding. The list quickly evolved into a platform for matching investors with startups looking to raise seed capital.

By 2013, AngelList had grown its network to include approximately 100,000 startups and 18,000 accredited investors.[48] In July of that year, it launched a new feature called syndicates, which enabled investors to collaborate with each other. How did this work? A lead investor would create a syndicate, which is typically organized around a theme or investment thesis, so inves-

AngelList—investment platform

tors know both who is leading the syndicate and the types of companies it will be investing in. The lead investor gets access to investment deals from startups and puts up part of the money for the investment. Other investors can then back a syndicate by agreeing to invest, on the same terms, alongside its lead investor. When you back a syndicate, you also get priority access on oversubscribed funding rounds.

This collaboration among investors helps smaller investors get in on deals they wouldn't be able to access otherwise. It also helps them find *quality* investments, as the lead is responsible for monitoring the performance of the investment and handling due diligence. In return, the syndicate lead gets a percentage of any profit that its backers make on the investment. By enabling this collaboration between users, AngelList has helped more startups get funded and opened up startup investing to many people who had never done it before.

Community

At the highest level of network effects, a platform encourages its users to go beyond self-interest and start taking ownership of the community. With both curation and collaboration, a platform encourages users to create additional value for each other by getting them to act selfishly. Curating or working collaboratively improves the platform *for me*. Self-interest is a powerful motivator, but here a platform's users become active participants in governing and maintaining the network rather than doing so merely as a by-product of pursuing their own interests. Wikipedia's lifeblood is its community of editors, who enable the platform to operate as a nonprofit while providing more than 36 million articles in 291 languages.[49] The English version of Wikipedia alone is enough to fill 7,473 encyclopedia-length volumes.[50] Even with such a large community, the platform operates without formal rules. In fact, one of Wikipedia's original pillars was "Wikipedia does not have firm rules." As the platform grew, its community took over for its founder, Jimmy Wales, who could no longer personally manage all of the activity as a "benevolent dictator."[51] Today, the community on Wikipedia creates and dictates the implicit rules and social mores that govern the network. They also are the ones who enforce these community standards by handling important administrative functions, such as deleting and blocking users who repeatedly make fraudulent or deceitful changes and protecting pages from underhanded editing. These users derive little direct benefit from this activity but feel a sense of ownership for the platform and its network. In an important sense, Wikipedia is theirs, not just the platform owner's.

However, this level of involvement isn't limited to nonprofits. Other great examples include Stack Overflow (a Q&A platform for developers) and Reddit, which both have highly engaged users that create and maintain the customs and standards that govern community behavior. Lyft, Uber's biggest competitor in the United States, places a similar emphasis on its driver community. Lyft founders Logan Green and Ryan Zimmer decided early on that actively building a community would be a priority for the platform. "Some people may think it's weird to build a community. The community should seem like it's just a natural thing," Green said. "Our feeling is that it is the right thing to do to build the community, because if you don't, your service can degrade into something like Chatroulette. By building the community you can create some community norms."[52] By building its driver community, Lyft has helped maintain driver quality as it has expanded across the United States. Lyft even has invested in regular offline events for its drivers in an effort to help them connect. "We host a lot of community events for our drivers," according to Ryan Fujui, former product lead on Lyft's growth team. "It really helps not only to bring everyone together to create that sense of community but also to help disseminate information and best practices. The best way to learn how to become a new driver is to actively engage with an existing driver."[53]

SCALING THE NETWORK EFFECT LADDER

The five steps of the Network Effects ladder are a reflection of a platform's ability to attract, activate, and empower its participants. Initially, a platform simply has to attract users to create connections. But to realize the potential value of these connections, the platform has to activate those users through communication. Once the network has been established and value is being exchanged, it can increase the strength of its network effects by empowering its users. By enabling curation and collaboration, it harnesses users' self-interest to improve quality within the network and create new types of value. Finally, a platform can enable its users to start taking ownership of the community by empowering them to help govern the network. By climbing each step in this ladder, the platform builds stronger network effects and creates a higher-quality network. The higher you go, the more valuable your network will be.

8

WHY PLATFORMS FAIL, AND HOW TO AVOID IT

People say it all the time: this product is so good that it sells itself. This is almost never true. These people are lying, either to themselves, to others, or both.

—Peter Thiel

"Every 10 years or so a company and a marketplace and an opportunity come together that's transformative. Not since Google have we seen this." That's how legendary venture capital firm Sequoia Capital reacted back in 2011 when it saw Color, a photo-sharing platform started by serial entrepreneur Bill Nguyen.[1] "No other app connects people like Color does," Sequoia Capital partner Douglas Leone said. What was Color? It was "an instant social network" that captured "experiences with those around you."[2] The platform had founders with impressive resumes and the ambitious goal of being "the Facebook of the smartphone era." Silicon Valley investors were foaming at the mouth. They didn't want to miss the next big thing.

Unlike Facebook, Color didn't require a user name or password to use. There was no "friending" or "following" on Color. Instead, photos taken by other Color users within 150 feet would appear automatically in what the company called an "elastic network," essentially a stream of photos that would change depending on where you were. The goal was to create a social network of people you didn't know, rather than ones you did. "I do think Facebook is broken," Nguyen said at the time.[3] Color would do what Facebook could not. The platform "intelligently identifies nearby smartphones, whether at a local park or at a concert, using advanced proximity algorithms," and instantly shares photos, videos, comments, and likes with them. Nguyen claimed that Color could ingest and analyze four times the amount of data that Google could in its early days.[4] Armed with this ambitious vision and a host of patents for the sophisticated-sounding technology designed by former LinkedIn chief scientist DJ Patil, Color raised $41 million. Nguyen dropped $350,000 for the URL Color.com and another $75,000 on Colour.com. The company garnered serious media attention, including profiles by *USA Today* and CNN. There was just one catch: Color hadn't launched yet.

The platform launched its iOS app on March 24, 2011, bizarrely choosing to go live a few days *after* über-tech conference SXSW ended, rather than before. (Twitter had launched its platform at SXSW in 2007 to great success.)

Thanks in part to the massive hype and widespread publicity, the app rocketed to number 2 in the App Store charts, the David to number-1 app Facebook's Goliath. But Color had a problem. "Within 30 minutes I realized, Oh my God, it's broken. Holy shit, we totally fucked up," Nguyen said.[5]

THE $41 MILLION MISTAKE

"What if you threw a $41 million party and nobody came?" That's how the *New York Times* began a June 2011 article on risky investments in tech startups. The app in question was, of course, Color. Color's problem was simple: If other people weren't using the app, the platform sucked. The app quickly was flooded with one- and two-star reviews in the App Store, most of which had a similar complaint. "First-time experience is terrible: it's totally blank. There's nothing to see," one user wrote. "It would be pointless even if I managed to understand how it works," another said.[6] For most of the people who downloaded the app, the platform was a ghost town. All of Color's technological wizardry and its "elastic network" showed them nothing. Because of its 150-foot proximity limit, the platform was useless outside of densely packed tech meccas. In order to get any value out of Color, you needed many other people nearby to be uploading photos. But with few people uploading photos at the start, new users had no incentive to stick around and upload photos. The app featured "ephemeral" photos (a feature Snapchat would later popularize), which meant that any existing photographs would disappear after 24 hours. The company tried to respond quickly. It put up a warning on its home page: "Don't use Color alone!" Nguyen eventually tried updating the app to relax the 150-foot limit in areas that weren't densely populated, but to no avail. Color became a tech-industry punch line. "Extremely-Hyped Startup Fails to Live Up to Extreme Hype," one headline joked.[7] "I wanna see that pitch deck," influential tech blogger Robert Scoble wrote. "It must have had some magic unicorn dust sprinkled on it."[8] The app quickly fell back down the App Store charts and faded into obscurity. After a failed attempt to pivot into being (ironically) a Facebook app, the company eventually shut down, with Apple "acquihiring" its tech team.

WHICH CAME FIRST?

That Color's seasoned execs failed to see this issue coming is shocking. The ghost town problem that brought down Color is hardly unique. Yet Color CEO Nguyen seemed confident that its sophisticated technology alone would "wow" users, even though the company did little external testing and had no discernible launch strategy. This if-you-build-it-they-will-come attitude is surprisingly common, even among experienced tech investors and executives. That's also why Color couldn't figure out how to jump-start its network. Technology alone isn't enough, especially when the platform has little value without the participation of other users. Color isn't the first platform to fail on these grounds, and it will certainly not be the last. In fact, this challenge is one that *every* platform, even the successful ones, must overcome at the start.

Why? Well, network effects are a double-edged sword. Successful platforms are very hard to compete against, but the same network effects that drive growth also make platforms much harder to build. Unlike a traditional, linear startup, a platform doesn't need to acquire just one group of customers. At a minimum it needs two, its consumers and its producers. Color needed some users to upload content in order for others to consume it. But without any content on the platform, there was no incentive for new users to add anything. Why bother populating a ghost town? Even successful platforms like Uber had the same problem when they first started. As we mentioned in chapter 5, building liquidity is an important goal of audience building. For example, Uber needed both drivers and passengers for the platform to work, so it had to build a liquid marketplace with both enough drivers and enough passengers for transactions to clear quickly. Liquidity is relative, so some markets with higher transaction frequency will be more liquid than those that have higher value but less frequent transactions. In either case, as a network grows over time, it builds greater liquidity and therefore facilitates more transactions. This is how platforms ultimately create more value as they grow: The larger their networks become, the more transactions they are able to facilitate.

Initially, however, for most users the cost of joining a platform exceeds the value they can get out of it. In fact, the value of joining the network is often *negative* early on—the cost to users of signing up and entering information is more than the value they receive for joining and being a part of the network. Joining the platform technically might be free, but other forms of transactions costs, such as time and effort spent signing up, still drive users away. If the network is sufficiently large, both consumers and producers would happily join. But most users on either side of the network aren't willing to join when the network is small.

The goal is to reach the point where the value of the network will exceed the cost of joining for most users. As we mentioned in chapter 3, this point is called critical mass. This dynamic is why most successful platforms have a hockey stick–shape growth curve (see Figure 8.1). It's easy to understand this shift from pre- to post-critical mass if you think of a network like a magnet. When a network is small, its magnetic force repels new users. But once the network reaches sufficient size, that magnet flips and reverses polarity. Suddenly it starts to pull in new users, and the platform's growth takes off.

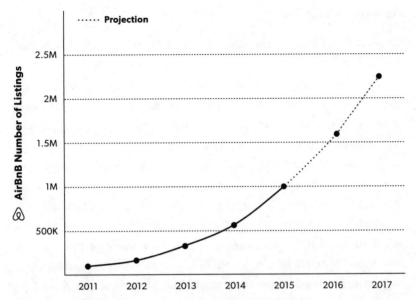

Figure 8.1.   Airbnb's hockey-stick growth curve. Source: Venturebeat

Platforms' struggles with early growth are the result of what economists call a coordination problem. If everyone on each side of the network could coordinate their behavior, they could all agree to join the network and everyone would benefit. But in practice, this almost never happens. That's where a platform's management of its network comes in. This coordination problem must be solved by incentivizing users to join. The main way platforms do this is by subsidizing participation for one or both user groups. In this way, the platform can get early users to join even when the value of the network is relatively low. The platform and its investors are betting that the eventual value of the network will exceed the cost of building it through subsidies. Once the network reaches maturity, it will provide enough value on its own that participation will no longer have to be heavily subsidized.

THREE WAYS TO SUBSIDIZE VALUE

There are three primary ways to subsidize value: monetary subsidies, product feature subsidies, and user sequencing.

Monetary Subsidies

Monetary subsidies are the most obvious way that platforms subsidize new users. These subsidies typically involve giving money directly to consumers or producers. One example of this is referral fees, which most platforms use to attract new users. For example, if you invite a friend to join Uber, you and your friend each get your next ride free, up to $30. PayPal built its network with a similar strategy, offering $10 both to the new user and to the referrer. Although this subsidy was expensive, it helped drive extremely high growth rates for PayPal's network in the early 2000s, with growth reaching as high as 7 to 10 percent *daily*.[9]

Another way to subsidize value is through price. Although less direct than handing out rebates and referral fees, lowering prices to one side of the platform is a very common way to subsidize participation. A great example of this is the console industry, where the Xbox One and Playstation 4 are sold at or below cost in order to get as many users as possible onto the platform. These platforms can then use their large consumer base to attract game developers, whom they charge licensing fees. Many platforms also provide guarantees to producers in order to get them to join. Heavy competition for drivers on ride-sharing platforms has led both Uber and Lyft to offer minimum-earnings guarantees to drivers who join. Handy also offers a guarantee to producers from other on-demand services marketplaces who join its network.

Product Features Subsidies

Another way to subsidize value is through product features. Many platforms create special functionality for power users in order to increase loyalty and usage among this prized user group. The goal here is to provide additional value to specific, high-value groups in order to get them to join the network.

One example of this is Instagram, which provided a great photo-taking app before it became the social network it is today. By offering this single-user utility, Instagram was able to attract many producers to its platform, which it then used to attract consumers and build a content platform around photos.

Another example is Twitter's Verified User program. You may have noticed a small checkmark next to some Twitter users' names. This icon means that user is a Verified Twitter user. Verified users get additional features, such as improved security and identity protection. They also get better customer service and the ability to view and talk only to other verified users. This feature typically is offered to high-profile users, such as celebrities and public figures, who attract a large number of followers. These are some of the most valuable users for Twitter, as they are the people that most users will want to follow and interact with. With this Verified program, Twitter creates product features that deliver value for a small subset of highly valuable users. As a result, Twitter can attract more celebrities and public figures. And if it gets more high-profile users to join, other users will want to join to follow and talk to them.

User Sequencing

Both monetary and feature subsidies should be guided by decisions on user sequencing, which is the third way to subsidize value. We covered this topic in greater detail in chapter 7. User sequencing involves deliberately prioritizing the acquisition of certain user groups that others will want to interact with. Then these high-value users can be used to attract a broader audience later on.

Combining these ways of subsidizing value allows a platform to offer enough value to early users to overcome the chicken-and-egg problem and reach the point where positive network effects to kick in and drive future growth. But what do these methods look like in action? Based on our experience working with countless platform start-ups and our extensive research into successful (and failed) platforms, we've documented seven essential strategies that combine these ways to subsidize value to overcome the chicken-and-egg problem and help a platform reach scale. These strategies are not all mutually exclusive; a platform can use any one of them on its own or it can use several at the same time, depending on its resources and goals. All of these strategies involve user-sequencing decisions, so we've sorted them by whether they primarily involve using monetary subsidies, product features, or both.

SEVEN WAYS TO SOLVE THE CHICKEN-AND-EGG PROBLEM

Monetary Subsidies

1. Provide Security through a Large, Up-front Investment
Significant up-front investment in a platform can signal that it's safe for producers to join the network. This strategy is especially common for development platforms, where developers incur considerable up-front costs to join a platform and high switching costs if they decide to leave. For the platform, making a big up-front investment signals that it isn't going anywhere, and producers become more comfortable making a long-term investment. A great example of this strategy was Microsoft's launch of the original Xbox. Microsoft made a big deal about its commitment to spend $500 million promoting the platform, thereby signaling that the company was fully committed to the platform for the long haul. This was an important way that Microsoft attracted third-party game developers, who then felt more comfortable developing games for the Xbox early on.

Another example comes from Chinese company Tencent, which wanted to increase adoption of its own payments platform to compete with Alibaba's Alipay. Tencent didn't accomplish this overnight. It seeded the platform's early activity through lots of promotion and investment. For example, in 2014, Tencent launched a campaign centered around the Chinese New Year where advertisers gave away 500 million RMB (about $81 million) of free cash to WeChat Payment users in a single day.

2. Cooperate with Industry Incumbents
Back in 2007, Google was in a precarious position. The company owned desktop search, but the mobile Internet was starting to take off. With the runaway early success of the iPhone, Google was worried that mobile would become Apple's walled garden. Luckily, it wasn't alone. Handset manufacturers and telecoms not named AT&T shared the same fear. So Google created the Open Handset Alliance, a group dedicated to advancing Google's Android operating system.

In essence, Google used a cooperative strategy. Rather than trying to build a network all on its own, it tapped into the existing sales channels of the companies in the Open Handset Alliance to spread Android to consumers. With Android enjoying more than 80 percent worldwide market share for mobile operating systems and having more than 1.8 million apps on its Play Store as of 2015, the strategy worked out pretty well.

Product Features

3. Act as a Producer

Fake it until you make it, or so the saying goes. This adage applies to many platform companies. Rather than trying to attract both consumers and producers at the same time, the platform acts as the producer to attract an initial group of consumers. It then uses its existing consumer base to attract producers. In essence, this strategy means you start out as a traditional linear business and then open up your network to producers once the platform has attracted enough consumers.

This tactic is a common one for kick-starting a network. For example, Uber started out by paying drivers to wait around until they got a call. Only once it had built up sufficient demand was the platform able to attract independent producers. Similarly, both Quora and Reddit seeded their platforms by curating and creating all of the original content themselves. Before Quora began attracting techies and venture capitalists, the company's founders, Charlie Cheever, Rebekah Cox, and former Facebook chief technology officer Adam D'Angelo, created most of the original questions and answers on the site. If you look at their Quora profiles, you can see dozens of questions they created early on. Quora's early employees and beta testers continued this trend until the amount of content and activity on the platform became self-sustaining. For Reddit, founders Alexis Ohanian and Steve Huffman used basically the same strategy. The two founded Reddit back in June 2005. It was one of the first startups out of Y Combinator, which today is widely recognized as the leading startup accelerator. The founders resorted to some old-school marketing to get their first users, printing out stickers and putting them up everywhere they traveled. But without any content on the site, no one was sticking around.[10] So Ohanian and Huffman started posting all the content themselves. However, they didn't stop there. They also created lots of fake profiles to post on, so it looked like the website had more activity than it actually did. Within a few months, they didn't have to submit content to fill the front page. Real users followed and took over production.

4. Tap into an Existing Network

Rather than trying to create a network from scratch, why not use one that's already there? The best way to do this is to tap into an existing large network to attract a subset of its users. In order to attract these users away from the existing network, your platform needs to provide incremental value compared to the existing solution. In essence, you've recognized that you're creating the next evolution of an existing network, and you're appealing to a portion of its existing network to help seed yours. As we mentioned in chapter 6, Airbnb used this strategy to help grow its ecosystem early on by tapping into Craigslist's network. Don't think you can get away with repeating this same Craigslist trick now, though. Craigslist was quick to ban Airbnb's tactic once it discovered what was going on. It has since banned any similar activity on its site, and violators may incur a potential fine of up to $25,000 a day.[11] Unlike the situation with a cooperative strategy, the existing network you're siphoning users from isn't likely to take kindly to your activities.

Digital networks aren't the only ones you should look for. Tinder kick-started its network by building on top of the existing social networks of Greek organizations on college campuses. Tinder co-founder Whitney Wolfe (who has since gone on to found Bumble, a competing dating platform) came up with the strategy, according to Joe Muñoz, one of Tinder's first engineers. "We sent [Wolfe] all over the country," Muñoz said. "Her pitch was pretty genius. She would go to chapters of her sorority, do her presentation, and have all the girls at the meetings install the app. Then she'd go to the corresponding brother fraternity—they'd open the app and see all these cute girls they knew." Tinder had fewer than 5,000 users when Wolfe started her trip. By the time she was done, Tinder had more than 15,000. "At that point, I thought the avalanche had started," Munoz said.[12]

Monetary Subsidies and Product Features

5. Attract High-Value or "Celebrity" Users

High-value users will help you attract other users who want to interact with them. As noted in chapter 7, the participation of "celebrity" users brings extra value to your ecosystem. That's why many platforms make special efforts to subsidize the participation of these high-value users. Dating websites are a classic example. Their populations tend to skew heavily male, so they often let women join for free. Some, like Coffee Meets Bagel, go even further, deliberately designing the experience to appeal to women with the knowledge that if women join, men will too.

As we mentioned earlier in this chapter, Twitter went out of its way to attract celebrities and public figures to its platform. In addition to creating features that catered specifically to these high-value users, it also built an emerging media team early on that was tasked with building relationships with stars, including actors, athletes, and musicians. These people were called VITs, or Very Important Tweeters, inside the company.[13] And as we covered in chapter 7, Sina Weibo and Youku Tudou followed similar strategies to attract celebrities, while top services marketplaces, such as Uber, Lyft, and Handy, all have programs that incentivize producers to take more jobs on the platform. These high-quality, full-time producers are especially valuable, as they help to improve both liquidity and quality.

However, perhaps the best example of this strategy is Yelp. Yelp's early competitors, Judy's Book and Insider Pages, had a big lead in reviews. They had more than ten times as many reviews as Yelp did, but they had a dirty secret: They were *paying* for reviews to seed content. Rather than be left behind, Yelp decided to join them. However, after experimenting with paying for reviews in a few cities, the platform quickly realized that the result would be thousands of crappy reviews and very few dedicated users. This wasn't a sustainable way to build a network. The local ratings and reviews platform then decided to get creative. It created the Yelp Elite Squad

Yelp—content platform

to incentivize its best users to create more and higher-quality reviews. The Elite Squad is made up of a select group of highly active Yelpers that the company picks because of their frequent, high-quality reviews. The process behind gaining admission to the Elite Squad is shrouded in mystery. Each year an elite council of Yelp staffers anoints new elites and decides whether existing members will have their elite status renewed. Inclusion in the tribe is closely guarded. Yelp cofounder Russel Simmons even lost his elite status a few years ago when he wasn't active enough on the platform to merit belonging. Clearly, you need to be one of the top Yelpers in your city to be considered. Once you're admitted, you get a nice shiny badge on your Yelp profile, and your reviews are highlighted for other users. But being part of the Elite Squad gets you the VIP treatment in the real world too. Yelp regularly hosts exclusive events and parties for squad members. By offering both digital and real-world swag to its top users, Yelp incentivizes them to stay active. In fact, the Elite Squad quickly became the backbone of Yelp's early marketing strategy. It's a great example of a company quickly scaling the network effects ladder to establish a strong sense of community where it matters most.

6. Target a User Group to Fill Both Sides

The idea behind this strategy is similar to number 3: Try to make a two-sided market one sided. The goal here is to find a user group that can fill both the consumer and producer roles. That way you no longer need to worry about attracting and balancing two separate user groups early on. This strategy was the recipe for success for handmade goods platform Etsy. Etsy's early research indicated that the people most likely to buy handmade goods were the people who also sold them, so the company decided to focus on this user group to fill out both sides of its marketplace before expanding to other audiences. The strategy worked pretty well, as Etsy went public in April 2015, raising $267 million in the process.[14] This strategy is also a natural fit for most social networks and communication platforms; rather than being two separate groups, consumers and producers have very high overlap. Almost every user will serve in each role at a different time. On Facebook, users both create their profile (producer) and view their friends' (consumer) profiles, while on Snapchat, the same user both sends (producer) and receives messages (consumer).

7. Provide Single-User Utility

Last but certainly not least is providing single-user utility. This is a come-for-the-tool-stay-for-the-network approach, as venture capitalist Chris Dixon says.[15] You attract one side of your multisided platform by offering that user group value even if the other side never shows up.

Many platforms that went this route were initially apps that provided their users with essential functionality even if the network never materialized. Early Instagram is a great example, as it provided its users with a way to take photos and make them look good long before it evolved into a full-fledged social networking platform.

Restaurant booking platform OpenTable used a similar strategy to get restaurants on board. The company realized that even the top restaurants in San Francisco didn't have back-end reservation systems. They were still using pen and paper to track reservations. OpenTable built a software application to handle electronic booking and targeted the top twenty restaurants in San Francisco, offering to help them set the system up. After these restaurants were on board, others soon became interested. Once OpenTable had this core group of restaurants, it was able to open its platform to allow for consumers to book restaurant reservations online.

Of course, a less subtle way to provide single-user utility is simply to find a way to pay users. Doing this can help remove any initial uncertainty users might have about a platform's value, because whether other users show up or not, they'll still get value from participating. But be careful, because these direct monetary subsidies can be hard to sustain long term. And once they go away, your users might too.

* * *

Those are the seven key strategies for getting your platform off the ground. While early customer acquisition is especially tough for platforms, creative use of these strategies should help you overcome the chicken-and-egg problem and attract your first users. After that, it's time to start climbing the network effects ladder to rev your long-term growth engine.

CONCLUSION

HOW TO SPOT THE NEXT BIG THING

The old doesn't go away, but it becomes less relevant.

—Benedict Evans, partner at
Andreessen Horowitz

Have you ever heard of Adyen? The Amsterdam-based payments company is the invisible engine of the platform economy. It handles payments for the likes of Airbnb, Booking.com, Dropbox, Facebook, Spotify, Yelp, and Uber, among many others. By focusing on partnering with global platform companies, Adyen has grown quickly. From 2013 to 2014, its revenue nearly doubled, from $95 million to $185 million, and in 2014, the company secured $250 million from investors, which valued it at $1.5 billion.[1]

Uber first started working with Adyen in 2012, when the transportation-network company first launched in the Netherlands. Adyen has since helped Uber expand to dozens of markets on six continents. It adapts its payments solution to regional differences in regulations and payments infrastructure, so that its client companies can accept payments in nearly 200 countries. "In the fast-moving, high-growth curve that unicorns go through, speed to market and removing complexity are paramount," Adyen CEO Pieter van der Does says. "The big advantage we can offer these businesses is time to market and ability to scale quickly. So when a Spotify or an Uber rolls out in countries such as Morocco or Poland, we can be powering local payments for them from day one."

International expansion is no easy feat for a global platform, especially from a payments perspective. Payment patterns vary greatly from region to region. For instance, in the United States and the United Kingdom, credit cards account for the lion's share of online transactions. But in the rest of the world, credit cards aren't nearly as popular for online purchases. "Consumers in different countries use an astonishing variety of payment methods to buy online," van der Does explains. "What we have done is revolutionized global e-commerce by enabling global companies to support all key payment methods in all markets around the world—Alipay, Tenpay, and UnionPay in China, SOFORT in Germany, QIWI in Russia, and Boletos in Brazil, to name but a few. This approach has been so successful that a number of our customers are taking a payments-first approach to global expansion, where they offer international shipping and key local payment methods before they actually set up local operations in the market."

Adyen also collects data on authorization rates and works with clients to minimize declined payments. So next time you take an Uber, or book an apartment on Airbnb, and your card doesn't get declined, now you know whom to thank.

However, Adyen faces unique challenges in partnering with platforms. The first is the ferocity and pace of growth these companies pursue. Second, platforms have to be able to transact with multiple customer groups simultaneously. "Our marketplace solution is the best example of how we work with platforms," van der Does says. "Adyen MarketPay enables marketplaces to automatically split payments between buyers, sellers, and their own accounts." This is a very powerful proposition for platform companies, since splitting payments normally consumes a great deal of internal resources, particularly when it comes to cross-border e-commerce. "With a single transaction, a customer may purchase three items supplied by three different sellers," van der Does says. "These transactions then need to be split twice, between payouts for each seller and the marketplace's own commission. This means that this single transaction is split a total of six times, between four different parties—creating enormous complexity in the process. We unshackle marketplaces from this complexity, enabling them to automate the payments process and focus on the hard work of international expansion."

"THIS IS A GOLD RUSH"

Adyen isn't the only company that's found success by solving problems for platform companies. With Airbnb's explosive growth, a host of independent service providers have sprung up around the platform, mostly catering to hosts. If you have an apartment you want to list but aren't sure how to create a good listing, then you're in luck. AirSpruce will connect you with a professional travel writer who will create your Airbnb listing for you. Not sure how much to charge for your room? Beyond Pricing will help you optimize the price on your listing by providing automatic, data-driven daily price adjustments. Competitors include Everbooked, Price Labs, and SmartHost, all of which offer similar services. Another startup called Keycafe offers to store your key at a local café. Then your guests can pick up their keys anytime the café is open. Another service, Urban Bellhop, offers to handle check-in, including personally delivering the key to guests. The company also offers listing management and cleaning services that focus on Airbnb hosts. Another startup called Pillow provides a similar service, as do Beyond Stays, GuestHop, Guesty, and many more.

Uber also has spawned its own ecosystem of support services. Many people who might want to drive an Uber part-time don't own a car. Well, thanks to Breeze, a San Francisco-based startup: no car, no problem. Breeze leases cars at $195 a week to aspiring Uber or Lyft drivers. In late 2013, Uber also began partnering with third-party lenders to offer vehicle financing to would-be drivers.[2] Insurance is another big opportunity. Both Uber and Lyft provide insurance coverage while drivers are on a job, but when they're not on the way to or driving a passenger, they are out of luck. Even worse, many personal auto insurance policies will cancel your policy if they find out you work for Uber (since the policy is not meant to cover commercial activity), and traditional commercial insurance options are prohibitively expensive for many part-time drivers.

Into that gap stepped insurance companies like Metromile, which offers per-mile insurance. The company gives drivers a device that plugs into their cars to track how far they drive. The more they drive, the more they pay. Even better, Metromile can track the driving and match up trips with Uber rides, so the insurance company can see which of miles are personal miles and which are commercial. Metromile charges users only for the personal miles, since Uber covers the car when drivers are with or en route to passengers. "The existing model for insurance hasn't been able to adapt [to Uber]," Metromile CEO Dan Preston said.[3] "We have a technology that drives the insurance product." More mainstream insurance companies, such as Geico and Progressive, have followed Metromile's lead by offering ride-share insurance that caters to Uber and Lyft drivers.

This phenomenon of derivative businesses being built around larger platform companies isn't new. The legion of search engine optimization experts that sprang up to help businesses grapple with Google's search engine are an obvious precedent, as are the legions of people and companies that hold some variation of the title "social media manager." All of these people owe their livelihoods to platforms like Facebook, LinkedIn, and Twitter. Likewise, YouTube has spawned scores of small businesses built around YouTube stars. Behind every YouTube star, such as Smosh or PewDiePie, is a host of people that support the stars and help them make money. App developers and the exploding mobile gaming industry are other examples. Both of these industries were built around development platforms, such as Apple's iOS and Google's Android. In fact, Applico, the company Alex founded in 2009, started out as an app development company. And by 2017, the app development industry alone will be a $77 billion market.[4]

Today, many investors who missed out on unicorns like Uber and Airbnb are looking to this second generation of companies to harness some of the growth potential of the core platforms. "This is a gold rush," one venture capitalist has said. "You can either mine for gold like Uber or Airbnb, or you can sell the pots, the pans, and the Levi jeans."[5] However, this approach is not without risk. The platform could extend its own products to incorporate features offered by independent service providers. It also could cut off access to the platform if third parties run afoul of its rules and standards. In either case, these businesses could find themselves out of business overnight. Some companies have learned this lesson the hard way.

BETTING THE FARMVILLE

After Facebook launched its developer platform at its F8 conference on May 24, 2007, another gold rush began. Developers flocked to the platform, hoping to capitalize on its "social graph"—basically a fancy name for the collection of data that articulates the network of social connections among Facebook's users. Mark Pincus was one of the first to see the social graph's potential. "What I thought was the ultimate thing you can do—once you bring all of your friends and their friends together—is play games," Pincus said. "And I've always been a closet gamer, but I never have the time and can never get all of my friends together in one place. So the power of my friends already being there and connected, and then adding games, seemed like a big idea."[6] The launch of Facebook's developer platform made Pincus's vision possible. He started a company called Presidio Media that would focus on developing Facebook games. Within two months, his company launched an online poker game on Facebook. Later that year, the company changed its name to Zynga Inc., after Pincus's bulldog. Then, in June 2008, the company released *Mafia Wars*, its first hit game. *Mafia Wars* was a multiplayer game in which users played as gangsters building their own gangs. The game was inherently social—you could fight or "rob" other players who were online, or ask for help to complete missions. However, there was a catch. *Mafia Wars* was one of the first of what are now known as freemium games, meaning the game itself was free to play but players had the option to purchase premium content or advance in the game faster for a small amount of money. (In an episode of *South Park*, one character jokes that the "-mium" in "freemium" is Latin for "not really.")

In June 2009, Zynga released *FarmVille*, a game that ostensibly copied an existing and already popular Facebook game called *Farm Town*.[7] Despite its lack of originality, *FarmVille* quickly became a mega-hit. Within two months of its release, it had over a million users active each *day*.[8] A month later, Zynga raised $29 million in a funding round led by stalwart venture capital firm Kleiner Perkins Caufield & Byers.

FarmVille also was a freemium game. In it, you could create your own farm and grow plants. But to continue advancing, you had to get friends to visit your farm and lend a hand. Or, of course, you could pay. Anyone who was on Facebook at the time will remember the result. The platform became flooded with requests from friends to help water their virtual crops or go on virtual missions. As is typical for freemium games, only about 3 to 5 percent of users were willing to pay to advance the game. Users who didn't want to pay to play resorted to spamming their friends' walls and Newsfeeds with invites and requests for help.

Facebook was caught off guard. It hadn't anticipated this kind of activity when it opened up its developer platform. It made the mistake of failing to set robust rules around how developers could connect with users. Zynga took advantage of this lack of foresight by getting its users to spam their friends. However, this spam mechanic worked only because the messages it sent out to other users were given the same priority as any other Facebook message users might receive from a friend. On March 1, 2010, Facebook changed its policy to limit notifications developers could send to users, and traffic for Zynga games fell sharply. *FarmVille* users declined by 26 percent within a month. Zynga considered leaving Facebook entirely and running all of its games on Zynga.com but ultimately decided against it and soldiered on. It released a new game, *CityVille*, which quickly became the company's most popular game, reaching more than 100 million monthly users within forty-three days.

In search of new growth channels after it reached near saturation on Facebook, Zynga went on an acquisitions spree, picking up eleven gaming companies in as many months between 2010 and 2011.[9] The online gaming industry is extremely hit based, so rather than try to keep manufacturing new hits, Zynga used its fundraising war chest to acquire other successful games (and their development teams) as a shortcut to revenue growth. As a result, in 2010, Zynga turned its first profit. But this success was short-lived. By 2011, Zynga's traditional growth channels on Facebook had started to dry up. Despite the warning signs, Zynga went public on December 16, 2011. It ended that year with its highest net loss ever: $404 million. The year 2012 saw the company continue its decline as Facebook further tightened the rules around its development platform, and Zynga failed to produce any new hit games. At the end of 2012, Zynga finally split with Facebook, ending what had been a close relationship.[10] Even though an estimated 80 percent of its revenue came from Facebook users, the company decided to move its games to its own gaming platform, which meant players would no longer be able to share their progress with their friends through Facebook.

The shift to mobile gaming also caught the company off guard. Zynga's largest competitors were no longer developing Facebook apps. iOS and Android were where the action was. Hits like *Temple Run, Clash of Clans,* and *Candy Crush* were the top titles on mobile, and Zynga couldn't replicate there the success it had enjoyed on Facebook. By June 2013, its number of daily active users had shrunk to 187 million, down from a height of 306 million just a year earlier. After a year of layoffs and losses, Pincus stepped down as CEO in 2013. The big party he envisioned had come to an end.

TERMINAL DECLINE

Zynga's rise and fall perfectly demonstrates the risk (and potential reward) of building around a dominant platform. The gaming company was quick to exploit the potential of Facebook's development platform, but when Facebook tightened the rules, Zynga's growth evaporated. Despite a spate of recent game releases, including a number of sequels to its original hits, the company hasn't recovered. Such a shift in fortunes isn't unusual. We covered how Twitter handled its development platform in chapter 6. Many developers built apps around Twitter, but once the platform decided it wanted to be the main provider of Twitter clients, a lot of these third-party developers were put out of business.

In both these cases, opportunistic developers found success by capitalizing on short-term opportunities. Zynga grew quickly by spamming Facebook users with invites to its games. And Facebook benefited hugely from Zynga's initial growth; Zynga accounted for 12 percent of Facebook's 2011 revenue.[11] The timing made this revenue contribution especially significant, since Facebook went public in early 2012. A big revenue boost at the time meant a higher IPO price and more cash in the bank. However, although Zynga enjoyed huge short-term growth, its success disappeared once Facebook (rightly) cut off its distribution mechanism. Similarly, Twitter benefited from developers providing third-party mobile apps back when the platform wasn't well established. But for Twitter to have a successful business, it had to own the core experience. And this meant owning the Twitter app. A number of developers found short-term success by selling Twitter apps for a dollar or two on the app store, but because they didn't align themselves with the platform's long-term goals, their revenue stream was short lived.

Of course, even businesses that align themselves with a platform's long-term vision don't always come out ahead. Just look at what's happened to several leading Android phone manufacturers. As we covered in the prologue, Google assembled an army of manufacturers and wireless carriers to help it launch Android. Both HTC and Motorola were instrumental in driving early Android phone sales. For Android's first few years on the market, HTC's myTouch and Evo smartphones were best sellers, as was Motorola's Droid. Yet by 2012, sales for both companies had tanked. HTC's sales shrank by 36 percent in 2012 compared to a year earlier.[12] Meanwhile, Motorola was already losing money. It registered a loss of $249 million for the fiscal year of 2011.[13] Faced with the prospect of continued decline, Motorola sold itself to Google in 2012 for $12.5 billion (though this acquisition included Motorola's $3 billion cash reserves, meaning the book value of the deal was only $9.5 billion). Even then, Google ostensibly acquired the company just for its patent portfolio, which helped Google defend Android against patent trolls and competitors. By the end of the year, Google already had sold off Motorola's Home division for $2.35 billion. Scarcely a year later, it sold Motorola's handset division for $2.91 billion to Lenovo. To add insult to injury, Lenovo decided to phase out the Motorola brand name entirely by the end of 2016. Fate hasn't been any kinder to HTC. In a six-month period at the end of 2011, HTC lost an incredible $27 billion of its market capitalization—or more than 75 percent of its peak value. In October 2012, HTC reported that its third-quarter revenue had declined by 48 percent while net income had declined by 79 percent compared to a year earlier.[14] By August 2015, HTC's market cap had declined to just 5 percent of its 2011 high. In fact, on August 9, 2015, HTC was trading *below* the value of its cash reserves. Investors valued the company at NT$47 billion ($1.5 billion at the time), less than the company's NT$47.2 billion cash on hand.[15] Aside from its cash reserves, HTC literally was worth *less than nothing*.

What happened to HTC and Motorola? The short answer is: Samsung. After toying with Windows Mobile, the consumer electronics giant decided to go with Android. (The company briefly dabbled with the idea of creating its own operating system for smartphones but mostly abandoned those plans in favor of building Android phones.) In June 2010, Samsung introduced its Galaxy S Android smartphone. A year later, it put its full weight behind Android. In November 2011, Samsung launched a massive marketing campaign that promoted its Galaxy S II smartphone while also attacking Apple and the iPhone. In 2012, Samsung's Galaxy S III Android smartphone officially passed Apple's iPhone by a comfortable margin as the best-selling smartphone on the planet. By the end of that year, Samsung's profits were up 76 percent, fueled by the growth of its smartphone division, which became the most profitable part of the company. On the heels of Samsung's success, the *Wall Street Journal* ran a feature in January 2013 titled "Has Apple Lost Its Cool to Samsung?"[16]

However, like its predecessors, Samsung's moment at the top didn't last. Although Android continued to grow—it's now the most-used mobile operating system in the world—Samsung has lost ground to new competitors. At the low-price end of the market, Chinese manufacturers have started to overtake Samsung. The decline was especially pronounced in China, where Samsung was once the best-selling smartphone vendor. However, it's since dropped below both Xiaomi and Huawei.[17] It's also fallen behind Apple, which started attacking Samsung's biggest advantage in the smartphone market when Apple company introduced the iPhone 6 and the even larger-screened iPhone 6 Plus on September 9, 2014. Big screens had long been one of the major factors driving Samsung's success at the high end of the market, and once Apple copied that feature, it quickly ate into Samsung's market share. After it launched the iPhone 6, Apple had what was then the most profitable quarter of *any company ever*.[18]

Meanwhile, Samsung's profits plunged 64 percent in the same quarter,[19] and its struggles have continued ever since. In July 2015, the company reported a profit decline for the seventh consecutive quarter. Within just a few years, Samsung's handset division had gone from the company's flagship to just flagging. Many analysts and investors have suggested that the once-dominant company is now in "terminal decline."[20]

THE TOP OF THE PYRAMID

What happened to Samsung, as well as to HTC and Motorola before it, is illustrative. The evolution of the smartphone industry is a microcosm of what's happening to the broader economic landscape. In this new world, platforms sit at the top of the economy. They have the most market power, the highest profits, and the most sustainable competitive advantage. As Samsung showed, it's still possible to build a valuable linear business, but its competitive advantage often evaporates quickly as products get commoditized and competitors copy features—leaving the originator continually scrambling to replace those strengths. Features are easy to emulate; networks aren't. Products get commoditized; platforms don't.

Samsung, long a linear business, realized its predicament several years ago and has been trying to transition to being a platform company. For the last couple of years, the consumer electronics manufacturer made a concerted effort to build support for its own development platform, Tizen, especially within newer device categories, such as wearable electronics and smart TVs. However, it hasn't had much success. Both Android and iOS already are moving into these categories, and Google and Apple aren't likely to lose their lead with developers to a hardware company. Samsung's decline is likely to continue. As *Market Makers* host Erik Schatzker said in a TV discussion with Alex on Samsung's struggles, "It's become clear that it's the platform companies where all the intelligence and power resides."[21]

If you're building a business today, platform businesses offer the biggest and most sustainable economic opportunity. However, you can't simply copy the business model of successful platforms like Facebook,

Uber, or Airbnb and expect it to work. The time to build a broad, desktop-based social network was in the early 2000s, when broadband access was becoming more widespread and the desktop Internet was growing. Similarly, the time to build a transportation marketplace like Uber was several years ago, when smartphones were just starting to spread to mainstream consumers and many of today's unicorn companies were just taking off. Trying to emulate the success of these businesses today without understanding the competitive landscape is a recipe for failure. In the rest of this chapter, we look at how you can spot potential platform opportunities, and where we expect platforms to have the biggest impact next.

I FOUGHT THE LAW, AND THE LAW WON

Before we jump in to the upside of potential platform opportunities, we want to cover the biggest risk associated with new platform business models: Dealing with existing laws and regulations. Because linear businesses dominated the economy for most of the twentieth century, most laws are still oriented around how these companies operate. The regulatory regime in most industries hasn't yet adapted to account for platforms. As a result, when a dominant platform business emerges for the first time in an industry, that platform often operates in a legal gray area. As Simon Rothman, a venture capitalist at Greylock Partners, has put it, "If your idea isn't big enough to warrant regulatory scrutiny, it might not be big enough."[22] (Rothman was also a founder and vice president at eBay Motors, where he helped build eBay's automotive marketplace.) Most incumbents will press the existing regulatory regime to their advantage to try to shut down the platform or limit its growth. The most prominent examples today are Airbnb and Uber, both of which have faced major legal obstacles. We briefly covered Airbnb's struggles with customer safety in chapter 6, and we looked at Uber's regulatory hurdles in Washington, D.C., and New York in chapter 4. Both companies also have other pending legal challenges—Airbnb with hospitality regulations and tax collection and Uber with regulations around the status of its "1099" contract workers—which we will get to in a minute. But these two platforms aren't alone. Almost every major platform company has faced major legal obstacles as it grew into a monopoly and challenged industry incumbents.

This trend goes all the way back to eBay in the dot-com era. In the late 1990s and early 2000s, eBay faced a spate of lawsuits from consumers who purchased fraudulent goods on its marketplace. The consumers sued eBay, alleging the company was responsible. eBay repeatedly argued that it merely operated as a marketplace for sales and could not be held liable for fraudulent transactions. Most cases were decided in eBay's favor.[23] More recently, after it went public in 2015, Alibaba began to face similar legal challenges over counterfeit goods sold through its Taobao marketplace. The U.S. government even stepped in to warn Alibaba that it must improve its process for removing fakes from its marketplaces.[24]

PayPal faced its own battle over its legal status in the early 2000s. PayPal didn't want its business to be classified as a commercial bank since the company didn't make loans or pay interest on account balances, as a commercial bank does. The issue came to a head just after PayPal filed for an initial public offering in January 2002, when regulators in California, Idaho, Louisiana, and New York all threatened to classify the company as a commercial bank. Louisiana even threatened to ban PayPal from the state. These moves were supported by banking industry lobbying groups such as the American Bankers Association.[25] However, the Federal Deposit Insurance Commission (FDIC) sent out a letter a few months later, advising that PayPal wouldn't be subject to federal banking laws.[26] Shortly thereafter, state regulators backed off.

Additionally, YouTube faced multiple lawsuits over its users' use of copyrighted content. The platform's growing legal risk was one of the motivating factors behind YouTube's decision to sell to Google in 2006. Mark Cuban, the renowned investor and star of hit TV show *Shark Tank,* even wrote a blog post at the time of the acquisition claiming that "Google would be crazy to buy YouTube" because of the risk of copyright lawsuits. "YouTube would get sued by the thousands of rights holders who will seek the maximum amount per download from YouTube for their content," Cuban wrote.[27] In a sense, Cuban was right. In March 2007, Viacom filed a copyright infringement suit against YouTube, seeking $1 billion in damages.[28] However, Google was able to use the safe harbor provision in the Digital Millennium Copyright Act (passed in 1998) to avoid liability.

The trend of new platforms facing legal challenges has only continued. Only a few years after the YouTube acquisition, peer-to-peer lending platform Lending Club faced its own legal obstacles. Founded in 2006, the company pioneered a different approach to making loans that met with regulatory resistance. Lending Club divided up consumer loans into small pieces so that individual lenders could take smaller chunks of many loans. This strategy enabled individual lenders to spread their risk across many smaller investments. However, the SEC decided that these loans weren't the same as any prior securities that it had approved. The SEC and Lending Club had to work together to define a new type of security, and the company had to register with the SEC. In 2008, Lending Club was shuttered for six months while it awaited SEC approval.[29] The company was eventually reopened after getting the okay from the SEC, but other peer-to-peer lending platforms, such as Prosper and Zopa (which briefly entered the U.S. market before withdrawing), have faced similar challenges from the regulatory agency.

As you can see, these legal and regulatory hurdles are very common for platform companies. Platform business models bring lots of advantages compared to linear businesses, but they also bring the potential downside of serious legal risk. Sometimes these legal troubles can nearly put the company out of business, as they almost did with Lending Club and Prosper. These issues should help put the controversy surrounding companies such as Airbnb and Uber in perspective. Challenging the legal status quo is well-established territory for platform companies.

In Airbnb's case, major companies in the hotel industry are unhappy that their platform competitor gets to skirt local hotel regulations and safety standards. They have pushed local regulators to crack down on Airbnb hosts, most notably in New York City. According to one report, as many as three quarters of Airbnb rentals in New York City, one of Airbnb's largest markets, are illegal.[30] Yet this hasn't stopped the company from continuing to grow, and it hasn't stopped many hosts in New York from continuing to do business. Another major legal issue concerns whether Airbnb is responsible for the safety of guests. The company has made big strides on customer safety, as we covered in chapter 6. But it still doesn't do much to ensure its hosts comply with local hospitality safety standards and regulations. The company attracted another wave of negative attention in November 2015, when a story came out about a guest who died while staying in an Airbnb.[31] The company is facing a number of similar lawsuits related to consumers' bad Airbnb experiences. As of the beginning of 2016, Airbnb's place within the existing regulatory regime for the hotel industry is anything but settled.

For Uber, the biggest legal issue is the classification status of its drivers. Uber drivers, which the company calls its "driver partners," are currently so-called 1099 contract employees, named for Form 1099 that these employees have to file with the IRS. This classification status means that Uber doesn't have to pay payroll taxes for these contractors and that it doesn't have to provide long-term benefits such as health insurance and workers' compensation. It also limits Uber's legal liability for the actions of its drivers. Most other services marketplaces, including Handy, Lyft, Instacart, and Postmates, classify all or some of their workers as 1099 contractors rather than W-2 workers or contractors. But every one of these companies is currently facing lawsuits alleging that they are misclassifying their workers. The potential legal fallout for each of these platforms is enormous. They could face hundreds of millions of dollars in damages and taxes owed if they lose these cases and have to reclassify their workers as W-2 employees. Because of the Affordable Care Act, most of these companies would then likely be responsible for providing health care for many of their workers. While it's possible to still operate a platform with W-2 contractors, the overhead involved in dealing with W-2 workers, as well as the additional tax obligations the companies would incur as a result, would severely limit the advantages of the model for services marketplaces. These platforms would lose a lot of flexibility and cost advantages, which are often passed on to consumers in the form of better prices. These pending legal challenges could have a big impact on which of these companies is able to survive long term.

As all these examples show, the upside of platform business models often comes with serious regulatory risk. Many platform businesses are effectively a call option on regulation: if the business can survive its regulatory and legal challenges and capture its market, it has enormous economic upside, both for investors as well as its users. However, if the platform can't overcome the legal status quo, it can very quickly be driven out of business. For example, if the leading services marketplaces lose their worker classification lawsuits, the less favorable unit economics of using W-2 workers may drive many of these marketplaces out of business in the United States. Even dominant platform companies, such as Airbnb and Uber, could lose value very quickly if they don't win their legal fights.

Finally, a quick word on the challenges of workers in the 1099 economy or the gig economy, as it's variously been called. The broader implications of this new model of flexible work are largely beyond the scope of this book. Many good books have and will be written on this topic alone. Further, these specific challenges around worker classification are primarily relevant only to one platform type—services marketplaces—which are only a part of the broader growth of platform businesses that we've described in this book. However, in order for these marketplaces to be both economically and socially viable long term, we may need to make some changes to the social safety net, particularly in the United States, that account for the changing nature of work.

Proposals that have gained traction include making the safety net portable (not tied to a particular job) and providing a basic income guarantee. These ideas seem like good starting points for the discussion. Workers' concerns about where they fit into the platform economy are certainly valid. But any changes should also take into account the unique needs of platform businesses and not try to fit a round (platform) peg into a square (linear) hole. At present, it's clear that many current policies and regulations are not a good fit for the platform economy. For the sake of both workers and platform businesses, we hope to see this change as platforms grow in economic and social influence.

ONE PLATFORM TO RULE THEM ALL?

To understand the future of the platform economy, we look once again to China. Alibaba has gotten most of the headlines in the wake of its record-setting IPO in September 2014. But when it comes to the bottom line, it's still outperformed by rival platform company Tencent. In 2014, Alibaba earned $3.73 billion in profit on $12.29 billion revenue, coming in behind Tencent's $3.90 billion in earnings from $12.90 billion in revenue. That also puts Tencent ahead of Facebook, the Western company it's most frequently compared to. Facebook brought in $2.94 billion in 2014 on $12.47 billion revenue.

What's most interesting is how Tencent makes its money. Like Alibaba with its Taobao and Tmall marketplaces, Tencent owns two major platforms: QQ and WeChat. QQ, which started as a clone of Western-based chat platform ICQ, is a desktop-based instant messaging platform. If you're not sure what that means, think AOL Instant Messenger, but with way more features. QQ had 815 million monthly active users in 2014. However, rather than just adapting QQ to mobile, Tencent decided to build a new platform from scratch. In January 2011, it released WeChat, known in Chinese as Weixin (微信), which translates literally as "micro message." By the middle of 2015, WeChat was the third most popular mobile messaging platform in the world; its 650 million monthly active users placed it behind only Facebook's WhatsApp and Messenger platforms.[32]

However, WeChat is the only one of these three messaging platforms that makes significant amounts of money. One industry estimate suggests that WeChat makes seven times more per user than WhatsApp, which makes only about $1 dollar per user through a yearly access fee.[33] And, unlike Facebook, Tencent generates only a small amount of revenue through advertising. More than 80 percent of the Chinese company's revenue comes from selling virtual goods, such as digital stickers, icons, emoticons, and avatars. The company also makes a lot of money by using its platforms to sell digital goods in its freemium games. (Imagine *Zynga* and *Candy Crush,* but in China; Tencent even has its popular own *FarmVille* clone, known as *QQ Farm*). In fact, in terms of revenue, Tencent is the largest gaming company in the world, with about 8 percent of the $70-billion-a-year global gaming market.[34]

Although games and virtual goods remain the biggest revenue generators for Tencent, that's not all you can do with WeChat. The platform has expanded over the last few years to include a growing number of marketplaces and services. In addition to playing games, users can pay bills, check their bank statements, send money to friends, donate to charity, read the news, find local shopping deals, buy movie tickets, and even book local services, such as doctors' appointments or taxis—all within the WeChat app. Another moneymaker for WeChat is "red envelope" gifting, a common practice among family and friends in China around the Chinese New Year and at special events such as weddings, where people give money in red envelopes. WeChat created the ability to gift digital cash-filled "red envelopes," which are deposited into the recipient's mobile banking account. On Chinese New Year's Eve (February 18) in 2015, an estimated 1 billion virtual red envelopes were sent using WeChat.[35]

WeChat—messaging platform

WeChat also added a development platform through what it calls "official accounts." These accounts, of which there are an estimated 10 million, function as mini-webpages, or "lightweight apps," within the WeChat app. Users connect with them the same way you would follow a business or a celebrity on Twitter. The uses for official accounts are broad, with celebrities, personal blogs, banks, hospitals, drugstores, media outlets, Internet startups, and more all on the platform.[36] Once they're approved by WeChat, these accounts are able to process payments, answer direct messages and voice messages, and access the location of users that have added them. WeChat even has search and an app store to help users sort through all of these apps. Think of these official accounts as mini-websites within WeChat or Facebook Pages on steroids.

WeChat, then, has become a kind of über-platform, a "platform to rule all platforms," as several outlets have described it. It supports a wide ecosystem of platforms and services outside of just messaging. WeChat's success in China has led many industry analysts to predict that this model eventually will take over in the West as well. So far, this hasn't been the case, but that could all be about to change.

In 2015, Facebook announced at its annual F8 conference that it plans to make Facebook Messenger into a development platform that will connect businesses and apps with consumers, much the way WeChat already does in China. One of the first companies to announce an official integration with Messenger was pro.com, one of the leading home-services marketplaces in the United States. Given Messenger's huge user base, other businesses will surely follow. However, given their bad experience with Facebook's last attempt at a development platform (remember what happened to Zynga), many developers are still wary.

Additionally, replicating WeChat's model in the United States will be a big challenge. In China, the app store market is very fragmented, with about a dozen such stores having market share of 5 percent or more. Other than Apple's iOS App Store, most of these app stores are operated by Android phone manufacturers in China. Because Google has very little presence there, Chinese phone manufacturers don't use Google's Android. This means they don't have access to Google Play Services, the set of apps and development services that Google owns and controls, and they don't use the Google Play store. Instead, almost all these manufacturers use open-source Android (what's known as AOSP, or Android Open Source Project). As a result, there are numerous Android app stores, each owned by a different company. The largest of these is Tencent's Myapp, which tops out at a market share of about 25 percent.[37] Other popular app stores include 360 Mobile Assistant, owned by Qihoo 360, Baidu Mobile Assistant, owned by search platform Baidu, and the MIUI App Store, owned by China's top Android phone maker, Xiaomi. In this fragmented environment, WeChat has stepped in to become a primary aggregator for other apps and businesses, both linear and platform alike. However, the situation in the United States is very different; Google's Play Store and Apple's App Store effectively enjoy a duopoly as the primary app development platforms. Facebook would love to leapfrog the operating system, the same way WeChat has, and become the primary platform where people interact with businesses and each other. (The abortive Facebook Home was the company's first attempt at accomplishing this goal, but Messenger seems much more likely to succeed.) However, given that Apple and Google already serve this role in the United States, Facebook will have a much harder time replicating WeChat's dominance domestically.

WeChat's success has also led some experts and entrepreneurs to suggest that the platform-of-platforms phenomenon will emerge in other sectors. Specifically, it is believed that the so-called on-demand economy, which includes companies such as Uber, GrubHub, Handy, and delivery platform Postmates, eventually will be aggregated within one "superplatform" that integrates all these platforms via their APIs.

However, in reality, this is unlikely to happen because rival platforms rarely play nice. When Twitter tried to build on Facebook's social graph by allowing users to import Facebook friends, Facebook revoked Twitter's access to that API. Similarly, in China, Alibaba and Tencent are locked in an ongoing platform war, with each shutting the other out of its ecosystem. This phenomenon isn't new. Back when eBay was first building its marketplace, several competitors tried to aggregate listings from eBay and other auction sites, but eBay cut off their access, and these aggregators quickly withered away.

Instead, it's most likely that separate platform ecosystems will develop. These ecosystems are the platform equivalent of old-school conglomerates. However, rather than buying up a number of companies in related industries, these ecosystems focus on creating businesses that cover multiple platform types. Google, for example, has Google Search (which encompasses both content and shopping, even if it doesn't do the latter particularly well), Android and the Google Play Store, Android Pay (as well as Google Wallet), Waze, Hangouts, and more. Its one glaring hole has been a social networking platform, which explains its repeat failed attempts at building one (e.g., Orkut, Google Wave, and Google+). Google has also experimented with services marketplaces, including Google Express, and is toying with the idea of an eventual Uber competitor that uses self-driving cars.

Similarly, Apple has iTunes, iOS and the App Store, Apple Pay, and iMessage, among others. And although Facebook started as a social networking platform, it has expanded to include content platforms (Instagram and Facebook Pages), messaging platforms (Messenger and WhatsApp), and development platforms, as well as a number of experiments with product and services marketplaces. Finally, Amazon has the Amazon Marketplace, Amazon Payments, Amazon Web Services, Fire TV, and the Kindle, which includes both a content platform (for books and digital content) and an Android-based development platform (for apps). The e-commerce company is also looking at expanding into services marketplaces with its Home Services marketplace.

In China, the outcome has been similar, with the dominant platform ecosystems controlled by Baidu, Alibaba, and Tencent, collectively referred to in China as BAT. Like their U.S. counterparts, each of these company's ecosystems includes many overlapping and competing platforms. In payments, for example, there's Alipay, Tenpay, and Baidu Wallet. And after Alibaba's acquisition of video platform Youku Tudou, each has its own streaming video platform as well. Meanwhile, Alibaba has created a WeChat competitor, Laiwang, while Tencent has invested heavily in JD.com, Alibaba's largest competitor in ecommerce. Similarly, each company has its own Android app store and its own investments in services marketplaces in China's rapidly growing on-demand economy. The result, as in the United States, is a collection of large but mostly incompatible platform ecosystems, each owned and orchestrated by a dominant platform holding company.[38]

Although each platform has an area where it effectively has a monopoly—Alibaba in ecommerce, Tencent in messaging and gaming, Baidu in search—the presence of these rival ecosystems means that each platform faces a constant competitive threat. But competition in a world dominated by platform monopolies looks very different from competition in the past. In the twentieth century, competition happened primarily between rival companies within one industry. Today, it happens *across* industries. The fiercest competition will be between incompatible, rival platform ecosystems and the networks of businesses they support. Platforms that fail to grow into their own larger ecosystems will slowly fade away, either by running into financial trouble (Foursquare, Groupon, Yelp), or becoming acquisition fodder for larger platform companies (OpenTable, Waze, Tumblr).

The upshot is that no one is safe for long. A platform that has a monopoly position within its industry is vulnerable to competitors that can tap into or steal away its network, even if these competitors operate in seemingly unrelated industries today. Google's entry from search into mobile operating systems with Android is just one example, but, as more platform ecosystems mature, there will be many more.

HOW TO SPOT PLATFORM OPPORTUNITIES

Our goal in chapters 1–4 was to convey the importance of platform companies in our economy, both today and in the future. In effect, we wanted to share with you the insight that drove us to transform Applico from a simple app developer into a Platform Innovation company, involved in all aspects of building and growing platform businesses. By now we hope we've accomplished that task.

We also wanted to share how platforms work and, just as important, how they differ from old ways of doing business. This was the focus of chapters 5–8. The next step is to start applying these insights to the world around you. To help you begin, we want to leave you with advice on how to spot potential platform opportunities. Whether you work at a large corporation, are working at or thinking of creating a startup, or just want to understand the evolution of the growing platform economy, these tips will help you see which industries platform business models are primed to disrupt next. As we covered in chapter 2, technological change is a big part of why platforms are so successful today. However, that doesn't mean that the next wave of technological change will lead to a shift away from platform business models. In fact, we would suggest the opposite. As we explain in more detail soon, the next generation of connected technologies will enable the creation of even *more* platforms, not fewer. Platforms are here to stay. Take advantage of what you've learned in this book, as well as the next tips, to use this knowledge to your benefit.

1. Look for Technology that Reduces Transaction Costs and Removes Gatekeepers

Look for industries where technology can reduce high transaction costs or remove high-cost gatekeepers. In many cases, you're looking for transactions that can be automated and run by algorithms. The more you can use technology to reduce transaction costs, the more opportunity you'll have to add value to both sides. The ultimate goal is to remove entire steps from the transaction. Remember, transaction costs aren't always about money. They also include time and effort, among other things. So if you can remove the need to (for example) make a phone call in favor of tapping a button on a smartphone, you're moving in the right direction. However, you're not just looking to make a product or service more convenient or easier to use; you're looking to make it cheaper too. The addressable market for a service that's more convenient at a higher price point is much smaller than the market for one that's both cheaper *and* more convenient.

As we covered in chapter 3, the healthcare industry is a great example. ZocDoc, a platform for booking doctor's appointments, was one of the earliest platform success stories in the industry. For doctors, ZocDoc reduces the need for back-office staff to handle patient scheduling. The platform makes it easy for doctors to manage their availability and offer open time slots to patients. Similarly, patients no longer need to call the doctor's office to make an appointment. They can make an appointment at any time with the push of a button. The platform also automates much of the paperwork involved (such as insurance information and medical history), so patients don't need to get to the office early to grab a clipboard and fill out a stack of forms.

Similarly, Uber removed the need for dispatchers to coordinate drivers and passengers. Uber's matching algorithm accomplishes this task far more efficiently. In some cases, technology will have a much bigger impact on one side of your network. For example, e-commerce in China existed before Alibaba. But its Taobao marketplace allowed merchants to set up a shop without having to build their own website or worry about attracting customers. Alibaba made both of these things easier and cheaper for its producers. In return, consumers got access to a wider variety of products, but the biggest reductions in transaction costs came on the producer side.

2. Look for Implicit or Underserved Networks

Now that you know the potential of networks, look for them everywhere you go. As LinkedIn CEO Reid Hoffman said, once you start to truly see networks, the way you operate changes.[39] However, building a network is hard work. So we suggest you cheat. Don't try to build a network out of nothing. Build on top of existing networks and behaviors, just as Facebook did in building a college-based social networking platform on top of its users' real-world relationships. Mark Zuckerberg built Facebook because he thought Harvard was too slow in making its (analog) student facebook available online. He capitalized on this huge but underserved network of students who wanted an easier way to connect with each other.

Another great example here is GrubHub. The food-delivery platform hit the jackpot by connecting hungry diners who don't want to get off the couch with restaurants that want more business. Consumers were already ordering out from restaurants, but GrubHub removed a lot of the friction from the transaction. No more hoarding stacks of menus. No more having to

GrubHub—services marketplace platform

worry if the person on the other end of the phone got your order right. No more wondering when you could expect your food to arrive. Grub-Hub took this implicit network of restaurants and diners and made it explicit through its platform. More recently, other platforms have continued this trend by taking a different angle and focusing just on delivery. Restaurants that don't have the staff to support delivery can partner with Postmates, for example, to let customers order remotely.

Another way to spot implicit networks is to look for untapped sources of supply. If you can take this unused supply and bring it into a formal community or marketplace, you can generate a lot of previously unrealized economic and social value. The more untapped supply you can bring into the market, the more value you can bring to your users by opening it up. Airbnb did this by enabling homeowners to rent out their unused home or apartment, or even just their couch. Because Airbnb built the market and grew the network, all of that unused space is now available, to the delight of travelers around the globe. Apple's iOS platform also brought untapped supply into its marketplace, though in a slightly different manner. Apple saw the potential of a network connecting app developers and consumers. But there was one key difference: This source of supply didn't exist yet.

Before iOS and the App Store, mobile apps didn't exist on a large scale. There was tremendous pent-up demand on the developer side, but Apple first had to recognize the value that third-party apps could bring to the table. After Apple made it easy for developers to create apps, its platform quickly vaulted ahead of the competition. Just as Apple did, you should look for potential complementary products that can add value to your core business, even if these complements aren't available yet.

3. Look for Large, Fragmented Sources of Supply

Finally, look for large, fragmented sources of supply. You want your potential supply to be large, because small industries often don't have enough scale to justify building out a network. And you want it to be fragmented, because the supply in consolidated industries won't see a need for you.

At the tail end of the dot-com bubble, business-to-business (B2B) marketplaces were all the rage. More than 1,500 B2B exchanges were established between 1995 and 2001.[40] Industry experts predicted astronomical success for these companies. In 2000, Gartner Group predicted that, by 2004, the total transaction volume handled by these marketplaces would reach \$7.3 trillion. Not to be left out, Goldman Sachs predicted that this number would be \$4.5 trillion by 2005.[41] With the music playing, the venture capitalists got up to dance, pumping hundreds of millions of dollars into various marketplaces, such as Chemdex (biotech), Ariba (corporate procurement), Covisint (automotive), Elemica (chemical), and Agentrics (retail). Yet by 2001, almost all of these marketplaces had collapsed. The lucky ones had survived by becoming linear software-based solutions for large companies. The predicted trillions of dollars in economic activity never materialized, and hundreds of millions in investment was wiped out almost overnight.

What happened? The suppliers never showed up. There was demand on the consumer side, but sellers in industries that were largely consolidated into a few dominant suppliers saw these marketplaces as superfluous. They were worried about comparison shopping driving down prices, and they saw no need to aggregate customers when they already had well-established channels to sell to many of them. Dell Marketplace, which opened in late 2000, was a typical example. Customers could buy Dell computers, servers, and related hardware as well as office products from selected suppliers. Yet months later, in February 2001, the marketplace closed down. Dell chalked it up to a lack of consumer interest, but that wasn't the real problem. Only three suppliers signed up to sell products to consumers in the four months that the marketplace was in operation.[42] Without suppliers, none of these businesses was able to build a liquid marketplace. They were stores without inventory.

Buyers showed up but quickly left when they found out there was little or nothing to buy.

The failure of these B2B marketplaces is a sharp contrast to the one major success story in B2B ecommerce from the dot-com era: Alibaba. Alibaba took a very different approach from these other marketplaces. Rather than going after large, consolidated industries, it went after small businesses. This strategy was the brainchild of Alibaba's founder and CEO, Jack Ma. Ma's vision was that "the revolutionary significance of the Internet is that it will enable small enterprises to operate independently." He wanted to be a savior to China's countless small and medium-sized enterprises by bringing them into the Internet era. "Asia is the largest supplier base in the world for exports," Ma said. "Among the great density of small companies here, most do not have channels to the large trading companies. Most have no way to reach a market. Simply by going through our Alibaba network, they can get access to all of America and Europe." He compared these businesses to "grains of sand on a beach. The Internet can glue them together. It can make them into an invincible force that is able to up against the big stones."[43] As it turned out, Ma was right. By unifying China's huge, fragmented small-business market, he was able to build a digital empire and grow the country's e-commerce sector. Similarly, a key part of Uber's success was that it went after an industry that had a large fragmented supply. By unifying all of this supply into one network, Uber made it much easier for consumers to get a ride and made it much simpler for drivers to find paying passengers. Passengers get to their destination faster, and drivers get more business.

However, one of the most interesting examples is ClassPass. Founded by current CEO Payal Kadakia, ClassPass originally started as a SaaS solution for local fitness venues, but early sales disappointed. The idea evolved into what ClassPass is today: a platform that allows users to pay a flat monthly subscription fee for access to fitness classes at any gym in the Class-Pass network. As the company's website puts it: "Thousands of classes. One Pass." ClassPass aggregated the many fragmented local fitness

ClassPass—services marketplace platform

options available to consumers and provided them with one platform to get access to all of them. A big part of how ClassPass built this network was by focusing on monetizing these gyms' spare inventory. Many fitness classes run at well below capacity. ClassPass allowed gyms to offers up this spare inventory to consumers through its platform. (Notice that the platform taps into multiple platform opportunities—it's also activating an underserved network by opening up previously untapped supply. This is a good sign.) Gyms get new business and consumers get access to lots of different classes for a much lower price than if they bought classes individually.

WHERE TO LOOK NEXT

Remember to look for these three factors when you're trying to spot platform opportunities: technology that reduces transaction costs and removes gatekeepers; implicit or underserved networks; and large, fragmented sources of supply. One of these factors can be enough to enable the growth of a successful platform business, but the more boxes you can tick off, the better. But remember that although the opportunity to build valuable platform businesses is real, timing matters. So where should you be looking to next? Well, there are a few industries where the three factors are starting to converge

The first industry is health care, which we've touched on at several points in this book. Here you have platforms connecting doctors and patients in new ways, like Doctor on Demand, Teladoc, and Zoc-Doc. However, these platforms are just going after the low-hanging fruit. There's still a tremendous amount of waste and inefficiency in the healthcare sector, especially in the United States. And wherever there's waste and inefficiency, there's a platform opportunity. For instance, although they're relatively popular with casual consumers, wearable health devices are just starting to make their way into formal health care. These devices offer tremendous potential for improving patient wellness. But in order for them to be useful, a platform will need to build a unified network of doctors and patients. Despite the recent entrance of Silicon Valley heavyweights Apple and Google, this market is still wide open.

Additionally, many more platforms focused on the enterprise healthcare market are likely to emerge as connected technology infuses the industry further. One example in this market is Figure 1, which is essentially Instagram but for doctors. It connects doctors with others who may have more expertise about a particular issue. Doctors get access to a large expert network; as a result, patients get better care. Regulations could significantly slow changes in health care, but the sector is clearly ripe for change. Fortunately, at least for now, user-generated content is not governed by HIPAA. As a result, we've seen greater innovation with platforms leveraging new data sources such as Apple Health and the aforementioned Figure 1. However, the FDA may be trying to expand HIPAA to also cover user-generated health data, which would severely limit the utility of many platforms in the sector. Still, as technology (and regulations) changes, there will be many more opportunities for platform business models to help improve patient outcomes.

The next sector where big changes are happening is the Internet of Things. If you're not familiar with it, the Internet of Things is an envisioned future where machines communicate directly with other machines rather than people. The idea is that Internet-enabled devices, such as cars, buildings, or electronics (really, any device you can imbed with a sensor), will exchange data directly with other devices. Any object could be connected and communicate with other devices in an intelligent manner. The hope is that devices will become context-aware and be able to respond or adjust dynamically to different users or situations. This idea has been hyped but not really solved. Security and privacy remain big issues. For example, there's a popular Twitter account whose name is "Internet of Shit." Its tagline is: "Have all of your best appliances ruined by putting the Internet in them!" One tweet jokes: "Wait endlessly while your toilet does software updates!" However, assuming these issues get ironed out (an admittedly large assumption), the industry has big potential. And wherever the Internet of Things is successful, you'll find platforms at the center of it. In order for all these devices to communicate, they need to be able to talk with one another and exchange information. This task is more complicated than it sounds, as there are myriad protocols, standards, and technologies that these devices use that are incompatible with each other. In other words, there are lots of devices that are all speaking different languages. A development platform is needed that can coordinate all of these fragmented resources and set the rules around machine-to-machine interaction. The challenge is getting most users to agree on one platform, as there are many platform competitors out there currently. (This situation is a classic example of excess fragmentation leading to lost value.)

The growth of the Internet of Things will have a big impact that spreads beyond just the platforms themselves. Insurance companies are starting to offer better rates based around users' ability to drive safely or their ability to monitor users' homes. Farther down the line, driverless cars will be a big part of the Internet of Things. And they will likely be connected by one or two dominant development platforms. Apple and Google have both made big moves in this space over the last year, so they are currently leading contenders. Uber is another. Travis Kalanick, the company's founder and CEO, has already said on the record that Uber intends to build on driverless car technology. To that end, in February 2015, Uber effectively bought out the entire robotics department at Carnegie Mellon University. (Yes, really.) The company likely will start by introducing driverless cars into its fleet to help prove out the market and construct a regulatory regime around the new technology. However, once Uber accomplishes this, it's unlikely that the company will simply own and operate its own armada of vehicles. It's not clear why a logistics and transportation platform would want to radically alter its business model in favor of owning a fleet of rapidly depreciating physical assets that also come with the downside of serious liability concerns.

The potential in the industrial sector of the economy to improve efficiency is enormous. Industry reports on the Internet of Things typically make astronomical predictions. For example, Gartner predicts that we'll have 25 billion connected "things" in use by 2020, not including PCs, laptops, and smartphones, which it predicts will make up an additional 7 billion devices. This total will be up more than 500 percent from an estimated 4.9 billion things at the end of 2015. Gartner also suggests that the Internet of Things will generate an additional $1.9 trillion in economic value by 2020, while market research and consulting firm

International Data Corporation places this number at a more sanguine $8.9 trillion.[44]

However, most of this value won't be created or captured by the makers of the "things" themselves. The real value will be in the platform that ties all of these things together. Interestingly, General Electric, the most linear of companies, is leading the way here by building out its own network to connect and monitor all of its hardware devices in the field. Given that this part of the economy typically is dominated by a handful of large companies in each industry, it may be a while before a winning development platform emerges. No company will want to use a competitor's platform for fear of getting "Samsunged" in the future as its products become commoditized and the platform grows in value.

Finally, we turn to finance. Finance is an industry that most people associate with large banks or money management firms. However, a host of platform startups have opened the industry to new kinds of consumers who haven't had access to sophisticated investment products before. In the startup realm are platforms such as AngelList, which enable people to invest in startups on a small scale. Many of these investors now have access to deals they never would have gotten in the past. Peer-to-peer lending is also big. Lending Club was the early success story in this area, but other more industry-specific competitors have emerged over the last couple of years. One example is SoFi (also called Social Finance), which focuses on peer-to-peer lending for student loans, mortgages, and personal loans. However, these platforms are just scratching the surface. The biggest potential disruption of the finance industry comes from the already-legendary Bitcoin.

What is Bitcoin? If you want to get into an argument with your tech-savvy friends, just start talking to them about this topic. The simple answer is that it's a new kind of digital money. But the reality is a lot more complicated than that. Bitcoin is controlled by a programming protocol that determines how new bitcoins enter circulation and how new transactions get verified. Bitcoin is usually considered a currency, but some economists think it looks more like a commodity—a sort of digital gold. Like a commodity, it's subject to wide swings in price based on speculators investing in the bitcoin market. And like gold, bitcoins are scarce. The Bitcoin protocol limits the number of new bitcoins that come into circulation each year. This number will automatically halve over time until a total of 21 million bitcoins are in existence. Then the issuance of new bitcoins will stop completely.

Additionally, unlike almost all currencies currently in existence, Bitcoin isn't controlled by any government. It's also completely anonymous. (Well, more accurately, it's pseudonymous—senders have to have an address to send bitcoins to.) As a result, many, particularly those who possess a more libertarian bent, view Bitcoin as the technological equivalent of the second coming. They see it as an "unregulated" currency that will help wrest economic control away from governments. It's unclear whether this actually will occur. We would suggest that such an outcome is unlikely. However, that doesn't mean Bitcoin doesn't have revolutionary potential.

Bitcoin the currency is based on a technology called the blockchain, although the two terms are often used synonymously. The blockchain is a novel way of transferring a digital message from one party to another, where both parties can count on the integrity of the message—even if they don't trust, or know, each other. Essentially, the blockchain is a ledger of transactions that keeps a record all previous transactions in one place. Each "block" in the blockchain requires a record of recent transactions as well as a string of letters and numbers (called a hash), which is produced using cryptographic algorithms.

People who generate these blocks are called miners. Miners are people (or, usually, people who own servers) that run the Bitcoin software and randomly generate hashes. Each miner is competing to produce a hash with a value below a certain target difficulty to complete a new block in the blockchain. The first miner to accomplish this task receives a reward, which is currently twenty-five bitcoins. Once the protocol stops issuing new bitcoins, miners likely will be supported by small transaction fees. This reward incentivizes people all over the world to spend time and money (the energy cost of running servers that mine for bitcoins is not insignificant) verifying transactions that they otherwise have no interest in.

Many Bitcoin enthusiasts view the blockchain as the solution to pretty much everything. They also see it as the undoing of today's dominant platform companies, because the blockchain makes its network's data open and portable to any other network. However, we think this crowd tends to overstate their case. The blockchain solves a very particular problem: It allows you to trust that the message you're sending will reach the intended recipient uncompromised. But it doesn't tell you whether you should trust that person in the first place. Or, if you're dealing with a physical product or service, whether that person will deliver what you're paying for. Or what to do if you need to resolve a dispute between the transacting parties. The blockchain solves only one small component of trust. As we've shown throughout this book, platforms play a very active role in constructing their marketplaces and communities, and in most cases the blockchain addresses only a very small part of what these platforms do.

Rather than ending the dominance of platforms, we would suggest that the growth of blockchain technologies will be accompanied by the emergence of many new platform companies. Like HTTP and the Web before it, the blockchain will create a decentralized infrastructure that provides the opportunity for new markets and communities to emerge. But most of these new opportunities won't take shape without a platform company orchestrating them and capitalizing on their potential. (Think about where the Web would be without a search platform like Google helping you make sense of it.) Some of these new companies may displace existing platform monopolies, but platforms will remain the dominant business model.

However, Bitcoin's impact still may be significant, especially within the world of finance. The blockchain cures the biggest issues that have traditionally haunted digital money: counterfeiting, double spending, and reliance on a central authority to process transactions. The blockchain turns the entire network of Bitcoin miners into a source of truth. Miners compete with each other to be first, and then others verify the result. In order to produce counterfeit transactions, you'd need to fool the majority of the network. Because the blockchain operates based on consensus, you'd need to control greater than 50 percent of the processing power in the entire network in order to produce a successful counterfeit block. Given the large (and growing) number of bitcoin miners out there, this is currently a borderline impossible task. If one miner were to gain control of a significant portion of the network, the entire blockchain would be endangered. But thus far this hasn't been a real threat.

Currently, Bitcoin is by far the largest blockchain network. However, many others (often collectively referred to altcoins) make small alterations to the Bitcoin protocol to adapt it for other uses. But as the nature of the blockchain suggests, a larger blockchain network is a more useful and more secure one. As a result, at present, Bitcoin is effectively the only game in town. However, there are signs that this could change in the near future. For one, Bitcoin experienced its first major governance crisis at the beginning of 2016. While governance of the Bitcoin network is putatively decentralized, the handful of individuals who have access to and the ability to modify Bitcoin's source code have an outsized influence. At the beginning of 2016, a few of these individuals resisted change to the Bitcoin protocol and effectively prevented changes that could increase the transaction capacity of Bitcoin's network. While this governance crisis could be resolved in the future, the lack of a formal governance model for changing the Bitcoin protocol could hamper Bitcoin's growth. Additionally, at the end of 2015 the Linux Foundation announced that it will begin work on a project, backed by a consortium of major firms including J.P. Morgan, Wells Fargo, and the London Stock Exchange, to develop an open-source blockchain designed specifically for use by global banking and financial institutions. It will likely take some time for this effort to gain steam, but given its backing it could become a competitor to the Bitcoin network in the future.

For now, the good news is that Bitcoin is effectively an open development platform. Anyone can create applications that tap into the Bitcoin network. This is a stark contrast to almost all existing payment protocols, such as Automated Clearing House (ACH), which are tightly regulated and inaccessible to developers. Bitcoin also is much quicker and more secure than most existing alternatives. Now, most of these financial regulations exist for good reason—for example, to prevent fraud, money laundering, and other criminal activities. But the blockchain could be the wedge that cracks open the overly concentrated financial sector. Because Bitcoin allows developers to build on top of the blockchain protocol, it enables countless new uses of the underlying technology. Just as Apple's iOS platform created a world where "there's an app for that," we may soon be in a world where "there's a Bitcoin app for that."

Today, there's an enormous ecosystem of blockchain-based startups that are building new applications tapping into Bitcoin's blockchain as a way of verifying transactions. But these startups also put the blockchain to radically new uses. Companies are working on everything from Bitcoin-based marketplaces and social networks to entirely new ways to record and track digital copyright on the Internet. And startups aren't the only organizations to see Bitcoin's potential. Recently, banks and financial services companies have started to get into the game. In June 2015, Santander Bank issued a report that estimated that blockchain technologies could reduce banks' infrastructure costs by as much as $20 billion a year by 2022.[45] But Santander isn't alone. Companies that have recently made investments in bitcoin startups or initiatives include Goldman Sachs, American Express, BBVA, Capital One, MasterCard, Nasdaq, the New York Stock Exchange, Citibank, and IBM.[46] This is in addition to the tsunami of venture capital money that has started pouring into blockchain-based startups.

With so many new players getting into finance and new technologies threatening to change the infrastructure underlying the entire industry, the highly concentrated financial sector could be in for a bit of turbulence. The potential to reduce transaction costs and remove high-cost gatekeepers is enormous, as is the opportunity to unify the more fragmented world of financial services professionals in one network or to activate untapped demand for more sophisticated investment opportunities. The next decade could see a number of as-yet-unknown platforms disrupt the industry in new and surprising ways. This future isn't guaranteed—both Bitcoin and most financial tech startups still face significant regulatory risk. And big banks have little incentive to play nice and no reason to not press the existing regulatory regime to their advantage. But for the first time in a long time, the opportunity for real change in the financial sector is here.

All of these sectors—health care, the Internet of Things, and finance—are already changing due to the influence of platform companies. But there are many more major platforms to come in each industry. We wish you the best of luck in making the most of this platformed future. Using the knowledge you've gained from reading this book, you will be well prepared to deal with whatever change comes your way.

We urge you to seek out platform opportunities wherever they lie. The biggest long-term opportunities are likely those that are impossible to identify today. Just as Bitcoin and the blockchain have created the possibility of change in the financial sector, new technologies will bring new chances for innovation. And, as always, platforms will be at the heart of it all.

APPLICO

A WORD FROM THE AUTHORS

Thank you for reading *Modern Monopolies*. We hope you enjoyed reading the book and learned a lot in the process. There's a lot more to say about platforms, as the platform economy is always evolving. To get the latest platform innovation news, visit our blog and subscribe to our weekly newsletter at http://www.applicoinc.com/.

We also hope that you will apply the knowledge you learned from this book to your own business. As a thank you for purchasing this book, and to help you on your own entrepreneurial journey, we offer a few free tools and resources for platform businesses at http://www.applico inc.com/modernmonopolies. There you can find a high-res version of the platform ecosystem diagram and other graphics from the book, a downloadable version of the glossary of platform terms, an updated and platform-specific version of the classic business model canvas that we created specifically to help our platforms clients, and more. We encourage you to use these tools to shape and organize your thinking around your platform business. Our clients have found them very helpful, and we hope you will too.

GLOSSARY OF PLATFORM TERMS

Audience Building—One of the four functions of a platform. A platform has to build a liquid network by attracting a critical mass of consumers and producers.

Chatroulette Rule of the Internet—When left unchecked, a network of sufficient size will naturally deteriorate in its quality of users and usage (e.g., naked men sitting in front of a camera).

Chicken-and-egg Problem—A coordination problem that makes it difficult for platforms to acquire their first users. Initially, for most users the cost of joining a platform exceeds the value they can get out of it. In fact, the value of joining the network is often *negative* early on. If the network were sufficiently large, both consumers and producers would happily join. But most users on either side of the network aren't willing to join when the network is small. There are seven ways to solve the chicken-and egg problem:

1. Provide Security through a Large, Up-front Investment
2. Cooperate with Industry Incumbents
3. Act as a Producer
4. Tap into an Existing Network
5. Attract High-Value or "Celebrity" Users
6. Target a User Group to Fill Both Sides
7. Provide Single-User Utility

Commoditization Level—The complexity of the core transaction within a given platform type. Within each type, platforms exist on a spectrum of commoditized to non-commoditized. Commoditization level has a big impact on platform design.

Communication Platform—See "Platform Type."

Connected Revolution—The economic and social transformation that occurred at the beginning of the twenty-first century with the spread of connected technology.

Content Platform—See "Platform Type."

Core Transaction—The set of actions consumers and producers must complete in order to exchange value. The core transaction on every platform includes the same four basic steps: create, connect, consume, and compensate.

Critical Mass—The point where the value of the network exceeds the cost of joining for most users. Once a network reaches sufficient size, its network effects starts to pull in new users and growth takes off.

Economies of Scale—Cost savings gained by increasing the volume of production, typically within a linear business. The idea was popularized in the 1970s by Bruce Henderson, founder of the Boston Consulting Group. The opposite of this idea, *diseconomies* of scale, arises when costs rise rather than decline as a business increases production.

Exchange Platform—A platform that provides value primarily by optimizing exchanges directly between a consumer and a producer. The matching intention for exchange platforms always has a limited, discrete value, typically 1:1. Exchange platforms include services marketplaces, product marketplaces, payments platforms, investment platforms, social networking platforms, communication platforms, and social gaming platforms.

Four Functions—The four activities that a platform engages in to support the core transaction. These are: audience building, matchmaking, creating rules and standards, and providing tools and services.

Indirect Network Effect—A network effect between two separate user groups, for example, consumers and producers. Also called a "cross-side" network effect. This effect creates a positive feedback loop between both sides of the network.

Investment Platform—See "Platform Type."

Linear Business—A company that creates a product or service and sells it to a customer. Value flows linearly and in one direction through the company's supply chain.

Liquidity—A term from financial markets that expresses how likely a market is to facilitate a transaction. A platform is considered liquid when there's enough overlap in supply and demand that most transactions can clear quickly.

Maker Platform—A platform that create values by enabling producers to create complementary products and broadcast or distribute them to a large audience. The matching intention for maker platforms is theoretically infinite, or 1:Many. Maker platforms include content platforms and development platforms.

Marginal Cost—The cost to a business of producing the next unit of inventory. Platforms benefit from near-zero marginal cost at scale.

Matching Intention—The maximum number of units of an item that a producer can exchange at a given time.

Matchmaking—One of the four functions. A platform has to connect the right consumers with the right producers in order to facilitate exchanges and interactions.

Metcalfe's Law—The theory that the value of a network is proportional to the square of the number of connected users in a system (roughly, network value = n^2). As more users join a network, the number of possible unique connections within the network grows according to the function: $(n^2-n)/2$, where n represents the number of users. As the number of possible connections gets very large, this mathematical function approaches a limit of n^2.

Monetary Subsidies—Giving money to consumers or producers to incentivize them to join a network, either directly or indirectly. One of the three ways platforms subsidize value for early users.

Network Effect—When the behavior of one user has a direct impact on the value that other users will get out of the same service. Network effects can be either positive or negative (see "Reverse Network Effect").

Network Effects Ladder—A framework for understanding how to grow quality systematically as a network expands. The network effects ladder consists of five "rungs:" Connection, Communication, Curation, Collaboration, and Community.

Path Dependence—A state that occurs when initial decisions and conditions affect subsequent decisions. For example, the types of users a network will attract in the future depend on the composition and behavior of that network's existing users. In other words, growth in networks isn't random. The path-dependent nature of networks makes platform design especially crucial early on.

Payments Platform—See "Platform Type."

Platform Business Model—A business model that facilitates the exchange of value between multiple user groups, consumers and producers.

Platform Type—A group of platforms in which the core transaction facilitates the same kind of value being exchanged. Figuring out which platform type a business model fits into is one of the first steps in platform design. There are nine platform types, which are listed below along with the type of value that defines their core transaction.

1. *Services marketplace:* a service
2. *Product marketplace:* a physical product
3. *Payments platform:* monetary payment
4. *Investment platform:* an investment (i.e., money exchanged for a financial instrument, be it equity or a loan, etc.)
5. *Social networking platform:* a double-opt-in (friending) mode of social interaction
6. *Communication platform:* 1:1 direct social communication (e.g., messaging)

7. *Social gaming platform:* a gaming interaction involving multiple users, either competing or cooperating
8. *Content platform:* a piece of content (a text article, photo, video, etc.)
9. *Development platform:* a software program

Product Feature Subsidies—Creating special functionality for power users in order to increase loyalty and usage among these users. One of the three ways platforms subsidize value for early users.

Product Marketplace—See "Platform Type."

Reverse Network Effect—When the behavior of one user negatively impacts or harms the experience of another user on a network.

Rules and Standards—One of the four functions of a platform. A platform sets guidelines and rules that govern which behaviors are allowed or encouraged and which are forbidden or discouraged.

Services Marketplace—See "Platform Type."

Social Gaming Platform—See "Platform Type."

Social Networking Platform—See "Platform Type."

Tools and Services—One of the four functions of a platform. A platform provides tools and services for users that support each step of the core transaction. Tools are self-service and decentralized while services are centralized and require continued involvement from the platform.

Tinderface—A term for a swipe-based user interface, similar to the one used by Tinder.

Transaction Cost—Costs incurred in making an exchange; the cost of participating in an interaction. Transaction costs fall broadly into three main categories. First is search and information costs, second is bargaining costs, and third is enforcement costs.

User Sequencing—Deliberately prioritizing the acquisition of certain user groups that others will want to interact with. One of the three ways platforms subsidize value for early users.

Value Chain—A tool for competitive analysis popularized by Michael Porter in his 1985 book, *Competitive Advantage.* The value chain is the set of activities that a linear business performs in order to deliver a valuable product or service to its customers.

Value Ecosystem—The set of activities that a platform designs and performs in order to support its network and facilitate transactions. The value ecosystem consists of the core transaction and the four functions of a platform.

ACKNOWLEDGMENTS

Much like building a platform, creating a book is a col-
laborative effort. Many individuals contributed to this book outside of
the two mentioned on the cover. First, the authors would like to thank
all of the brilliant people at Applico who bring platform innovation to
life each and every day. Without your hard work, we would have had
nothing to write about. This book is truly the product of a team effort
and it belongs to all of us. A few individuals merit mention in particular for their extraordinary contributions during the writing and editing
process. A special thanks goes to Greg Battle for his insight and contributions to the book. Greg was one of the main inspirations for chapter 7
and the original source for the framework that we introduce at the end
of that chapter. His input during the editing process was also a huge
help, and this book is significantly better thanks to his insights and suggestions. We would also like to thank Nathaniel Malka and Erik Zam-
brano for their input throughout the writing process. Their intellectual
capital and comments greatly improved the final product.

Outside of Applico, we would like to thank all of the entrepreneurs
who were kind enough to offer us their time for interviews and conversations. This book was greatly improved thanks to the contributions of
these individuals. Thanks also goes to Glen Weyl for his insights into
the economics of platform markets. Our conversations with Glen at the
beginning of this process helped refine our thinking. Glen was also the
inspiration for what became chapter 2 of this book and is the source for
the most insightful parts of that chapter. His work on platform economics and pricing is brilliant and we recommend it highly. Andre Veiga

also deserves a mention. Our conversations and work with him helped refine the sections of this book that focus on platform economics.

We would like to thank everyone at St. Martin's Press for bringing this book to life. Foremost among this group was our editor, Emily Carleton. Emily believed in us from the beginning and took a chance on two first-time authors. For her belief in us and help throughout this process, we are eternally grateful. This book was significantly improved thanks to her input and edits. There isn't a page within it that doesn't bear the fruit of her efforts. We would also like to thank Laura Apperson, Donna Cherry, Laura Clark, Karlyn Hixson, and Annabella Hochschild for their contributions at various stages of the publishing process. As first-time authors, we were blessed to have a great team to work with who helped make this process smooth, quick, and productive. To all of those we mentioned, and to the many we didn't have the good fortune to meet who contributed to this book's publication, we offer our gratitude.

Last but certainly not least, is our agent, William Clark. William believed in us from the very beginning and saw the power of platforms to change the world. He took a chance on us and helped find this book a fantastic home. The impact of his support throughout the last year and a half as we navigated publishing our first book cannot be overstated. We thank him for his trust and his support.

Each of the authors would like to thank a few more people who helped them on their respective journeys.

From Alex—

Thank you to my mom, without whom none of this would be possible. You always put me before yourself and set the right example for me. You taught me what it meant to work hard and to earn success. Even today, you're the most selfless person I know and continue to lead by example. You inspire me to do better and to never give up. This book is a testament to everything I learned from you. Your love and support are what made it all possible. To my sister, Christina, thank you for always motivating me to do my best. You continue to challenge me and drive me to do better. I couldn't have accomplished everything I have today without you.

To Will Roush and George Hornig, thank you for believing in me from the beginning. Both of you stuck with me through thick and thin. This book is a milestone for Applico that we all share, and the beginning of even greater things for the company you helped create. Additionally, I would like to thank the select group of advisors and investors who have helped Applico along its journey. The company would not have succeeded without your contributions, and we would not be here today to celebrate this book. While I don't have the space to name each of you here, you know who you are. Thank you.

Finally, to Lindsey Wellenstein, thank you for being my partner. You keep me focused, even when it means listening to me rant about the latest platform idea that has me excited. Thank you for your patience and support.

From Nicholas—

Thank you to my parents, who at various points housed me, fed me, put up with me, and gave me their input throughout the writing process. Their support kept me sane and productive. For your unconditional love and support and perhaps inadvisable decision to have a second child I am forever grateful. Thank you also to my sister, Natalie. You are an inspiration. Your kindness, passion, hard work, and dedication drives me to try do better every day. I couldn't ask for a better role model and big sister. I'm sorry for being the baby of the family and stealing your thunder. But in fairness, it wasn't my call.

A special thank-you deservedly belongs to Eric Weiner. Eric saw something in a kid fresh out of college, and he became a mentor and a great friend. He has taught me many good habits and a few bad ones. His help, from concept to book proposal and all the way through to the finished product, played a key part in this book making it to print.

Finally, thank you to Tiffany Tsai. Your help throughout the publishing process was vital. Thanks for maintaining my sanity and making sure I got everything done on time. You were always willing to go the extra mile for me, whether it was helping with research, making sure I actually ate food, or keeping me focused. This book wouldn't have gotten done without your support.

NOTES

Quotes that are not cited in the text come from either interviews the authors conducted or direct conversations with those persons.

PROLOGUE: THE BURNING PLATFORM

1. Quoted in Andrew Hill, "Inside Nokia: Trying to Revive a Giant," *Financial Times*, April 11, 2011, http://www.ft.com/intl/cms/s/0/20137ef0-6480-11 e0-a69a-00144feab49a.html#axzz417XSTdSN.
2. "Full Text: Nokia CEO Stephen Elop's 'Burning Platform' Memo," *Wall Street Journal*, February 9, 2011, http://blogs.wsj.com/tech-europe/2011/02/09/full -text-nokia-ceo-stephen-elops-burning-platform-memo/.
3. Quoted in Andrew Hill, "Inside Nokia: Rebuilt from Within," *Financial Times*, April 13, 2011, http://www.ft.com/intl/cms/s/0/9ec857b6-65f7-11e0 -9d40-00144feab49a.html#axzz3wUbbzzoW.
4. Ritsuko Ando and Bill Rigby, "Microsoft Swallows Nokia's Phone Business for $7.2 Billion," *Reuters*, September 3, 2013, http://www.reuters.com/article /us-microsoft-nokia-idUSBRE98202V20130903.
5. Donald Melanson, "Fortune Names RIM Fastest Growing Company. in the World," *Engadget*, August 18, 2019, http://www.engadget.com/2009/08/18 /fortune-names-rim-fastest-growing-company-in-the-world/.
6. Quoted in Charles Arthur, "RIM Chiefs Mike Lazaridis and Jim Balsillie's Best Quotes," *Guardian* (UK), June 29, 2012, http://www.theguardian.com /technology/2012/jun/29/rim-chiefs-best-quotes.
7. Quoted in Al Sacco, "RIM's CEO: What Went Wrong and Where Black-Berry Goes from Here," *InfoWorld*, July 10, 2012, http://www.infoworld.com /article/2617392/blackberry/rim-s-ceo—what-went-wrong-and-where -blackberry-goes-from-here.html.
8. Quoted in Jesse Hicks, "Research, No Motion: How the BlackBerry CEOs Lost an Empire," *The Verge*, February 21, 2012, http://www.theverge .com/2012/2/21/2789676/rim-blackberry-mike-lazaridis-jim-balsillie-lost -empire.
9. Quoted in Ian Austen, "Research In Motion Eyes a Rebound," *New York Times*, April 10, 2011, http://www.nytimes.com/2011/04/11/technology /companies/11rim.html?_r=0.

10. Andy Rubin, "Where's My Gphone?," November 5, 2007, https://googleblog .blogspot.com/2007/11/wheres-my-gphone.html.

11. Jim Dalrymple, "Apple Reaches iPhone Goal, Reports $1.14B Profit," *Macworld*, October 22, 2008, http://www.macworld.com/article/1136282/apple earnings.html.

12. "Apple Reports Fourth Quarter Results," press release, October 21, 2008, https://www.apple.com/pr/library/2008/10/21Apple-Reports-Fourth -Quarter-Results.html.

13. Matt Hartley, "With New BlackBerry, RIM Ramps Up Smart-phone War," *Globe and Mail*, March 31, 2009, http://www.theglobeandmail.com /technology/with-new-blackberry-rim-ramps-up-smart-phone-war/article 1065647/.

14. "iPhone App Store Downloads Top 10 Million in First Weekend," press release, July 14, 2008, http://www.apple.com/pr/library/2008/07/14iPhone -App-Store-Downloads-Top-10-Million-in-First-Weekend.html.

15. Zach Spear, "App Store Daily Download Rates Now Double December Volumes," *Apple Insider*, January 16, 2009, http://appleinsider.com/articles /09/01/16/app_store_daily_download_rates_now_double_december_vol umes.html.

16. App Store and Google Play statistics can be found at http://www.statista. com.

17. Quoted in Erick Shonfeld, "RIM CEO Jim Balsillie To Steve Jobs: 'You Don't Need An App For The Web,'" *Techcrunch*, November 16, 2010, http:// techcrunch.com/2010/11/16/rim-ceo-balsillie-jobsapp-web/.

18. John Gruber, "WWDC 2007 Keynote News," June 11, 2007, http://daring fireball.net/2007/06/wwdc_2007_keynote.

19. Quoted in Jonathan S. Geller, "Open Letter to BlackBerry Bosses: Senior RIM Exec Tells All as Company Crumbles Around Him," June 30, 2011, http://bgr.com/2011/06/30/open-letter-to-blackberry-bosses-senior-rim -exec-tells-all-as-company-crumbles-around-him/.

20. Quoted in Hicks, "Research, No Motion."

CHAPTER 1: PLATFORMS ARE EATING THE WORLD

1. Marc Andreessen, "Why Software is Eating the World," *Wall Street Journal*, August 20, 2011, http://www.wsj.com/articles/SB100014240531119034809 04576512250915629460.

2. Danny Wong, "In Q3, Facebook Drove 4X More Traffic than Pinterest," *Shareaholic Reports*, October 27, 2014, https://blog.shareaholic.com/social -media-traffic-trends-10-2014/.

3. Henry Blodget, "Google's Crash Took 40% of Internet Traffic Down with It," *Business Insider*, August 18, 2013, http://www.businessinsider.com/google -goes-down-2013-8.

4. "Top Sites in the United States," Alexa.com, http://www.alexa.com/topsites /countries/US.

5. Brenda Goh, "Chinese Rivals Snap at Alibaba's Heels in Cross-Border e-Commerce Race," *Reuters*, February 25, 2015, http://www.reuters.com/arti cle/us-china-retail-internet-idUSKBN0LT2FK20150226.

6. Cecilia, "Yu'E Bao Exceeded 578.9 Bln Yuan in 2014," *China Internet Watch*, January 7, 2015, http://www.chinainternetwatch.com/11837/yue-ba os-2014/.

7. W. Brian Arthur, *Increasing Returns and Path Dependence in the Economy* (Ann Arbor: University of Michigan Press, 1994).

8. For example, see David Goldman, "10 Big Dot-Com Flops," *CNN Money*, November 6, 2015, http://money.cnn.com/gallery/technology/2015/03/02 /dot-com-flops/index.html.

9. Adam Cohen, *The Perfect Store: Inside eBay* (New York: Little, Brown, 2002).

10. Julia Ferris, Dr. Mike Goldsmith, Ian Graham, Sally MacGill, Andrea Mills, Isabel Thomas, and Matt Turner, *Big Ideas that Changed the World: Incredible Inventions and the Stories behind Them* (New York: DK Publishing, 2010).

11. Cohen, *The Perfect Store*.

12. Ibid.

13. Daniel Gross, "My eBay Job," *Slate*, May 21, 2008, http://www.slate.com /articles/business/moneybox/2008/05/my_ebay_job.html.

14. Cohen, *The Perfect Store*.

15. "The World's Most Valuable Brands," *Forbes*, http://www.forbes.com/power ful-brands/list.

16. Red Hat finance information, Google Finance, https://www.google.com /finance?q=NYSE:RHT.

17. Rip Empson, "Led by Former Microsofties, GitHub Brings the Party to En- terprise with New Windows Client," *TechCrunch*, May 21, 2012, http://tech crunch.com/2012/05/21/github-launches-windows-client/.

18. You can view our GitHub here: https://github.com/applico.

19. GitHub statistics, CrunchBase, https://www.crunchbase.com/organization /github.

20. Cade Metz, "How GitHub Conquered Google, Microsoft, and Everyone Else," *Wired*, March 12, 2015, http://www.wired.com/2015/03/github-con quered-google-microsoft-everyone-else/.

21. For more, visit our open-source platform database at www.platforminnova tion.com

CHAPTER 2: HAYEK VERSUS THE MACHINE

1. Credit for this analogy goes to Paul Boag, "Are We Thinking about Digital All Wrong?," *Smashing Magazine*, March 14, 2014, http://www.smashing magazine.com/2014/03/14/are-we-thinking-about-digital-all-wrong/.

2. Royal Swedish Academy of Sciences, press release, October 14, 1975, http:// www.nobelprize.org/nobel_prizes/economic-sciences/laureates/1975/press .html.

3. Friedrich Hayek, *Individualism and the Economic Order* (Chicago, IL: Univer- sity of Chicago Press, 1948). Subsequent quotes by Hayek are from this book.

4. Ibid.

5. Credit for this analogy goes to Microsoft senior researcher E. Glen Weyl.

6. Ronald Coase, "The Institutional Structure of Production," in Nobel Lec- tures, *Economics 1991-1995*, ed. Torsten Persson (Hackensack, NJ: World Sci- entific Publishing, 1997).

7. Martin Reeves, George Stalk, and Filippo L. Scognamiglio Pasini, "BCG Classics Revisited: The Experience Curve," *BCG Perspectives*, May 28, 2013, https://www.bcgperspectives.com/content/articles/growth_business_unit _strategy_experience_curve_bcg_classics_revisited/.

8. Oskar Lange, "The Computer and the Market," in *Socialism, Capitalism and Economic Growth: Essays Presented to Maurice Dob*, ed. C. F. Feinstein (Cambridge, UK: Cambridge University Press, 1967). Subsequent quotes by Lange are from this book.

9. This story and the specific details about the encyclopedia business comes from Philip Evans and Thomas S. Wurster's excellent 1999 book, *Blown to Bits: How the New Economics of Information Transforms Strategy* (Boston, MA: Harvard Business Review Press).

10. Paul Krugman, "Why Most Economists' Predictions Are Wrong," *Red Herring*, June 1998.

11. SINTEF, "Big Data, for Better or Worse: 90% of World's Data Generated Over Last Two Years," May 22, 2013, *ScienceDaily*, www.sciencedaily.com /releases/2013/05/130522085217.htm.

12. John F. Gantz, Stephon Minton, Vernon Turner, and David Reinsel, "The Digital Universe of Opportunities: Rich Data and the Increasing Value of the Internet of Things," IDC whitepaper, April 2014.

13. Ming Zeng of Alibaba, *Big Data Is the Future of the Internet*, February 21, 2014, https://www.youtube.com/watch?v=yOIkB0mxqxs.

14. Mark Zuckerberg, Facebook post, August 27, 2015, https://www.facebook .com/zuck/posts/10102329188394581.

15. According to Alibaba's quarterly earnings report, "Alibaba Group Announces March Quarter 2015 and Full Fiscal Year 2015 Results," May 7, 2015, http:// www.alibabagroup.com/en/news/press_pdf/p150507.pdf.

16. Peter Thiel with Blake Masters, *Zero to One: Notes on Startups, or How to Build the Future* (New York: Crown Business, 2014). Subsequent quotes by Thiel are from this book.

17. Edward Tse, *China's Disruptors: How Alibaba, Xiaomi, Tencent, and Other Companies are Changing the Rules of Business* (New York: Penguin, 2014).

CHAPTER 3: THE ZERO-MARGINAL-COST COMPANY

1. Fred Wilson, tweet, July 30, 2014, https://twitter.com/fredwilson/status/49 4485051607089153.

2. This story and all related quotes come from "The Dentist Office Software Story," *AVC* (blog), July 30, 2014, http://avc.com/2014/07/the-dentist-office -software-story/.

3. Quoted in Sramana Mitra, *Billion Dollar Unicorns: Entrepreneur Journeys* (Amazon Digital Services, 2014), Kindle eBook.

4. Brian Horowitz, "EHR Adoption to Hit 80 Percent in Health Care Market by 2016: IDC," *eWeek*, June 1, 2012, http://www.eweek.com/c/a/Health -Care-IT/EHR-Adoption-to-Hit-80-Percent-in-Health-Care-Market-by -2016-IDC-515677.

5. "Telehealth Companies See Investor Funding Jump in 2014—The Doctor Is Always In," *CB Insights* (blog), August 17, 2014, https://www.cbinsights .com/blog/telehealth-financing-record/.

6. See Erin McCann, "Google Testing Telehealth Waters," *HealthCare IT News,* October 13, 2014, http://www.healthcareitnews.com/news/google -testing-telemedicine-waters.

7. Bill Gurley, "All Revenue Is Not Created Equal: The Keys to the 10X Revenue Club," *Above the Crowd* (blog), May 24, 2011, http://abovethecrowd.com /2011/05/24/all-revenue-is-not-created-equal-the-keys-to-the-10x-revenue -club/.

8. Josh Constine, "Facebook Beats in Q2 with $4.04B Revenue, User Growth Slows to 3.47% QOQ to Hit 1.49B," *TechCrunch,* July 29, 2015, http://tech crunch.com/2015/07/29/facebook-earnings-q2-2015/

9. Our calculations were based off of publicly available market data as of June 2015.

10. See, for example, Talia Goldberg and Jeremy Levine, "Valuations: What Is Happening and Does It Matter?," *Slideshare,* February 2015, http://www .slideshare.net/taliagold/valuation-presentation-blog-version; Boris Wertz, "How We Determine Valuations for Marketplaces," *Version One,* July 20, 2015, http://versionone.vc/how-we-determine-valuations-for-marketplaces/; Barry Libert, Yoram Wind, and Megan Beck Fenley, "What Airbnb, Uber, and Alibaba Have in Common," *Harvard Business Review,* November 20, 2014, https://hbr.org/2014/11/what-airbnb-uber-and-alibaba-have-in-common.

11. All S&P 500 data is calculated as of third quarter 2014 using publically available market data. We calculated the net income generated in the third quarter of 2014 by the ten true platform companies in the S&P 500. We compared their collective net income to the aggregate of all the S&P 500 companies and extended these ratios with our projections to account for the estimated number of platform companies that will be in the S&P 500 over the next twenty-five years based on our trend line.

12. Data on unicorn companies is as of July 29, 2015, and is drawn from CB Insight's Unicorn List (https://www.cbinsights.com/research-unicorn-compa nies) and the *Wall Street Journal's* "Billion-Dollar Startup Club" (http://graph ics.wsj.com/billion-dollar-club/), along with our own proprietary research.

13. IDC, "Worldwide Smartphone Shipments Increase 25.2% in the Third Quarter with Heightened Competition and Growth beyond Samsung and Apple, Says IDC," press release, October 29, 2014, http://www.idc.com/get doc.jsp?containerId=prUS25224914.

14. This idea has also been supported by research from Libert, Wind, and Fenley, "What Airbnb, Uber, and Alibaba Have in Common."

15. The first quote is from Dennis Schaal, "Interview: OpenTable CEO on How Its Game Changes within Priceline," *Skift,* September 29, 2014, http://skift.com/2014/09/29/interview-opentable-ceo-on-how-its-game -changes-within-priceline/. The second quote is from "OpenTable CEO Matt Roberts Talks Restaurants_," July 11, 2012. YouTube, https://www.you tube.com/watch?v=BJy3wrjzLJk.

16. Ellen Huet, "What Really Killed Homejoy? It Couldn't Hold on to Its Customers," *Forbes,* July 23, 2015, http://www.forbes.com/sites/ellenhuet/2015/07/23 /what-really-killed-homejoy-it-couldnt-hold-onto-its-customers/.

17. Mae Anderson, "Amazon Launches Etsy Rival 'Handmade At Amazon,'" Associated Press, October 8, 2015, http://www.huffingtonpost.com/entry /handmade-at-amazon_561668d1e4b0e66ad4c689ca.

CHAPTER 4: MODERN MONOPOLIES

1. Ming Zeng, speaking at the July 25, 2014, Platform Strategy Summit at MIT.
2. Quoted in Chris Nuttall and Mure Dickie, "Ebay's Strategy in China Shattered," *Financial Times*, December 19, 2006, http://www.ft.com/intl/cms /s/0/7d963794-8f8b-11db-9ba3-0000779e2340.html#axzz3j7J7sRPL.
3. Quoted in Porter Erisman, *Crocodile in the Yangtze: The Alibaba Story* (Talus-Wood Films, 2012).
4. Porter Erisman, *Alibaba's World: How a Remarkable Chinese Company is Changing the Face of Global Business* (New York: Palgrave Macmillan, 2015).
5. Quoted in Helen H. Wang, "How EBay Failed in China," *Forbes*, September 12, 2010, http://www.forbes.com/sites/china/2010/09/12/how-ebay-failed -in-china/.
6. "Standard Oil Company and Trust," *Encyclopaedia Britannica*, http://www .britannica.com/topic/Standard-Oil-Company-and-Trust.
7. Zeng, MIT Platform Strategy Summit.
8. Josh Dawsey, "War With Uber Hurt de Blasio with Allies," *Wall Street Journal*, July 30, 2015, http://www.wsj.com/articles/war-with-uber-hurt-de-blas io-with-allies-1438304186.
9. Edward T. Walkers, "The Uber-ization of Activism," *New York Times*, August 6, 2015, http://www.nytimes.com/2015/08/07/opinion/the-uber-ization-of -activism.html.
10. Kalanick was speaking at a *TechCrunch* event later that year. Video can be found here: http://techcrunch.com/2012/09/12/ceo-travis-kalanick-says-ub erx-numbers-are-probably-at-or-above-lyft/.
11. See, for example, E. Glen Weyl and Alexander White, "Let the Right 'One' Win: Policy Lessons from the New Economics of Platforms," *Social Science Research Network*, December 8, 2014, http://papers.ssrn.com/sol3/papers.cfm ?abstract_id=2524368. In the interest of full disclosure, E. Glen Weyl has acted as an advisor to Applico in the past.
12. David Plouffe, "Uber and the American Worker," *Medium*, November 5, 2015, https://medium.com/@davidplouffe/uber-and-the-american-worker-bdd499 ec5323#.24uxoctyq.
13. Georgios Zervas, David Prosperio, and John Byers, "The Rise of the Sharing Economy: Estimating the Impact of Airbnb on the Hotel Industry," May 7, 2015, http://papers.ssrn.com/sol3/papers.cfm?abstract_id=2366898.
14. Paul Carsten, "Alibaba's Singles' Day Sales Surge 60 Percent to $14.3 Billion," *Reuters*, November 11, 2015, http://www.reuters.com/article/us-ali baba-singles-day-idUSKCN0SZ34J20151112.
15. See, for example, this 2014 report on Taobao villages in rural China: Eunice Yoon, "Inside a Taobao Village," CNBC, September 17, 2014, http://www .cnbc.com/2014/09/17/inside-a-taobao-village.html. See also a report on the growing number of Taobao villages in China: Xu Wenwen, "'Taobao Villages' Soar Past 200," *Shanghai Daily*, December 30, 2014, http://www.shanghai daily.com/hangzhou/Taobao-Villages-soar-past-200/shdaily.shtml.
16. To be clear, this is not an argument for unrestrained deregulation and "free trade"—as we show in chapter 5, a key part of the way platforms create value is by introducing rules and standards that structure their marketplaces to help facilitate trade.

17. Tim Wu, "In the Grip of the New Monopolists," *Wall Street Journal*, November 13, 2010, http://www.wsj.com/articles/SB1000142405274870463570457 5604993311538482.

18. See Fred Vogelstein, *Dogfight: Apple and Google Went to War and Started a Revolution* (New York: Sarah Crichton Books, 2013).

CHAPTER 5: DESIGNING A BILLION-DOLLAR COMPANY

1. Quoted in Jana Kasperkevic, "Airbnb Founder: Best Way to Get Inside Your Customers' Heads," *Inc.*, May 3, 2013, http://www.inc.com/jana-kasperkevic /joe-gebbia-airbnb-99u-empathize-users-storyboard-their-experience.html.

2. We're talking about heterosexual couples in this example, although all of these platforms are open to gay and lesbian users as well. We focus here on heterosexual relationships because most published articles and statistics about these companies do as well. However, from our anecdotal knowledge, the type of relationship doesn't change the situation much on platforms like OkCupid; many users still are inundated with messages while others often receive no reply.

3. Tomasz Tunguz, "If You Chase Two Rabbits . . . ," *Tomasz Tunguz* (blog), July 28, 2015, http://tomtunguz.com/if-you-chase-two-rabbits/.

4. Lada A. Adamic, Orkut Buyukkokten, and Eytan Ada, "Orkut: A Social Network Caught in the Web," *First Monday* 8, no. 6 (June 2003), http://firstmonday.org/article/view/1057/977.

5. David Kirkpatrick, *The Facebook Effect* (New York: Simon and Schuster, 2010).

6. Ibid.

CHAPTER 6: THE VISIBLE HAND

1. The ratio is a ballpark number based on the limited amount of data on Uber drivers and customers that's publicly available. Most notably, we used Uber's self-funded report by Jonathan V. Hall and Alan B. Krueger, "An Analysis of the Labor Market for Uber's Driver-Partners in the United States," January 22, 2015 (http://dataspace.princeton.edu/jspui/bitstream/88435/ds p010z708z67d/5/587.pdf), which we collated with leaked customer numbers from: Nitasha Tiku, "Leaked: Uber's Internal Revenue and Ride Request Numbers," *Valleywag*, December 4, 2013, http://valleywag.gawker.com /leaked-ubers-internal-revenue-and-ride-request-number-1475924182. Another source, "Uber Spearheads Growth of the Shared Economy in Mexico," *Global Delivery Report*, July 9, 2014 (http://globaldeliveryreport .com/uber-spearheads-growth-of-the-shared-economy-in-mexico/), puts the driver/passenger ratio at about 1 to 8, but exact, up-to-date data is not publicly available.

2. Tom Cheredar, "Airbnb Admits Gaming Craigslist, Blames Rogue Contractors," *Venture Beat News*, June 2, 2011, http://venturebeat.com/2011/06/02 /airbnb-admits-gaming-craigslist/.

3. Alex Moazed, "5 Things You Can Learn From One of Airbnb's Earliest Hustles," *Inc.*, June 30, 2015, http://www.inc.com/alex-moazed/cereal

-obama-denver-the-recipe-these-airbnb-hustlers-used-to-launch-a-unicorn
.html.

4.   Eric M. Jackson, *The PayPal Wars* (Los Angeles: World Ahead, 2004).

5.   Ibid.

6.   Brian X. Chen, "App-Powered Car Service Leaves Cabs in the Dust," *Wired*,
April 5, 2011, http://www.wired.com/2011/04/app-stars-uber/all/.

7.   "Statistics," YouTube, https://www.youtube.com/yt/press/statistics.html, accessed June 2015.

8.   Quotes from Cristos Goodrow are from Jillian D'Onfro, "The 'Ter-
rifying' Moment in 2012 when YouTube Changed Its Entire Philosophy," *Business Insider*, July 3, 2015, http://www.businessinsider.com/you
tube-watch-time-vs-views-2015-7.

9.   Eric Meyerson, "YouTube Now: Why We Focus on Watch Time," *YouTube
Creator Blog*, August 10, 2012, http://youtubecreator.blogspot.com/2012/08
/youtube-now-why-we-focus-on-watch-time.html.

10. "Twitter Usage Statistics," Internet Live Stats, http://www.internetlivestats
.com/twitter-statistics/, accessed November 2015.

11. David Kirkpatrick, *The Facebook Effect*.

12. "The Twitter Platform's Inflection Point," *AVC* (blog), April 7, 2010, http://
avc.com/2010/04/the-twitter-platform/.

13. Staci D. Kramer, "Bill Gross on Ubermedia, the Power of Twitter and Why
He's Acquiring," *Gigaom*, February 12, 2011, https://gigaom.com/2011/02/12
/419-bill-gross-on-ubermedia-the-power-of-twitter-and-why-hes-acquiring/.

14. Quoted in Juan Carlos Perez, "Twitter Clamps Down on Client Apps," *PC
World*, March 11, 2011, http://www.pcworld.com/article/222045/article
.html.

15. Quoted in Michael Sippey, "Delivering a Consistent Twitter Experience" *Twitter Blogs* (blog), June 29, 2012, https://blog.twitter.com/2012
/delivering-consistent-twitter-experience.

16. Yoree Koh, "Only 11% of New Twitter Users in 2012 Are Still Tweeting," *Digits*, March 21, 2014, http://blogs.wsj.com/digits/2014/03/21/new
-report-spotlights-twitters-retention-problem/; and Jim Edwards, "The
Number of People Actively Using Twitter May Actually Be in Decline,"
Business Insider, April 27, 2015, http://www.businessinsider.com/twitter
-users-may-be-in-decline-2015-4?r=UK&IR=T.

17. Nick Bilton, *Hatching Twitter: A True Story of Money, Power, Friendship, and
Betrayal* (New York: Portfolio/Penguin, 2013).

18. Bill Gurley, "You Don't Have to Tweet to Twitter," *Above the Crowd* (blog),
November 15, 2011, http://abovethecrowd.com/2011/11/15/you-dont-have
-to-tweet-to-twitter/.

19. "Twitter Boss Admits Firm Is Failing Victims of Trolling," *BBC News*, February 5, 2015, http://www.bbc.com/news/technology-31146659.

20. Alyson Shontell, "Here's What the First Hires at Apple, Google and Other
Top Tech Companies Are Doing Now," *Entrepreneur*, November 1, 2014,
http://www.entrepreneur.com/article/239115.

21. Jackson, *The PayPal Wars*.

22. Quoted in Liz Gannes, "Airbnb Now Wants to Check Your Government ID," *All Things*, April 30, 2013, http://allthingsd.com/20130430
/airbnb-now-wants-to-check-your-government-id/.

23. Katie Roof, "Checkr Is Raising $30M+ For Its Background Checking API, Y Combinator Investing," *TechCrunch*, October 13, 2015, http://techcrunch .com/2015/10/13/checkr-series-b/#.e9v15e:kySL.

24. To be fair, this problem isn't unique to platforms. It's a hiring risk for any business. The risk just becomes more obvious when you're dealing with a huge decentralized network rather than a smaller, centralized linear business.

25. Liz Gannes, "After Home-Trashing Incident, Airbnb Builds an In-House Enforcer Team," *All Things*, July 16, 2013, http://allthingsd.com/20130716 /after-home-trashing-incident-airbnb-builds-an-in-house-enforcer-team/.

26. Ibid.

27. Bilton, *Hatching Twitter*.

28. You can find more information about our Platform Modeling process on our website, http://www.applicoinc.com/services/.

CHAPTER 7: LET THE NETWORK DO THE WORK

1. Nick Bilton, "The Surreal World of Chatroulette," *New York Times*, February 20, 2010, http://www.nytimes.com/2010/02/21/weekinreview/21bilton .html.

2. Sam Anderson, "The Human Shuffle," *New York*, February 5, 2010, http:// nymag.com/news/media/63663/.

3. Michelle Kessler, "Webcam 'Chatroulette' Generates Conversation—and Controversy," *USA Today*, February 23, 2010, http://content.usatoday.com /communities/technologylive/post/2010/02/webcam-chatroulette-generates -conversation—and-controversy/1#.VpbDF4QnaHk.

4. Michael Arrington, "Chatroulette Enlists Shawn Fanning in the Fight against the Masturbators," *TechCrunch*, June 13, 2010, http://techcrunch.com/2010 /06/13/chatroulette-enlists-shawn-fanning-in-the-fight-against-the-mastur bators/.

5. Erick Schonfeld, "Chatroulette Quadruples to 4 Million Visitors in February," *TechCrunch*, March 29, 2010, http://techcrunch.com/2010/03/29 /chatroulette-4-million-visitors/; Andrew Lipsman, "Chatroulette Takes the College Crowd by Storm," *comScore*, March 16, 2010, http://www.com score.com/ita/Insights/Blog/Chatroulette-Takes-the-College-Crowd-by -Storm; Jennifer Valentino-DeVries and Lauren Goode, "Chatroulette, by the Numbers," *Digits*, March 2, 2010, http://blogs.wsj.com/digits/2010/03/02 /chatroulette-by-the-numbers/.

6. Robert J. Moore, "Chatroulette Is 89 Percent Male, 47 Percent American, And 13 Percent Perverts," *TechCrunch*, March 16, 2010, http://techcrunch .com/2010/03/16/chatroulette-stats-male-perverts/.

7. Mary Elizabeth Williams, "R.I.P. Chatroulette, 2009–2010," *Salon*, June 29, 2010, http://www.salon.com/2010/06/29/requiem_for_chatroulette/.

8. "Finding Love Online, Version 2.0," *Bloomberg Business*, June 10, 2003, http:// www.bloomberg.com/bw/stories/2003-06-09/finding-love-online-version -2-dot-0.

9. Quoted in Julia Angwin, *Stealing Myspace: The Battle to Control the Most Popular Website in America* (New York: Random House, 2009).

10. Fast Company Staff, "A Cautionary Tale," *Fast Company*, May 1, 2007, http:// www.fastcompany.com/59447/cautionary-tale.

11. Max Chafkin, "How to Kill a Great Idea," *Inc.*, June 1, 2007, http://www.inc.com/magazine/20070601/features-how-to-kill-a-great-idea.html.

12. Gary Rivlin, "Wallflower at the Web Party" *New York Times,* October 15, 2006, http://www.nytimes.com/2006/10/15/business/yourmoney/15friend.html?pagewanted=2&_r=2.

13. danah boyd, "None of This Is Real: Identity and Participation in Friendster," in *Structures of Participation in Digital Culture,* ed. Joe Karaganis (New York: Social Science Research Council, 2007).

14. Chafkin, "How to Kill a Great Idea."

15. Angwin, *Stealing Myspace;* Stuart Dredge, "MySpace—What Went Wrong: 'The Site Was a Massive Spaghetti-Ball Mess,'" *Guardian* (UK), March 6, 2015, http://www.hitc.com/en-gb/2015/03/07/myspace-what-went-wrong-the-site-was-a-massive-spaghetti-ball-me/.

16. Angwin, *Stealing Myspace.*

17. Felix Gillette, "The Rise and Inglorious Fall of Myspace," *Bloomberg Business,* June 22, 2011, http://www.bloomberg.com/bw/magazine/content/11_27/b4235053917570.htm#p2.

18. Quoted in ibid.

19. Ibid.

20. Kirkpatrick, *The Facebook Effect.*

21. Carolyn, "Welcome to Facebook Everyone," Facebook note, September 26, 2006, https://www.facebook.com/notes/facebook/welcome-to-facebook-everyone/2210227130.

22. Rob Hof, "Facebook Declares New Era for Advertising," *Bloomberg Business,* November 6, 2007, http://www.businessweek.com/the_thread/techbeat/archives/2007/11/facebook_declar.html.

23. "Number of Active Users at Facebook over the Years," Associated Press, May 1, 2013, http://finance.yahoo.com/news/number-active-users-facebook-over-years-214600186—finance.html.

24. For example, in a 2012 interview, Zuckerberg suggested that Facebook's initial limited ambitions (starting out only at Harvard and expanding from school to school) played a big part in its eventual success. "It took a year for us to get to one million users and we thought it was incredibly fast," he said. "I think having that time to baby was really helpful for us." "Mark Zuckerberg at Startup School 2012," YouTube, October 25, 2013, https://www.youtube.com/watch?v=5bJi7k-y1Lo.

25. Luz Lazo, "Uber Turns 5, Reaches 1 Million Drivers and 300 Cities Worldwide. Now What?" *Washington Post,* June 4, 2015, https://www.washingtonpost.com/news/dr-gridlock/wp/2015/06/04/uber-turns-5-reaches-1-million-drivers-and-300-cities-worldwide-now-what/.

26. Kirkpatrick, *The Facebook Effect.*

27. Angwin, *Stealing Myspace.*

28. Gillette, "The Rise and Inglorious Fall of Myspace."

29. Ibid.

30. That is, until Facebook came in a few years later and kneecapped it on its home turf. Google shut down Orkut entirely in 2014.

31. Seth Fiegerman, "Inside the Failure of Google+, a Very Expensive Attempt to Unseat Facebook," *Mashable,* August 2, 2015, http://mashable.com/2015/08/02/google-plus-history/.

32. We borrow the term "reverse network effect" from Bernard Lunn, "Is There a Reverse Network Effect with Scale?" *readwrite*, March 16, 2009, http://readwrite.com/2009/03/16/is_there_a_reverse_network_effect_with_scale.

33. Kevin Maney, "'First Mover Advantage' No Longer an Advantage," *USA Today*, July 18, 2001.

34. Steve Blank, "Steve Blank: Here's Why the First-Mover Advantage Is Extremely Overrated," *Business Insider*, October 19, 2010, http://www.business insider.com/steve-blank-first-mover-advantage-overrated-2010-10.

35. For more detail, see David S. Evans, "Governing Bad Behavior by Users of Multi-Sided Platforms," *Berkeley Technology Law Journal* 27, no. 2 (Fall 2012).

36. Angwin, *Stealing Myspace.*

37. Xu Lin, "First Impressions Count," *China Daily*, http://www.chinaculture.org/chineseway/2012-05/17/content_433892.htm, accessed July 2015.

38. Nancy Jo Sales, "Tinder and the Dawn of the "Dating Apocalypse," *Vanity Fair*, August 31, 2015, http://www.vanityfair.com/culture/2015/08/tinder-hook-up-culture-end-of-dating.

39. Julia Greenberg, "Tinder Completely Freaked Out on Twitter," *Wired*, August 11, 2015 http://www.wired.com/2015/08/tinder-completely-freaked-twitter/.

40. These quotes come from a series of interviews Zuckerberg gave at Y Combinator's Startup School from 2009 to 2013. You can find videos of the events online here: https://www.youtube.com/user/siwuzzz/videos.

41. Nick Summers, "Facebook's 'Porn Cops' Are Key to Its Growth," *Newsweek*, April 30, 2009, http://www.newsweek.com/facebooks-porn-cops-are-key-its-growth-77055.

42. For more, see danah boyd, "White Flight in Networked Publics? How Race and Class Shaped American Teen Engagement with MySpace and Facebook," in *Race after the Internet*, ed. Lisa Nakamura and Peter A. Chow-White (New York: Routledge, 2011).

43. Tim Arango, "Hot Social Networking Site Cools as Facebook Grows," *New York Times*, January 11, 2011, http://www.nytimes.com/2011/01/12/technology/internet/12myspace.html?_r=0.

44. Shane McGlaun, "Microsoft Spends 1 Billion on Exclusive Xbox One Games," *Dailytech*, May 30, 2013, http://www.dailytech.com/Microsoft+Sp ends+1+Billion+on+Exclusive+Xbox+One+Games/article31656.htm.

45. Josh Halliday, "Twitter Founders Launch Two New Websites, Medium and Branch," *Guardian* (UK), August 15, 2012, http://www.theguardian.com/technology/blog/2012/aug/15/twitter-founders-new-branch-medium.

46. Liz Gannes, "The Secret Behind Pinterest's Growth Was Marketing, Not Engineering, Says CEO Ben Silbermann," *All Things D*, October 20, 2012, http://allthingsd.com/20121020/the-secret-behind-pinterests-growth-was-marketing-not-engineering-says-ceo-ben-silbermann/.

47. Credit for the insights behind this framework goes to Applico principal Greg Battle.

48. Ramana Nanda and Liz Kind, "AngelList," Harvard Business School Case 814-036, September 2013 (revised November 2013).

49. According to "List of Wikipedias," September 2015, https://meta.wikimedia.org/wiki/List_of_Wikipedias.

50. Michael Mandiberg, "7,473 Volumes at 700 Pages Each: Meet Print Wikipedia," *Wikimedia Blog*, June 19, 2015, http://blog.wikimedia.org/2015/06/19/meet-print-wikipedia/.

51. Andrew Lih, *The Wikipedia Revolution: How A Bunch of Nobodies Created The World's Greatest Encyclopedia* (New York: Hyperion, 2009).

52. Comments made at 2013 SXSW panel discussion.

53. "Episode 45—Ryan Fujiu, Product Lead on Lyft's Growth Team," *500 Start-ups Podcast,* http://www.stitcher.com/podcast/500-startups/e/episode-45-ry an-fujiu-product-lead-on-lyfts-growth-team-35017106.

CHAPTER 8: WHY PLATFORMS FAIL

1. Ty McMahan, "Sequoia to Color Labs: Not Since Google Have We Seen This," *Wall Street Journal, Venture Capital Dispatch,* March 11, 2011, http:// blogs.wsj.com/venturecapital/2011/03/24/sequoia-to-color-labs-not-since -google-have-we-seen-this/.

2. Quoted in Jefferson Graham, "Color App for iPhone Lets Others Peek at Your Photos, Video," *USA Today,* March 23, 2011, http://usatoday30.usa today.com/tech/news/2011-03-23-iphone-photo-sharing.htm.

3. Quoted in Danielle Sacks, "Bill Nguyen: The Boy in the Bubble," *Fast Company,* October 19, 2011, http://www.fastcompany.com/1784823/bill-nguyen -the-boy-in-the-bubble.

4. Mike Melanson, "Color CEO: The Tech Justifies the $41 Million," *read write,* March 24, 2011, http://readwrite.com/2011/03/24/color_ceo_the _tech_justifies_the_41_million.

5. Quoted in Sacks, "Bill Nguyen."

6. Melanson, "Color CEO"; Claire Cain Miller, "Investors Provide Millions to Risky Startups," *New York Times,* June 20, 2011, http://www.nytimes .com/2011/06/20/technology/20color.html.

7. Adrian Chen, "Extremely-Hyped Startup Fails to Live Up to Extreme Hype," *Gizmodo,* http://gizmodo.com/5813600/extremely-hyped-startup-fa ils-to-live-up-to-extreme-hype.

8. Robert Scoble, "Why Color's Bad First Experience Will Always 'Color' This Company in App Stores," *Scobleizer* (blog), March 24, 2011, http:// scobleizer.com/why-colors-bad-first-experience-will-always-color-this-com pany-in-app-stores/.

9. Jackson, *The PayPal Wars*; Visakan Veerasamy, "The Original #Growth-Hackers: How PayPal Achieved 7–10% Daily Growth in the Early 2000s," *ReferralCandy,* January 23, 2014, http://www.referralcandy.com/blog/paypal -referrals/.

10. Carly Page, "Android Hits 83.6 Percent Marketshare while iOS, Windows and BlackBerry Slide," *Inquirer,* November 3, 2014, http://www.theinquirer .net/inquirer/news/2379036/android-hits-836-percent-marketshare-while -ios-windows-and-blackberry-slide.

11. Thoshi, "Chicken & Egg Problem: How Quora & Reddit Got Their First Users," *Byte Campaign,* January 6, 2015, http://www.bytecampaign.com /how-quora-and-reddit-got-first-users/.

12. Jeff Roberts, "Craigslist Cracks Down on Outside Services, Says Violators Must Pay '$0.10 per Server Request,'" *Gigaom,* August 19, 2014, https:// gigaom.com/2014/08/19/craigslist-cracks-down-on-outside-services-says -violators-must-pay-0-10-per-server-request/.

13. Nick Summers, "The Truth About Tinder and Women Is Even Worse Than You Think," *Bloomberg Businessweek,* July 2, 2014, http://www.bloomberg.com /bw/articles/2014-07-02/tinders-forgotten-woman-whitney-wolfe-sexism -and-startup-creation-myths.

14. Bilton, *Hatching Twitter.*

15. Matt Egan, "Etsy Now Worth Over $3 Billion. Stock Jumps 88% after IPO," *CNN Money,* April 16, 2015, http://money.cnn.com/2015/04/15/investing /etsy-ipo-16-a-share-wall-street/.

16. Chris Dixon, "Come for the Tool, Stay for the Network," cdixonblog, January 31, 2015, http://cdixon.org/2015/01/31/come-for-the-tool-stay-for -the-network/.

CONCLUSION: HOW TO SPOT THE NEXT BIG THING

1. Alex Moazed, "3 Growth Lessons From the Billion-Dollar Company That Handles Payments for Facebook and Uber," *Inc.,* September 16, 2015, http://www.inc.com/alex-moazed/3-growth-lessons-from-the-billion -dollar-company-that-handles-facebook-and-uber-.html.

2. Ryan Lawler, "Uber Strikes Deal to Lower the Cost of Car Ownership for Drivers," *TechCrunch,* November 24, 2013, http://techcrunch.com/2013 /11/24/uber-driver-car-financing/.

3. Jennifer Van Grove, "New Industry Piggybacking on Uber, Airbnb," *San Diego Union Tribune,* August 8, 2015, http://www.sandiegouniontribune.com /news/2015/aug/08/pillow-zendrive-breezee-sharing-startups/.

4. Catherine Clifford, "By 2017, the App Market Will Be a $77 Billion Industry," *Entrepreneur,* August 26, 2014, http://www.entrepreneur.com/art icle/236832.

5. Charlie Wells, "Piggybackers' Hitch Themselves to Airbnb, Uber," *Wall Street Journal,* February 18, 2015, http://www.wsj.com/articles/piggy backers-hitch-themselves-to-airbnb-uber-1424305849.

6. Cyrus Farivar, "How Zynga Went from Social Gaming Powerhouse to Has-Been," *Ars Technica,* September 12, 2013, http://arstechnica.com/business /2013/09/how-zynga-went-from-social-gaming-powerhouse-to-has-been/1/.

7. Nick O'Neill, "Zynga Launches 'FarmVille.' Does It Look Familiar?" *Social Times,* June 22, 2009, http://www.adweek.com/socialtimes/zynga-farm ville/309484.

8. Vikas Shukla, "Zynga Inc: The Rise and Fall," *ValueWalk,* May 28, 2014, http://www.valuewalk.com/2014/05/zynga-inc-rise-and-fall-infographic/.

9. Farivar, "How Zynga Went from Social Gaming Powerhouse to Has-Been."

10. "Facebook and Zynga to End Close Relationship," BBC News, November 30, 2012, http://www.bbc.com/news/technology-20554441.

11. Dean Takahashi, "Zynga Accounted for $445M, or 12 Percent of Facebook's Revenue, in 2011," *Venture Beat,* February 1, 2012, http://venture beat.com/2012/02/01/zynga-accounted-for-12-percent-of-facebooks-reven ue-in-2011/.

12. Terrence O'Brien, "HTC Revenues Continue to Drop at Alarming Rates, Down 61% From Last October," *Engadget,* November 6, 2012, http://www .engadget.com/2012/11/06/htc-revenues-continue-to-drop-at-alarming -rates/.

13. Chris Velazco, "Motorola Mobility Closes Out Q4 2011 with an $80 Million Net Loss," *TechCrunch*, January 26, 2012, http://techcrunch.com/2012/01/26/motorola-mobility-closes-out-q4-2011-with-an-80-million-net-loss/.

14. Tim Culpan, "HTC Posts Record Profit Drop as Samsung, Apple Grab Sales," *Bloomberg Business*, October 8, 2012, http://www.bloomberg.com/news/articles/2012-10-08/htc-posts-record-profit-drop-as-samsung-apple-grab-sales.

15. Tim Culpan, "HTC Trading below Cash Leaves Smartphone Brand with No Value," *Bloomberg Business*, August 9, 2015, http://www.bloomberg.com/news/articles/2015-08-10/htc-trading-near-cash-leaves-a-smartphone-brand-with-no-value.

16. Ian Sherr and Evan Ramstad, "Has Apple Lost Its Cool to Samsung?" *Wall Street Journal*, January 28, 2013, http://www.wsj.com/articles/SB10001424127887323854904578264090074879024.

17. David Gilbert, "Samsung Loses 50% of Its China Smartphone Market Share as Apple Dominates," *International Business Times*, May 11, 2015, http://www.ibtimes.co.uk/samsung-loses-50-its-china-smartphone-market-share-apple-dominates-1500636.

18. Greg Kumparak, "Apple Just Had the Most Profitable Quarter of Any Company Ever," *TechCrunch*, January 27, 2015, http://techcrunch.com/2015/01/27/apple-just-had-the-biggest-quarterly-earnings-of-any-company-ever/.

19. Daniel Eran Dilger, "Samsung's Mobile Profits Plunge 64.2% after Apple's iPhone 6 Devastates Premium Galaxy Sales," *Apple Insider*, January 28, 2015, http://appleinsider.com/articles/15/01/28/samsungs-mobile-profits-plunge-642-after-apples-iphone-6-devastates-premium-galaxy-sales.

20. See, for example: Joe Minihane, "Why Samsung's Smartphone Business's Decline Could Be Terminal," uSwitch.com, July 30, 2015, http://www.uswitch.com/mobiles/news/2015/07/why_samsung_s_smartphone_business_decline_could_be_terminal/; Ben Thompson, "Smartphone Truths and Samsung's Inevitable Decline," *Stratechery*, July 8, 2014, https://stratechery.com/2014/smartphone-truths-samsungs-inevitable-decline/.

21. "Smartphone Wars: Why Is Samsung Losing Momentum?," *Bloomberg*, September 3, 2015, http://www.bloomberg.com/news/videos/b/be2c2a0b-7b24-4115-8fda-e69df9e388c6.

22. Simon Rothman, tweet, November 13, 2015, https://twitter.com/GreylockVC/status/665212984445296640. Rothman was speaking at the "Next Economy: What's the Future of Work?" conference.

23. For example, see Lisa Guernsey, "EBay Not Liable for Goods That Are Illegal, Judge Says," *New York Times*, November 13, 2000, http://www.nytimes.com/2000/11/13/business/ebay-not-liable-for-goods-that-are-illegal-judge-says.html.

24. Carlos Tejada, "U.S. Warns Alibaba Again about Selling Counterfeit Goods," *Wall Street Journal*, December 17, 2015, http://www.wsj.com/articles/u-s-warns-alibaba-again-about-selling-counterfeit-goods-1450406612.

25. Jackson, *The PayPal Wars*.

26. "Feds: PayPal Not a Bank," *CNET*, May 19, 2002, http://www.cnet.com/news/feds-paypal-not-a-bank/.

27. Mark Cuban, "Some Thoughts on YouTube and Google," *Blog Maverick: The Mark Cuban Weblog,* October 7, 2006, http://blogmaverick.com/2006/10/07 /some-thoughts-on-youtube-and-google/.

28. Anne Broache, "Viacom sues Google over YouTube clips," *CNET,* March 13, 2006, http://www.cnet.com/news/viacom-sues-google-over-youtube-clips/ ; The Viacom case was later settled out of court.

29. David Bogoslaw, "Peer-to-Peer Lending: Problems and Promise," *Bloomberg,* April 6, 2009, http://www.businessweek.com/investor/content/apr2009 /pi2009043_811816.htm.

30. Hari Sreenivasan, "Why Is New York City Cracking Down on Airbnb?" *PBS,* August 1, 2015, http://www.pbs.org/newshour/bb/will-new-york-city -shut-airbnb-2/.

31. Zak Stone, "Living and Dying on Airbnb," *Medium,* November 8, 2015, https://medium.com/matter/living-and-dying-on-airbnb-6bff8d600c04.

32. Steven Millwar, "WeChat's Growth Continues, Hits 650 Million Users," *Tech In Asia,* November 10, 2015, https://www.techinasia.com/we chat-650-million-monthly-active-users.

33. Lily Kuo, "WeChat Is Nothing Like WhatsApp—and That Makes It Even More Valuable," *Quartz,* February 20, 2014, http://qz.com/179007 /wechat-is-nothing-like-whatsapp-and-that-makes-it-even-more-valuable/.

34. Jeff Grub, "Research Firm: China's Tencent Is Now a Bigger Gaming Company than Microsoft and Activision," *Venture Beat,* March 10, 2014, http://venturebeat.com/2014/03/10/research-firm-chinas-tencent -is-now-a-bigger-gaming-company-than-microsoft-and-activision/.

35. Eric Savitz, "5 Things You Need to Know about Chinese Social Media," *Forbes,* October 25, 2012, http://www.forbes.com/sites/davidyin/2015/02 /19/tencents-wechat-sends-1-billion-virtual-red-envelopes-on-new-years -eve/.

36. Connie Chan, "When One App Rules Them All: The Case of WeChat and Mobile in China," *Andreessen Horowitz* (blog), August 6, 2015, http://a16z .com/2015/08/06/wechat-china-mobile-first/.

37. "Top 10 Android App Stores | China," *Newzoo,* http://www.newzoo.com /free/rankings/top-10-android-app-stores-china/, accessed July 2015.

38. However, there are a few exceptions. Most notably, Tencent-backed Didi Dache merged with Alibaba's Kuiadi Dache in February 2015 in order to consolidate their market share and stave off Uber, a recent entrant into China. And in October 2015 China's top group-buying sites, Meituan and Dianping, announced a $15 billion merger, even though they are backed by Alibaba and Tencent, respectively.

39. Reid Hoffman, "The Information Age to the Networked Age: Are You Network Literate?" June 13, 2014, http://reidhoffman.org/information-age -networked-age-network-literate/.

40. A. Harrington, "The B2B Super Markets," *Management Consultancy,* May 7, 2001.

41. Erin Griffith, "In B2B E-commerce, Alibaba Has Solved the One Problem Amazon Can't," *Fortune,* September 8, 2014, http://fortune.com/2014/09/08 /alibaba-amazon-b2b-ecommerce/.

42. David S. Evans and Richard Schmalensee, "Failure to Launch: Critical Mass in Platform Businesses," *Review of Network Economics* 9, no. 4 (2010).

43. Quoted in Liu Shiying and Martha Avery, *Alibaba: The Inside Story Behind Jack Ma and the Creation of the World's Biggest Online Marketplace* (New York: HarperCollins e-books, 2009).

44. Gitta Rohling, "Facts and Forecasts: Billions of Things, Trillions of Dollars," *Pictures of the Future,* October 1, 2014, http://www.siemens.com/innovation/en/home/pictures-of-the-future/digitalization-and-software/internet-of-things-facts-and-forecasts.html.

45. Yessi Bello Perez, "Santander: Blockchain Tech Can Save Banks $20 Billion a Year," *CoinDesk,* June 16, 2015, http://www.coindesk.com/santander-blockchain-tech-can-save-banks-20-billion-a-year/.

46. "The March of Financial Services Giants into Bitcoin and Blockchain Startups in One Chart," *Insurance Tech Insights,* November 3, 2015, https://www.cbinsights.com/blog/financial-services-corporate-blockchain-investments/.

INDEX

Adyen, 203–5
Airbnb: Adyen and, 203–4; automated tools, 149–50; compensation and, 116; consumption and, 115; cost and, 37, 87–89; Craigslist and, 129–31, 198; creation of, 109, 129–31; customer safety and, 146, 155, 615–15; growth, 104, 193, 205; investment and, 82, 206; legal issues, 213, 215–17; matching intention and, 43–45; monopolies and, 102; platform business model, 6, 29–30, 41, 114, 213; platform modeling, 156; problems facing, 151–52, 215; reputation and, 100, 144–45; success, 32; untapped sources of supply, 225; Urban Bellhop and, 205
AirSpruce, 205
Alibaba: Alipay, 19, 75, 96–97, 99, 196, 204, 222; B2B and, 227; Baidu and, 105; compared to linear businesses, 87; competition and, 103–4; counterfeiting and, 144, 155, 214; data and, 70–72; economy and, 75; as exchange platform, 47; growth, 30, 87; investment and, 19, 217–18; market dominance, 101; platform battles and, 99–100, 221; platform split and, 41; Taobao, 19, 95–100, 104, 114–15, 183, 214, 218, 224; Tencent and, 196, 221–22; Tmall, 19, 99, 218; as "unicorn" company, 84
Alphabet Inc. *See* Google
Amazon, 6, 18–19, 29–32, 79, 93, 97–98, 100, 105, 114–15, 132, 134–35, 154, 221
American Management Association, 1
American Well, 80
Anderson, Robert, 155

Andreessen Horowitz, 36, 203
Andreessen, Marc, 17–18
Android: Android Pay, 221; BlackBerry and, 8; China and, 84, 220; competition and, 106–7; derivative business and, 206; development and, 221–22; Google and, 154; iPhone and, 1–4; as maker platform, 41, 47; mobile gaming and, 209; Open Handset Alliance and, 196–97; open source and, 33, 220; platform business model, 6, 94; platform capitalism and, 99; platform modeling and, 156; RIM and, 8, 10–15; terminal decline and, 209–12; *see also* Google
Apple: App Store, 6, 10–12, 14–15, 19, 140, 190–91, 220–21, 225; iOS, 2, 4, 6, 13, 15, 31, 38, 41, 99, 104, 156, 168, 190, 206, 209, 212, 220–21, 225; iPhone, 1–2, 8–14, 38, 141, 196, 211; iTunes, 6, 11, 221; Worldwide Developers Conference (WWDC), 14
Applico, 13, 15–16, 35, 45, 121, 206, 222
Arthur, W. Brian, 21
AT&T, 11, 106–7, 196
athenahealth, 79
Auction Web, 21
Auctionata, 15
audience building: defined, 239; do-or-die nature of, 132; explained, 126–27; hacking networks for growth, 129–31; importance of, 154; liquidity and, 132; Operation SLOG, 192; Operation SLOG, 127–29; PayPal and, 131–32; platform category and, 47; Uber and, 152

Baidu, 19, 30, 95, 97–99, 105, 220–22
Balsillie, Jim, 7–11, 13–15

BAT, 221
Beanie Babies, 28
Benchmark, 81, 142
Benioff, Marc, 79
Best Buy, 23
Best Use of Resources, The (Kantorovich), 52
Bilton, Nick, 142, 159–60
Bing, 99; *see also* Microsoft
BlackBerry, 7–15, 81, 141; App World, 13; Storm, 12–13
Booking.com, 203
Boston Consulting Group, 56, 240
Breeze, 205
"bring your own device" (BYOD) policies, 9
Buffet, Warren, 80
burning platform, 2–5, 7
business models, explained, 22–25
Büyükkükten, Orkut, 122, 173

capitalism: competition and, 74–75; platform capitalism, 99–100
CD-ROMs, 62, 67
central planning, 52–55, 60–61, 70, 72–73
Chatroulette, 159–61, 164, 167, 169, 174, 186, 239
Chesky, Brian, 130–31, 150
chicken-and-egg problem: monetary subsidies, 196–97; monetary subsidies and product features, 199–201; product features, 197–98
cloud computing, 32–33, 66, 77, 79–80
Club Nexus, 122, 173
Coase, Ronald, 36, 55–56, 58, 60, 69–70
Cold War, 74
collaboration, 184–86
Color, 189–90
Comcast, 18, 102
commoditization, 44–47, 212, 231, 239
communication, 183
community, 185–86

competition, 53, 66, 74–75, 90–91, 99, 103, 106, 222
Competitive Advantage (Porter), 58
"Computer and the Market, The" (Lange), 61
connection, 30, 39–41, 46, 69, 74, 87, 101, 112, 116–17, 127, 161–62, 166–72, 183
connectivity, 64–66, 70
coordination cost, 36, 59
core tools and services, 40, 126, 146–57
core transaction: compensate, 115–16; connect, 114; consume, 114–15; create, 113–14; diagram, 39; exchange platforms, 118; explained, 39, 111–12; four actions of, 113; maker platforms, 118–19; platform types and, 43–47; steps, 116–17; Tinder and, 119–20
Costolo, Dick, 141, 143
Craigslist, 129–31, 198
Crocodile in the Yangtze, 97
curation, 183–84

data analytics, 66
decentralization, 34, 52–56, 61, 63, 66, 68, 70, 72–74, 89, 146, 233–34
democratization of processing power and storage, 65–66
Dentasoft, 77–79
Dentistry.com, 78
Didi Kuaidi, 99
digital advertising, 106
Doctor on Demand, 80, 228
Dorsey, Jack, 142
dotBank, 131
dot-com era, 20–22, 26, 29, 31–32, 63–64, 67, 79, 175, 214, 226–27
Dropbox, 82, 203

EachNet, 96
eBay, 6, 19, 21–22, 27–30, 41, 70, 95–100, 116, 131–32, 144, 150, 213–14, 221
eClinicalWorks, 79
e-commerce, 19, 29, 96–99, 104, 204, 221, 224, 227
economies of scale, 56, 59–60, 68, 72, 75, 86, 103, 240
ecosystems: competition and, 13, 221–22; enterprise software and, 79; monetary subsidies and, 199; open, 10; value and, 69, 92, 111, 152–54; war of, 3, 7, 15

efficiency, 18, 24, 52, 55–56, 79, 86, 89, 103, 147–48, 228, 230
electronic medical record (EMR) systems, 79–80
Elop, Stephen, 1–5, 7
Encarta, 62, 68; *see also* Microsoft
Encyclopaedia Britannica, 62, 67–68, 85
encyclopedias, 62, 68, 85
enterprise software, 78–80
entrepreneurship, 63, 77, 109–10, 146, 157, 175, 181, 189, 220
Epic Systems Corp., 79
Erisman, Porter, 97–98
Etsy, 19, 77–78, 93, 115, 200
European Union, 100
Evans, Benedict, 203
Evans, David S., 95
expanding markets
ExxonMobil, 22, 60

Facebook: Adyen and, 203; competition and, 74, 174; core transaction and, 118; data and, 70. 72; derivative businesses and, 206; Facebook Home, 220; GitHub and, 35; growth, 67, 224; identity and, 178–80; Messenger, 218–20; network effects, 170–74, 183; open source and, 33; privacy and, 106–8, 155; simplicity and, 122–23; success, 18–19, 30, 81, 164–67, 212; terminal decline and, 209–10; transactions and, 37, 149, 153–54; value, 30; Twitter and, 139, 142–44; Zynga and, 207–9
Farmville, 207–8, 218
Financial Times, 3
firm, theory of, 55–61
Flickr, 18, 155
Force.com, 79; *see also* Salesforce
Ford, 7, 14, 24–25, 60, 112
fragmentation, 103, 220, 226–28, 230, 235

Garden.com, 64
Gebbia, Joe, 109, 131
General Electric, 22, 60, 231
General Motors (GM), 22, 24–25, 60
GitHub, 35–38, 41
Glamsquad, 15, 45, 156
Gooden, Dave, 130

Goodrow, Cristos, 135–36
Google: Gmail, 129, 174; Google Ventures, 15; Nest, 6; Orkut, 122, 173, 221; Play Store, 12, 197, 220–21; Search, 6, 73, 135, 151, 154, 221; *see also* Android
government regulations, 80, 101–2, 106, 108, 152, 203, 213–17, 229–30, 232, 234–35
graphical user interfaces (GUIs), 35
Greenspan, Aaron, 123
Gross, Bill, 141
Gurley, Bill, 81, 93, 142–43

Handy, 30, 32, 45–46, 90–93, 116, 145, 149–51, 156, 181, 194, 199, 216, 220
Hanrahan, Oisin, 90
harassment, social media and, 143
Harlow, Jo, 2–3
Hatching Twitter (Bilton), 142
Hayek, Friedrich, 53–55, 59, 61, 63, 70–73
Heins, Thorsten, 7–8
Henderson, Bruce, 56–60, 69, 72
Homejoy, 91–92, 177
houseSYSTEM, 122–23, 147
Hyatt, 87

IBM, 33, 71, 235
information goods, 85
infrastructure-as-a-service (IaaS), 79
inputs/outputs, 58, 111–12, 117
Instacart, 32, 147–49, 216
Instagram, 30, 46–47, 81, 107, 114, 119, 144, 146, 194, 201, 221, 229
investors, 21–22, 63, 77, 81–83
iPhone, 1–2, 8–14, 38, 141, 196, 211; *see also* Apple
IPOs, 20–22, 29–30, 154, 209, 217
iTunes, 6, 11, 221; *see also* Apple

Jackson, Eric M., 132
James Bond, 49, 54
Jobs, Steve, 11, 13–15
J.P. Morgan, 23, 234

Kalanick, Travis, 102, 134, 230
Kantorovich, Leonid, 52–53
Keynes, John Maynard, 107
Kickstarter, 30, 77–78, 114, 183
Kozmo.com, 64, 175

Krugman, Paul, 64, 67

LakePlace.com, 130
Lange, Oskar, 61, 63, 71, 73
Lazaridis, Mike, 7–11
Lean Startup movement, 175
Lending Club, 46, 77–78,
   113–14, 215, 231
Lenovo, 23, 210
Lessin, Sam, 122–23
linear business model:
   competition and, 68, 74–75;
   connection and, 112, 114;
   data and, 100; defined,
   240; explained, 22–24;
   investment and, 81–82;
   legal issues and, 213; market
   size and, 93; monopolies
   and, 103; platforms and,
   29, 31–33, 109–11, 116,
   192, 215; privacy and, 108;
   Samsung and, 212; supply
   chain, 24–25; transactions
   and, 116–17; U-shaped
   economies of scale curve for,
   60; value and, 39, 84–85,
   152, 231; zero-marginal-
   cost and, 85–89
LinkedIn, 17–18, 30, 46, 82,
   87, 118, 120–21, 155, 190,
   206, 224
Linux, 33–35, 139, 234
liquidity, 121, 130, 132, 135,
   181, 192, 199, 240
local knowledge, 54–55, 59,
   70, 73
Lyft, 30, 45, 121, 127, 152, 181,
   186, 194, 199, 205–6, 216

Ma, Jack, 96–98, 227
margins, 89–90, 93, 95
market size, 87–88, 93
matching intention, 41–42,
   47, 241
matchmaking: collaborative
   filtering, 134–35;
   commoditization and,
   46; core transactions and,
   47, 126; creating rules
   and standards, 136–38;
   explained, 126; measuring
   success, 135–36; overview,
   132–33; preventing
   unintended consequences,
   143–46; Twitter and,
   138–43; Uber and, 133–34;
   Yahoo and, 135–36
McLuhan, Marshall, 51
MDLIVE, 80
"Meaning of Competition,
   The" (Hayek), 53

Medium, 41–42, 116, 125, 181
MeeGo, 1–2
Mehta, Apoorva, 147–49
Metcalfe's Law, 168–70, 175,
   183, 241
Metromile, 206
Microsoft, 1, 3, 15, 18,
   29–31, 35, 62, 68, 99, 106–7,
   180–81, 196
MIT, 62, 165
mobile technology, 65, 67
monetary subsidies: attracting
   high-value users, 199–200;
   cooperating with industry
   incumbents, 196–97;
   providing security through
   large, up-front investment,
   196; providing single-user
   utility, 201; targeting user
   groups, 200–1
monopolies: business model
   and, 97–99; competition
   and, 105–8; government-
   sponsored, 74–75; old vs.
   new, 100–3; overview,
   95–97; platform capitalism,
   99–100
Moore, Gordon, 61
Moore's Law, 61, 174
Motorola, 10, 210–12
MySpace, 144, 162–65, 167,
   169, 172–76, 179–80,
   183

Navani, Girish, 79–80
Net neutrality, 18
Netflix, 100
network ecosystem, 69
network effects ladder:
   collaboration, 184–85;
   communication, 183;
   community, 185–86;
   connection, 183; curation,
   183–84; diagram, 182;
   overview, 182–83
Nokia, 1–8, 11, 14–15, 81, 106
Nosek, Luke, 131

Obama, Barack, 130–31
Omidyar, Pierre, 21–22, 27
on-demand, 29, 32, 45, 80, 90,
   147, 150, 194, 220, 222, 228
Open Handset Alliance
   (OHA), 10
open source, 10, 33–36, 38, 78,
   107, 220, 234
OpenTable, 89–90, 201, 222
opt-ins: double, 43, 118–19,
   122, 152–53, 165, 241;
   single, 118–20
Oracle, 23, 79

PayPal, 18, 37, 74, 131–32, 149,
   159, 194, 214
perfect information, 36, 52–54
Pets.com, 20–22, 27, 29, 32,
   64, 175
Pinterest, 30, 82, 106, 181–82
Pishevar, Shervin, 160
platforms: anatomy of, 39–41;
   competition between,
   99–100, 103, 106, 222;
   computing, 32; costs,
   36–37; definition, 29;
   design, 46–47; examples,
   29–31; exchange, 41, 43–44;
   expansion of markets,
   103–5; industry, 32; maker,
   41, 44; matching intention
   and, 41–43; monopolies,
   99–101; platform capitalism,
   99–100; product, 32; as
   service, 32; types, 43–46
Porter, Michael, 57–60, 69,
   72, 86, 97–98, 110, 112,
   131, 242
Preston, Dan, 206
Preston-Warner, Tom, 35
privacy, 108, 155, 174, 179, 229
processing power, 29, 61–63,
   65–67, 70, 233
product features: acting as
   producer, 197–98; attracting
   high-value users, 199–200;
   providing single-user utility,
   201; tapping into existing
   network, 198; targeting user
   groups, 200–1
profitability, 22, 29, 107, 211
ProGit, 36

QQ, 19, 154, 218
QWERTY keyboards, 8, 11

Rakuten, 30
recommendations, 100, 116
Red Cross, 132
Red Hat, 33–34
Redpoint Ventures, 120, 138
Reidman, Hoff, 78
repeat business, 91–92
reputation, 96, 100, 107, 116,
   129, 144–45, 154, 160, 164,
   174, 177–78, 180, 183–84
Research in Motion (RIM),
   7–15; see also BlackBerry
restaurants, 89–90, 201,
   225; see also GrubHub;
   OpenTable
rewards, 115–16
Riedel, Josh, 144
Road to Serfdom (Hayek), 53
Roberts, Matthew, 90

Rubin, Andy, 10
rules and standards, 136–38

Salesforce, 79
Samsung, 10, 84, 94, 211–12, 231
Sandberg, Sheryl, 139
SAP, 79
Sarver, Ryan, 138–41, 145
Scoble, Robert, 191
search, 6, 18, 37, 45–46, 73, 95, 97–99, 105–7, 116, 130, 133, 135–36, 154, 196, 206, 208, 219–22, 233; see also Alibaba; Baidu; Google
showrooming, 50
simplicity, 122–23, 147
Skype, 18, 42, 114
smartphones
Snapchat, 30, 38, 81–82, 114, 191, 201
Social Finance (SoFi), 30, 231
social networking, 18, 35, 43, 46, 67, 74, 81, 118–22, 142, 153, 161, 163–67, 170, 172–74, 176, 189–90, 194, 198, 200–1, 213, 221, 224, 235
software as a service (SaaS), 23, 33, 79, 85, 227
software development kit (SDK), 13–14
SoundCloud, 77
Spotify, 184, 203–4
Square, 18, 30
Standard Oil, 22, 100–2, 107
startups, 15, 22, 30–31, 46, 74, 77, 80, 83–85, 97, 107, 120–21, 129–30, 147, 156, 172, 175, 177, 184–85, 190–92, 195, 197, 205, 219, 223, 231, 235
Steel, Anna, 151–52
storage, 66, 68, 79
Super Bowl ads, 20
supply chain, 4, 18, 22–26, 29, 69, 89
Symbian, 1–2, 4, 32

Taobao. See Alibaba, Taobao
Target, 23
targeting, 22–24, 166, 171, 178, 200
TaskRabbit, 45–46
Teladoc, 80, 228
telemedicine, 80
Tencent, 19, 30, 84, 99, 154, 196, 217–18, 220–22
terminal decline, 209–12

Ternovskiy, Andrey, 160
Thiel, Peter, 74, 104, 159, 189
Time Warner Cable, 102
Tinder, 38, 46, 114, 119–20, 152, 177–78, 198, 242
Tmall, 19, 99, 219; see also Alibaba
TOM Online, 97
Torvalds, Linus, 33–34
Toyota, 22, 24–25
transaction costs, 36–38, 41, 44, 56–58, 60, 62–63, 72, 126, 223–24, 228, 242
Tumblr, 77–78, 222
Tungus, Tomasz, 120–21
Twitch, 30, 42, 143
Twitter: creating rules and standards, 136–38; future of, 141–43; growth of business, 139–41, 154–55, 173; managing, 138–39; preventing unintended consequences, 143–46; user sequencing and, 180–81; Verified User program, 195

Uber: capital costs of, 87; competition and, 6, 99, 186, 221; connection and, 6, 112; core tools and services, 146–47, 149–53, 155; curation and, 184; as exchange platform, 47; growth, 104, 120–21; imitators, 32; impact of, 75; Internet of Things and, 230; investment and, 82; legal issues, 101–2, 213, 215–17; liquidity and, 192; matching and, 42–43, 44, 133–35; monetary subsidies, 194, 199; network effects, 170–71, 181; Operation SLOG, 127–28; product features, 197, 199; reputation and, 144–45; success of platform, 29–30, 203–6, 213, 227; transactions and, 37–39, 90, 112, 114–16, 118, 224; value and, 73, 112
UberEATS, 121, 153
UberMedia, 141
UberRUSH, 121
ubiquitous connectivity. See connectivity
unicorn companies, 83–85, 191, 203, 206, 213
Union Square Ventures (USV), 77–78

UnionPay, 75, 204
Urban Bellhop, 205
U.S. Steel, 22, 60, 100
"Use of Knowledge in Society, The" (Hayek), 53
user sequencing, 180–82, 195

value chain, 57–60, 62–63, 68–69, 72, 75, 82, 86, 110–12, 152, 242
value proposition, 10, 37–38, 79, 138
value, subsidizing: monetary subsidies, 194; product features subsidies, 194–95; user sequencing, 195
version control, 34
video streaming, 68, 222

Walmart, 18, 22–23, 87
Wangwang, 96
Watson, 33; see also IBM
Waze, 30, 221–22
Webvan, 64
WeChat, 19, 99, 154, 196, 218–20, 222
Wenger, Albert, 78
WhatsApp, 30, 81, 107–8, 118, 218, 221
Whitman, Meg, 21, 96
Wikipedia, 35, 67–68, 86, 185–86
Williams, Ev, 125, 142, 181
Wilson, Fred, 77–81, 93, 140
Windows Phones, 2–3, 99; see also Microsoft
Wu, Tim, 105

Xbox, 181, 194, 196
X.com, 131
Xiaomi, 84, 211, 220

Yahoo, 29, 98–99, 132
Yelp, 171, 199–200, 203, 222
Youku Tudou, 180, 199, 222
YouTube, 29, 41–42, 46–47, 67–68, 70, 87, 113–16, 118–19, 135–36, 143, 145–46, 149, 171, 174, 180–81, 206, 214–15

Zeng, Ming, 71, 95, 101
zero-marginal-cost companies, 85–89
Zero to One (Thiel), 74, 104
Zuckerberg, Mark, 109, 122–23, 139, 146–47, 165–67, 178–80, 224
Zynga, 207–10, 220